'This collection is a rich resource for exploring theoretical issues related to tasks. At the same time, concrete design and practice are always close at hand. The authors tackle the practical issues of tasks in classrooms and invent ways to construct task environments that systematically foster student independence, introduce students to strategies for becoming productive learners, and thereby enable students to accomplish challenging and significant work... There is much to be learned from this team about task design and enactment, about classrooms' activity systems, about learning and development, about subject pedagogy, and about realising curriculum potential. These factors are essential considerations in any attempt to understand and promote teaching quality.'

*from the Foreword by Professor Walter Doyle, University of Arizona, USA*

# DESIGNING TASKS IN SECONDARY EDUCATION

Engaging students in learning about their subject is a central concern for all teachers and teacher educators. How teachers view and use the pedagogic potential of different tasks to engage pupils with knowledge in different subjects is central to this endeavour.

*Designing Tasks in Secondary Education* explores models for effective task design, and demonstrates how to translate the curriculum into appropriate tasks and activities that facilitate developmental or higher-level understanding of curriculum content.

Written by experts in the field of education from a range of subjects and including a foreword written by renowned author Professor Walter Doyle, this book spans an international context and offers a refreshing alternative of how to plan and design tasks that will not only intellectually stimulate but improve teaching quality. Key topics explored include:

- designing tasks that engage learners with knowledge
- policy perspectives on task design
- designing cognitively demanding classroom tasks
- task design issues in the secondary subjects.

*Designing Tasks in Secondary Education* offers essential insight into task design and its importance for enhancing subject understanding and student engagement. It will challenge and support all education professionals concerned with issues of curriculum design, subject knowledge, classroom organisation, agency in the learning process and teaching quality.

**Ian Thompson** is Associate Professor of English Education at the University of Oxford, UK.

# DESIGNING TASKS IN SECONDARY EDUCATION

Enhancing subject understanding and student engagement

*Edited by Ian Thompson*

Routledge
Taylor & Francis Group
LONDON AND NEW YORK

First published 2015
by Routledge
2 Park Square, Milton Park, Abingdon, Oxon OX14 4RN

and by Routledge
711 Third Avenue, New York, NY 10017

*Routledge is an imprint of the Taylor & Francis Group, an informa business*

© 2015 Ian Thompson

The right of Ian Thompson to be identified as the author of the editorial material, and of the authors for their individual chapters, has been asserted in accordance with sections 77 and 78 of the Copyright, Designs and Patents Act 1988.

All rights reserved. No part of this book may be reprinted or reproduced or utilised in any form or by any electronic, mechanical, or other means, now known or hereafter invented, including photocopying and recording, or in any information storage or retrieval system, without permission in writing from the publishers.

*Trademark notice*: Product or corporate names may be trademarks or registered trademarks, and are used only for identification and explanation without intent to infringe.

*British Library Cataloguing in Publication Data*
A catalogue record for this book is available from the British Library

*Library of Congress Cataloging in Publication Data*
Designing tasks in secondary education : enhancing subject understanding and student engagement / edited by Ian Thompson.
pages cm
1. Education, Secondary--Curricula. 2. Learning, Psychology of. 3. Task analysis.
I. Thompson, Ian (Frederick Ian), editor of compilation.
LB1628.D47 2014
373.19--dc23
2014012821

ISBN: 978-0-415-71233-0 (hbk)
ISBN: 978-0-415-71234-7 (pbk)
ISBN: 978-1-315-75543-4 (ebk)

Typeset in Bembo
by Fish Books Ltd.

# CONTENTS

*List of illustrations* ix
*List of contributors* x

Foreword xiii
Walter Doyle

**PART I**
**The background** 1

1 Introduction: tasks, concepts and subject knowledge 3
  *Ian Thompson*

2 Designing tasks which engage learners with knowledge 13
  *Anne Edwards*

3 Policy perspectives on task design: classroom learning
  and the national curriculum 28
  *Mark Chater*

**PART II**
**Learning from the subjects** 45

4 The interplay between mathematics and pedagogy:
  designing tasks for mathematics teacher education 47
  *Gabriel J. Stylianides and Anne Watson*

5  Disciplinary knowledge: task design in geography  70
   *Roger Firth*

6  Communication, culture and conceptual learning:
   task design in the English classroom  86
   *Ian Thompson*

7  Practical theorising: designing tasks for science explanations  107
   *Ann Childs and Jane McNicholl*

8  Designing tasks to promote learning in the foreign language classroom  129
   *Trevor Mutton and Robert Woore*

9  Negotiating knowledge: task design in the history classroom  152
   *Jason Todd*

10 Insiders and outsiders: task design in learning about religions  170
   *Nigel Fancourt*

## PART III
## Looking forward  **189**

11 Designing the task of teaching novice teachers:
   how to design instructional tasks  191
   *Peter Smagorinsky*

*Index*  207

# ILLUSTRATIONS

## Figures

| | | |
|---|---|---|
| 2.1 | A model of task sequencing to promote learning | 21 |
| 4.1 | Mathematical task about the sum of interior and exterior angles of convex polygons | 52 |
| 4.2 | Analysis of student work on a related mathematical task | 54 |
| 4.3 | Proof by mathematical induction | 55 |
| 4.4 | Discussion of different task formulations | 56 |
| 4.5 | Example of a tetramino on a 7 x 7 counting grid | 60 |
| 4.6 | Example of a tetramino on a two-variable grid | 62 |
| 8.1 | A dialogical approach to foreign language task design | 139 |
| 9.1 | Examining the First World War on different levels | 160 |
| 10.1 | Insiders and outsiders in religious education | 172 |
| 10.2 | Vygotskian model of concept formation | 177 |
| 10.3 | A Vygotskian approach to conceptual development in religious education | 179 |

## Tables

| | | |
|---|---|---|
| 4.1 | The two prompts to which prospective teachers responded at the end of the session | 51 |
| 4.2 | Coding of prospective teachers' responses to Prompt 1 in the first task sequence | 58 |
| 4.3 | Coding of prospective teachers' responses to Prompt 2 in the first task sequence | 58 |
| 4.4 | Structure and purpose of the second task sequence | 60 |
| 4.5 | Coding of prospective teachers' responses to Prompts 1 and 2 in the second task sequence | 65 |

# CONTRIBUTORS

**Dr Ian Thompson** is an Associate Professor of English Education at the University of Oxford. He is a joint convenor of the Oxford Centre for Sociocultural and Activity Theory Research (OSAT) and leads the secondary English initial teacher education course. He previously taught English for 16 years in secondary schools. In his current research, he focuses on English pedagogy, collaborative learning, initial teacher education, and social justice in education from a Vygotskian theoretical perspective.

**Dr Mark Chater** is a qualified teacher who has worked in schools and universities as a trainer and researcher, and in the UK civil service as a senior curriculum adviser. He now works in the third sector directing a charity promoting research, development and innovation in RE.

**Dr Ann Childs** is an Associate Professor of Science Education at the University of Oxford and Director of the Master's in Teacher Education (Science and Maths). Her main research interests are science teachers' professional knowledge and the ways in which this is developed in and by different contexts, and how technology can be used to enhance teaching and learning in secondary school contexts.

**Walter Doyle** is a professor in the Department of Teaching, Learning and Sociocultural Studies at the University of Arizona. He has published extensively in the areas of classroom processes, curriculum theory, and teacher education. His most recent work is focused on curriculum events in classrooms and teacher-curriculum relationships.

**Anne Edwards** is Professor of Education and a former Director of the Department of Education at the University of Oxford. She joined the Department in

2005 after holding chairs at Birmingham and Leeds and currently jointly convenes the Oxford Centre for Sociocultural and Activity Theory Research. She has researched pedagogy and the professional learning of teachers over the last thirty years. Her most recent research draws on Vygotskian theory to examine the exercise of what she terms relational expertise and relational agency in collaborations across practice boundaries.

**Dr Nigel Fancourt** is the course director of the Master's in Learning and Teaching at the University of Oxford where he is also involved in developing a range of teachers' professional development projects. He lectures and tutors on the religious education initial teacher education course. Nigel's research interests are in teacher education and religion in education.

**Dr Roger Firth** is an Associate Professor of Education (Geography) at the University of Oxford where he leads the secondary geography initial teacher education course. His research interests are curriculum and pedagogic development in geography and environmental education; education for sustainable development; knowledge and its impact on curriculum and pedagogy; curriculum change, theory and policy; and social and cultural theory.

**Dr Jane McNicholl** is an Associate Professor of Science Education at the University of Oxford. Her principal teaching responsibilities are in initial teacher education. Her main research interest involves science teachers' professional knowledge and the ways this is developed in and by different contexts. Her research draws largely on sociocultural theoretical perspectives.

**Trevor Mutton** is the Postgraduate Certificate in Education (PGCE) Course Director at the University of Oxford and an Associate Professor of Modern Foreign Languages. He also teaches on the modern languages initial teacher education course and on the Master's in Learning and Teaching. His research focuses on teacher education, with a particular interest in the learning of beginning teachers.

**Peter Smagorinsky** is Distinguished Research Professor of English Education at The University of Georgia and winner of the 2012 Sylvia Scribner Award from Division C of the American Educational Research Association and 2013 David H. Russell Research Award for Distinguished Research in the Teaching of English from the National Council of Teachers of English.

**Dr Gabriel J. Stylianides** is an Associate Professor of Mathematics Education at the University of Oxford. He convenes the Subject Pedagogy Research Group and leads the secondary mathematics initial teacher education course. His research focuses on issues related to the meaningful engagement of students of all levels of education in fundamental mathematical activities – notably mathematical reasoning, proving, problem solving and algebraic thinking.

**Jason Todd** is a Teacher Education Research Fellow in History Education at the University of Oxford. He has previously worked as a history teacher in a variety of London schools, including middle management and senior management roles. Jason currently works as a curriculum tutor in history initial teacher education.

**Emeritus Professor Anne Watson** has two mathematics degrees and a DPhil in Mathematics Education. She taught mathematics in challenging schools for 13 years before becoming an academic at the University of Oxford. Her research interests include task design, promoting mathematical thinking and relational understanding, and social justice through raising achievement.

**Dr Robert Woore** is a lecturer in Applied Linguistics at Oxford University Department of Education (OUDE). He is the lead tutor on the modern languages initial teacher education course. He previously taught French and German at secondary school level. His principal research interest is print-to-sound decoding in a second language, particularly in relation to beginner and near-beginner learners in modern foreign languages classrooms in the UK.

# FOREWORD

*Walter Doyle*

Teacher quality is a dominant theme in contemporary scholarship on teaching, reflecting a long tradition in the field. The pursuit of quality, however, often has at least two consequences: (1) a tendency to focus inquiry on how a teacher acts in public and (2) a push toward quantification. Both of these pathways mask important teaching processes that are not always readily apparent when one is watching a lesson but are essential in constructing a plausible understanding of how teaching works and in promoting quality curricular experiences for students.

The idea of task opens a wide lens on fundamental processes in teaching. The tasks a teacher defines for a lesson or unit shape how pupils engage intellectually with the content of the curriculum, what tools and strategies they learn to use with this content, and what learning capacities they take away from these curriculum encounters. Teacher actions, regardless of their inherent 'quality', that do not have an instrumental connection to the tasks students are working on are unlikely to have much effect on learning and development. Tasks, in other words, instantiate the curriculum in a classroom. They are the curriculum in motion – the actual curriculum that is taught – and they embody a teacher's understanding of the content as educative experience. Task design and enactment, then, are at the core of the work of teaching.

Despite their central importance, tasks are not the first thing an observer sees when entering a classroom. Words and actions dominate the scene. Interactions and relationships are ubiquitous. Materials, displays, and colours are everywhere. So it is not always easy to find the tasks amid this complex array, explaining in part why observers often overlook the task on the floor, especially novices who are likely to focus on personal attributes and behaviour.

Research on classroom tasks suggests that there is often congruence between predictable, routine tasks and the challenges teachers face in maintaining orderly classroom systems. As a result, challenging work that promotes deeper understanding and student independence is often rare in classrooms. Moreover, tasks that elicit student thinking and decision making are frequently proceduralised over time as students negotiate issues of ambiguity and risk that surround classroom tasks. Indeed, high stakes government accountability systems narrow curriculum precisely because they typically constrain the range of tasks that are perceived to be appropriate for classrooms.

The papers in this collection are a comprehensive and courageous attempt to take seriously the power of tasks in classrooms and to confront the issues that this perspective on teaching brings into focus. Overall, the authors share a common, but not necessarily uniform, framework for examining tasks and a commitment to use this framework to unravel systematically the issues and dilemmas that have been shown to be associated with task design and enactment.

The chapters have three important features. First, they bring a sociocultural perspective to understanding tasks and their consequences. Tasks can easily be seen primarily from a cognitive standpoint, which extracts schoolwork from the activity systems in which it occurs and minimizes the importance of resources, effort, purpose and culture in schooling. Students are not 'learners' in some disembodied, abstract sense, but agents in a complex task environment, interpreting goals and demands, appropriating resources, designing products, and negotiating accountability. The chapters in this collection acknowledge this complexity and employ powerful tools to help make it intelligible.

Second, the analyses are embedded in school subjects. As many contemporary scholars have emphasized, the subject matters. These papers demonstrate the importance of this view – there are subtle but crucial differences along several dimensions of tasks across fields of study.

Finally, there is an emphasis on both understanding and action. The collection is certainly a rich resource for exploring theoretical issues related to tasks. At the same time, concrete design and practice are always close at hand. The authors and their graduate students work closely with practicing teachers – many are practicing teachers themselves – to tackle the practical issues of tasks in the classroom and invent ways to construct task environments that systematically foster student independence, introduce students to strategies for becoming productive learners, and thereby enable students to accomplish challenging and significant work.

One issue that is frequently underscored in task studies is that of safety. True learning in any setting is often accompanied by perplexity, mistakes and setbacks. In many classrooms, however, these experiences are problematic rather than productive, in large part because the way accountability plays out increases the personal cost of confusion and mistakes. The problem is not simple. Eliminating accountability can make work in classrooms pointless except for those with high interest in the subject at hand. Students also expect credit for their efforts, which can mean that all work becomes part of the summative evaluation and, therefore, carries consequences. Creating classroom cultures in which students are challenged but also feel safe to explore tentative responses without undermining the integrity of the work system is not easily done. These authors are certainly aware of the complexity of this issue and offer some intriguing and tangible ways to think about and address it.

There is much to be learned from this team about task design and enactment, about classroom activity systems, about learning and development, about subject pedagogy and about realising curriculum potential. These factors are essential considerations in any attempt to understand and promote teaching quality.

Walter Doyle

# PART I
# The background

# 1
# INTRODUCTION
## Tasks, concepts and subject knowledge

*Ian Thompson*

Douglas Barnes (1976) prefaced his aptly titled book *From Communication to Curriculum* by pointing out that orthodox curriculum theory analyses curriculum process from the teacher's objectives rather than learners' understandings. Engaging students in learning about their subject is a central concern for all teachers and teacher educators. The issue of task design in secondary education, how teachers view and use the pedagogic potential of different tasks to engage pupils with knowledge in different subjects, is central to this endeavour. Subject task design relates to the ways teachers translate the curriculum into the tasks and activities that they ask their pupils to do in order to facilitate developmental or higher-level understanding of curriculum content. This involves identifying the goal or purpose of the task, the resources available in a given setting, and the forms of instruction and intervention that allow pupils to process the information as they negotiate the task activities.

The background to this book on task design is that for the past 25 years the curriculum in the UK, and subsequently teaching, has been dominated by the introduction and implementation of government national strategies. In the secondary school environment this has often led to teaching through narrow and restrictive versions of 'teaching objectives' and patterns of assessment that focus on product and external examinations rather than process and student development. This pattern of curriculum imposition is not unique to the UK of course and educators in many other settings and contexts will recognise the same pressures on teaching and learning. The danger is that pedagogic practices that promote students' learning and knowledge transformation through active participation can be largely shelved (or hidden) in favour of a passive form of knowledge acquisition through transmission assessed by recall of knowledge gleaned from others or the mastery of technical skills.

One of the aims of this book is to help re-professionalise teachers and question approaches to curriculum imposition. The emphasis is on enhancing students' learning, and prospective and experienced teachers' practice, through a focus on curriculum design, classroom subject knowledge, subject task design, classroom organisation, assessment, student engagement and questions of agency in the learning process. We aim to help to develop an understanding of task design as a pedagogic tool that will provide insights for teacher training and teacher development in enhancing subject understanding and student engagement.

The focus on task design stems from many years of conversation: in the Department of Education at the University of Oxford (OUDE); in our innovative internship initial teaching education (ITE) programme (Benton 1990: McIntyre 1997); in sessions of our Master's in Learning and Teaching course; and in talks with both prospective and practicing teachers. The Oxford Internship scheme was set up by OUDE in 1987 in collaborative partnership with the Oxfordshire Local Education Authority and its local secondary schools. The commitment to school-based and research led teacher training was underpinned by 'sustained critical dialogue between the different kinds of expertise which teachers and university lecturers could bring as equal partners to considerations of teaching expertise' (Hagger and McIntyre 2006: 15). The educational landscape may have changed, particularly in school governance and the role of local educational authorities, but the collaborative partnership between OUDE and Oxfordshire schools remains strong in both initial teacher education and in educational research.

## Subject knowledge and concept acquisition

Mercer (2000) identifies three methods that good teachers use when they teach well:

1. They use question-and-answer sequences not just to test knowledge, but also to guide the development of understanding.
2. They teach not just 'subject knowledge', but also procedures for solving problems and making sense of experience.
3. They treat learning as a 'social, communicative process'.

*(Mercer 2000: 160)*

In other words good teaching is as much to do with the processes of pupils' learning as it is to do with the outcomes of that teaching. The act of learning for the secondary school student takes place within a constructed classroom zone (Newman, Griffin, and Cole 1989): instruction and learning within this zone involves both mediated activity and the participants' cultural contexts and past histories. Pedagogy, in this definition of learning, has to attend to both the cognitive and affective processes involved in learners' development. Teachers, to borrow Vygotsky's metaphor, have to conduct the classroom environment whilst attending to the following questions regarding task design in the different motives and varied sub-practices of school subjects:

- What matters in my subject?

- How does task design relate to subject knowledge?
- What is meant by task demand?
- How do tasks/activities help students conceptualise?

Viv Ellis characterises subject knowledge 'as a form of expertise that exists amongst people who engage in the same kind of practice' (Ellis 2007: 167). Ellis rightly warns against a potential pitfall involved in using metaphors of subject knowledge or pedagogical content knowledge:

> The effect of such metaphors (intended or otherwise) is to distinguish between certain high-status kinds of knowledge that are fixed and universal (subjects or disciplines) and lower status forms of (albeit valued and valuable) 'professional' knowledge that depends on 'use-value' and context.
>
> *(Ellis 2007: 167)*

Pedagogy involves both knowledge about subject and knowledge about how to learn the subject. If the teacher or teacher educator as subject specialist is the all knowing master, then the apprentice could be viewed as being merely a spectator in their own learning. Learning is more complex and requires the learners' active involvement in the dialectical relationship of appropriation and internalisation. At the same time, it would be dangerous to ignore the importance of teachers' knowledge of their subject and the ways in which to teach what Schwab (1978) described as the substantive (key concepts) and syntactic (ways of knowing and representing) knowledge required in a particular subject. Egan argues that the task of teaching is to help learners to engage with the symbolic representations of knowledge that remain hidden without the acquisition by learners of the cultural and social tools needed to translate them:

> The educational task, then, involves the resuscitation of knowledge from its suspended animation in symbolic codes. The task is to convert, reanimate, transmute the symbolic codes into living human knowledge in students' minds.
>
> *(Egan 2005: 95)*

Designing classroom tasks to enable learning requires the teacher to attend to both the design of the learning environment and to conceptual design (see Derry 2013). Vygotsky (1998) and his colleague Shif extended Vygotsky's (1988) theories of scientific and spontaneous concept development to the field of education. Vygotsky argued that scientific concepts have their origins in the structured academic activity of classroom instruction. Schools introduce scientific, logically defined concepts to students. Spontaneous concepts, on the other hand, emerge from the student's own reflections of everyday experience. The relationship between the two types of concept formation is dialectical: spontaneous concepts develop upwards towards greater abstractness just as scientific concepts develop downwards towards greater concreteness. Only when both concepts merge do students develop mature understanding.

Barnes (1976) argues that: 'Many of the tasks set in schools do not make it easy for pupils to utilize their everyday knowledge' (Barnes 1976: 29). Barnes describes everyday knowledge as 'action knowledge' as opposed to 'school knowledge' rather than spontaneous or scientific knowledge but the interrelation between the two forms of knowledge is the same. In setting the activities for classroom tasks, teachers need to attend to the following questions:

- How are students' everyday understandings used in the learning?
- What part does talk and language play and what is the role of the teacher in relation to this classroom talk?
- What areas of substantive and syntactic knowledge are learners engaged with?
- What kinds of support are built into different activities in the task sequence?
- What are the different support demands on the teacher, peers, or other adults?
- What are the different assessment demands?
- Do the activities allow opportunities for formative assessment so that support can be adjusted?
- Does the assessment of outcome allow assessment of the teaching objective?

## Classroom task design

One of the first questions for teachers to ask when designing a classroom task is: what is the educational function of the task and how should its design maximise the learning potential? Alexander (2000) makes the following distinction between 'task' and 'activity'.

> The 'task' dimension of a learning assignment is concerned with cognitive demand, ways of knowing and kinds of learning while 'activity' connotes the ways these are packaged for teaching purposes.
>
> *(Alexander 2000: 535)*

Task design involves both elements of teachers' understanding task demand and a focus on the design of the activities and classroom organisation in which the task demands are played out. Vygotsky's followers Davydov (1990) and Elkonin (1999) used the phrase 'learning activity' to describe the design of activities that address the development of students' grasp and use of higher order theoretical concepts. The students in this sort of classroom are active agents in their own learning through social collaboration with their teacher and peers. It is in this same context that Vygotsky described the teacher as the conductor of the social environment: both integral to the activity but reliant on social interaction for the symphony to be played.

Doyle and Carter (1984), building on Doyle's (1979) earlier conceptual framework of task analysis for integrating the academic and managerial aspects of classroom activity, argue that an academic (school) task has three elements: (1) a goal or product; (2) a set of resources or 'givens' available in the situation; and (3) a set of operations that can be applied to the resources to reach the goal or generate the product. Doyle (1983: 162) wrote, 'task is more than just content. It also includes the situation in which content is embedded'. Doyle goes on to argue that task accomplishment has two consequences:

> First, a person will acquire information – facts, concepts, principles, solutions – involved in the particular task that is accomplished. Second, a person will practice operations – memorising, classifying, inferring, analysing – used to obtain or produce the information demanded by the task.
> *(Doyle 1983: 162)*

It is important to add that the situation in which these operations take place is a social one – the classroom environment. Shavelson and Stern (1981) argue that task design should consider the following:

- content – the subject matter to be taught
- materials – the things that learners can observe/manipulate
- activities – the things the learners and teacher will be doing in the lesson
- goals – the teacher's general aim for the task (these are more general and vague than objectives)
- students – their abilities, needs and interests are important
- social community – the class as a whole and its sense of 'groupness'

*(Shavelson and Stern 1981: 478)*

The question remains: does the design of linked tasks clearly highlight what is to be learnt – both substantive and syntactic knowledge? In considering what is to be learnt, we need now to consider how that learning is supported by task design.

## Designing contingent support for concept development

One of Vygotsky's (1998) key theoretical points is that we learn through mediated activity. As Wertsch states of Vygotsky:

> In his view a hallmark of human consciousness is that it is associated with the use of tools, especially 'psychological tools' or 'signs.' Instead of acting in a direct, unmediated way in the social and physical world, our contact with the world is indirect or mediated by signs.
> *(Wertsch 2007:178)*

But our contact with the world is also mediated through our interaction with more 'expert' others: more expert in their use of socially, culturally, and historically acquired and developed psychological tools. From the work of Wood, Bruner and

Ross (1976), the concept of 'scaffolding' developed as a metaphor to describe the wide range of strategies such as modelling, suggestion or structuring by which an adult or more expert peer could help an emergent learner. The concept of assisted learning through scaffolding has been extensively discussed (e.g. Langer and Applebee, 1986; Tharp and Gallimore 1988) in attempts to identify the type and nature of assistance that may usefully be provided through scaffolding.

However, scaffolding as a concept has been criticised by Vygotskian and other sociocultural researchers as a potentially reductive way of viewing learning as being merely the supported transference of knowledge from teacher to learner rather than a collaborative act of learning between teacher and pupil. Newman, Griffin and Cole (1989) argue that the scaffold metaphor suggests a 'unilateral action' by the teacher rather than 'the notion of a social distribution of the task' in the zone of proximal development (ZPD) (Newman, Griffin and Cole 1989: 153). There is division of labour within the task, but the 'task – in the sense of the whole task as negotiated between the teacher and child – remains the same' (ibid). Some Vygotskian theorists (for example Newman and Holzman 1993; Valsiner and Van der Veer 2000) position the ZPD as a symbolic space for emergent interaction and communication. Nevertheless, both Chaiklin (2003) and Edwards (this volume) go back to Vygotsky's own writings in order to warn against the simplification of regarding the ZPD as simply a property of the child alone or a metaphoric space for learning. Rather, the ZPD is an indication of students' emerging psychological functions that can be the basis for useful pedagogic interventions that focus on leading development. Assisted performance needs to be seen as one of the strategies within task design rather than the whole point of teaching.

Harry Daniels (2007) suggests an inherent danger in the lack of theoretical clarity in the use of the term 'scaffolding' that can render the term meaningless in the context of teaching. Daniels identifies four essential task design features for assisted support in the context of mediated and reciprocal learning:

1  The recruitment by an adult of a child's involvement in a meaningful and culturally desirable activity beyond the child's current understanding or control.
2  The 'titration' of the assistance provided using a process of 'online diagnosis' of the learner's understanding and skill level and the estimation of the amount of support required.
3  The support is not a uniform prescription – it may vary in mode (e.g. physical gesture, verbal prompt, extensive dialogue) as well as in amount.
4  The support provided is gradually withdrawn as control over the task is transferred to the learner.

*(Daniels 2007: 323)*

It is interesting that Daniels uses the scientific term 'titration' for assistance suggesting that the assistance given needs to transform the learner's conceptual development. Assisted performance should not be seen as a prop to hold up current development but as one of the mediational tools through which students develop their ability to engage with tasks at more complex levels. As Edwards (2010) argues:

> Resourceful teaching for resourceful learning is therefore more than curriculum delivery and teaching for successful test performance. It involves guiding the agency of the learner to actions that strengthen their understanding of tasks and their impact on them. That in turn means emphasising decoding alongside encoding so that the complexity of tasks is revealed and the potential for artefacts and ideas is recognised.
> *(Edwards 2010: 73)*

## An overview of the chapters

The chapters in this book take different perspectives on task design although all share a concern with the social and cultural aspects of learning. Most of the authors work in initial teacher education (ITE) either at the University of Oxford or in the USA. Chapter 2 has a strong theoretical basis and explains some of the key concepts to be drawn on in the chapters that follow. Chapter 3, written by a former Qualifications and Curriculum Authority (QCA) advisor, addresses the politics of a crisis in curriculum design. Chapters 4–10 are subject-based chapters from each of our curriculum areas on our ITE courses at OUDE. However, these subject chapters are not written exclusively for subject experts as they are part of the general argument about curriculum and classroom task design, student learning, subject knowledge, and classroom engagement. There is much to learn from the different sub-practices and varied motives for task design of other subjects. The final chapter presents a model for conceptual unit design.

In Chapter 2 Anne Edwards poses the questions: what kinds of learners do we need for what kind of society and what kinds of teachers do we need to help develop them? Her argument is that the learning processes that underpin the move from partial understanding to confident use of ideas involve careful task design. It will be argued that task design not only includes enabling a grasp of key ideas and of ways of thinking and acting in a knowledge domain; but also sustaining student engagement and self-regulation or metacognitive awareness. From a Vygotskian theoretical perspective she introduces a quadrant model of task design as a heuristic device that enables teachers to focus on the Vygotskian emphasis on internalisation and externalisation alongside the demands of mastery of a subject.

In Chapter 3 Mark Chater argues that task design and curriculum design are political issues. The chapter critically examines the discourses and structures that thread between classroom learning and national curriculum policy. Using the English educational system as a case study and a warning, the chapter shows how neo-liberal policy approaches have given contradictory messages to a national system by combining a strategy of marketization and centralisation with a discourse of collaboration and autonomy.

In Chapter 4 Gabriel Stylianides and Anne Watson describe their work with prospective secondary mathematics teachers in which they encourage an interplay between mathematical and pedagogical ideas. Task design and implementation is at the core of their approach to this issue. Stylianides and Watson illustrate the role of tasks in promoting the interplay between mathematics and pedagogy with two examples of task sequences from their work with prospective teachers. They argue that helping these students to explore connections between mathematics and pedagogy facilitates the development of a deeper understanding of the complexities of mathematics teaching.

In Chapter 5 Roger Firth explores task design that takes into account the epistemic nature of disciplinary knowledge in geography. The chapter explores ways in which the epistemic can be brought more explicitly into view and made an object of consideration through instructional planning. To set the scene Firth discusses the limitations of current constructivist conceptions of geography pedagogy (teaching, learning and assessment) before considering an approach to task design that is not only concerned with the learner, the learning process and the subject content (what is known by geography) but also how the discipline of geography has come to arrive at such knowledge. It emphasises the need for a more disciplinary, constrained approach to subject pedagogy.

In Chapter 6 Ian Thompson addresses the question, how do students acquire the conceptual understandings that allow them to engage with and act on the cultures of literate practices? The chapter argues that task design in the English classroom can often focus on the teacher's objectives for task completion produced under the pressure of teaching to examinations rather than the developmental demand for learners. Conceptual learning in the English classroom involves a task design focus on both the theories and practices of communicative activity. The challenge for English teachers and teacher educators lies in designing demanding classroom communicative tasks that create the conditions for learning to occur through social and cultural interaction. This challenge is addressed with two examples of collaborative learning tasks for writing and reading.

In Chapter 7 Ann Childs and Jane McNicholl focus upon task design in relation to explaining concepts in science and the kinds of tasks which might be used in such science explanations. The chapter begins by looking at an important body of literature in science education on pedagogical content knowledge (PCK) to look in detail at the knowledge teachers have to design appropriate tasks to facilitate pupil learning of important concepts in science. The chapter then examines the process of practical theorising in the contexts of an initial teacher education programme through which prospective science teachers develop their knowledge and understanding about how to explain science to learners and to build a repertoire of tasks in order to do this.

In Chapter 8 Trevor Mutton and Robert Woore argue that the design of language learning tasks for the foreign language classroom must draw on knowledge from a wide range of sources. The chapter develops the ideas that language learning differs from the learning which takes place in some other subjects in important respects and that the knowledge sources that inform task design should include an understanding of how languages are learnt. Designing effective tasks for the languages classroom is viewed as an intellectual exercise rather than imitating experienced practitioners or implementing pre-existing tasks. Beginning teachers need opportunities to engage with the complexities of task design for language learning.

In Chapter 9 Jason Todd argues that prospective history teachers need to draw knowledge from different quarters in order to design tasks in the classroom. This includes knowledge about history as a discipline, knowledge about how pupils learn, and knowledge about specific forms of history subject pedagogy. Todd argues that unhelpful binaries, such as the debate between knowledge that is contingent and knowledge that is evidence-based, can distract teachers from a central focus on the importance of the context of children's learning both within and outside of school and of the disciplinary tradition with history. This chapter explores how the concept of phronesis might help reconcile this dualism and help prospective teachers negotiate the complex processes involved in task design in the history classroom.

In Chapter 10 Nigel Fancourt makes the point that in many countries religious education has moved from a mono-religious focus to the study of several world religions. Students are asked to understand different belief systems, such as Christianity or Buddhism, which may not be theirs, and with which they may disagree. This chapter explores an important distinction between insiders and outsiders that raises some challenges for task design in religious education. These challenges are examined using Vygotsky's distinction between generic and everyday concepts.

Finally, in Chapter 11 Peter Smagorinsky presents a case for prospective teachers learning the skill of designing instructional tasks through conceptual units. His structured process approach is founded in the idea that students learn well when actively engaged with things that interest them. In this chapter Smagorinsky exemplifies the long-term, process-oriented, workshop-based approach he has developed to serve the needs for prospective learners in learning the task of designing instructional tasks. The design of conceptual units typically includes the following: a rationale, goals, assessments, lessons, activities, discussions, texts, tools and compositions. Smagorinsky's argument for the instructional, task-based design of a learning structure and appropriate activities is based on almost 40 years of experience and thought as an English teacher, teacher educator and academic in the United States.

## References

Alexander, R. (2000) *Culture and Pedagogy: International comparisons in primary education*. Oxford: Blackwell.
Barnes, D. (1976) *From Communication to Curriculum*. Harmondsworth: Penguin.
Benton, P. (ed.) (1990) *The Oxford Internship Scheme*. London: Calouste Gulbenkian Foundation.

Candlin, C.N. (1987). Towards task-based learning. In C.N. Candlin & D. Murphy (eds) *Lancaster Practical Papers in English Language Education. Vol. 7. Language Learning Tasks.* Englewood Cliffs, NJ: Prentice Hall, 5–22.

Chaiklin, S. (2003) The zone of proximal development in Vygotsky's analyses of learning and instruction. In A Kozulin, B. Gindis, V. Ageyev and S. M. Miller (eds) *Vygotsky's Educational Theory in a Cultural Context.* Cambridge: Cambridge University Press.

Daniels, H. (2007) Pedagogy. In H. Daniels, M. Cole and J. Wertsch (eds) *The Cambridge Companion to Vygotsky.* New York: Cambridge University Press.

Davydov, V. V. (1990) *Types of Generalisation in Instruction.* Reston, VA: National Council of Teachers of Mathematics.

Derry, J. (2013) *Vygotsky Philosophy and Education.* London: Wiley Blackwell.

Doyle, W. (1979) Making managerial decisions in classrooms. In D. L. Duke (ed.) *Classroom Management: 78th yearbook of the National Society for the Study of Education, part 2.* Chicago: University of Chicago Press.

Doyle, W. (1983) Academic work. *Review of Educational Research,* 53: 159–99.

Doyle, W. and Carter, K. (1984) Academic tasks in classrooms. *Curriculum Inquiry,* 14: 129–49.

Edwards, A. (2010) Vygotsky, his legacy and teacher education. In V. Ellis, A. Edwards and P. Smagorinsky (eds) *Cultural-historical Perspectives on Teacher Education and Development.* Abingdon: Routledge.

Egan, K. (2005) *An Imaginative Approach to Teaching.* San Francisco: Jossey-Bass.

Elkonin, D. B. (1999) Towards the problem of stages in the mental development of children. *Journal of Russian and East European Psychology,* 37: 11–29.

Ellis, V. (2007) *Subject Knowledge and Teacher Education.* London: Continuum.

Hagger, H. and McIntyre, D. (2006) *Learning Teaching from Teachers: Realising the potential of school-based teacher education.* Maidenhead and New York: Open University Press.

Langer, J. A. and Applebee, A. N. (1986) Reading and writing instruction: toward a theory of teaching and learning. *Review of Research in Education,* 13: 171–94.

McIntyre, D. (1997) *Teacher Education in a New Context: The Oxford Internship Scheme.* London: Paul Chapman Publishing.

Mercer, N. (2000) *Words and Minds: How we use language to think together.* London: Routledge.

Newman, D., Griffin, P. and Cole, M. (1989) *The Construction Zones: Working for cognitive change in school.* Cambridge: Cambridge University Press.

Newman, F. and Holzman, D. (1993) *Lev Vygotsky: Revolutionary scientist.* London: Routledge.

Schwab, J. (1978) *Science, Curriculum and Liberal Education: Selected essays, Joseph Schwab* (eds I. Westbury and N. Wilkof). Chicago: University of Chicago Press.

Shavelson, R. J. and Stern, P. (1981) Research on teachers' pedagogical thoughts, judgements, decisions and behaviour. *Review of Educational Research,* 51: 455–98.

Tharp, R. and Gallimore, R. (1988) *Rousing Minds to Life.* Cambridge: Cambridge University Press.

Valsiner, J. and Van der Veer, R. (2000) *The Social Mind.* Cambridge: Cambridge University Press.

Vygotsky, L. S. (1988) *The Collected Work of L S Vygotsky. Vol. 1.* New York: Plenum Press.

Vygotsky, L. S. (1998) *The Collected Work of L. S. Vygotsky. Vol. 5 Child Psychology.* New York: Plenum Press.

Wertsch, J. V. (2007) Mediation. In H. Daniels, M. Cole and J. Wertsch (eds) *The Cambridge Companion to Vygotsky.* New York: Cambridge University Press.

Wood, D., Bruner, J. and Ross, G. (1976) The role of tutoring in problem-solving. *Journal of Child Psychology and Psychiatry and Allied Disciplines,* 17: 89–100.

# 2
# DESIGNING TASKS WHICH ENGAGE LEARNERS WITH KNOWLEDGE

*Anne Edwards*

## Introduction

Never take seriously anyone who suggests that teaching is simply a matter of knowing the subject you teach. Of course subject knowledge and a love of the subject are important when teaching; but enabling learning requires far more from the teacher. In brief, it involves engaging students as learners, whatever their age, who enjoy working in and on the subject. These topics: engaging students as learners and working in an on the subject are the major themes in this chapter. I shall keep a dual focus on learners and the knowledge and knowledge practices into which they are inducted by teachers. The connections between these parallel focuses will be made by examining the design of learning activities and the actions taken by teachers in these activities in order to enable student learning.

A key question for an education system has to be: what kinds of learners will be needed to create the kind of society we would like to have? Policy communities will provide a variety of answers; but teachers, in state-funded systems at least, are pretty consistent in their responses. Teachers come into teaching to open up pupils' life chances and have a positive influence on how children and young people can approach the opportunities available to them. Theirs is a social inclusion argument, attempting to ensure that all pupils are helped to engage with knowledge that is culturally powerful and are able to contribute to society in productive ways.

As explanations of how learning occurs in educational settings have become more robust we are increasingly able to sustain a parallel focus on learners and what is to be learnt and to translate that into guidelines for teaching. You will note the loose term 'guidelines'. Successful teaching can never be a prescriptive and predetermined delivery of a curriculum. Instead it involves sensitive reciprocity, in which the teacher attempts to understand the learner's perspective on a classroom task: both their current grasp of the demands of the task and their motives for engaging with it. Using those insights the teacher draws on her knowledge of the subject to highlight what the child needs to know and to calibrate her engagement with it.

Bruner once wrote, with what seems a sense of exasperation, about the need for teachers to connect their understandings of child development with emphases on knowledge and instruction.

> The heart of the educational process consists of providing aides and dialogues for translating experience into more powerful systems of notation and ordering. And it is for this reason that I think a theory of development must be linked to both a theory of knowledge and to a theory of instruction, or be doomed to triviality.
>
> *(Bruner 1966: 21)*

This was written at a time when education had discovered Piagetian developmental theory, which was never meant to be a pedagogical theory, hence his emphases in this extract. Almost 50 years later, the extract offers a succinct introduction to the lines to be pursued in this chapter. It states firmly that teachers have an important and complex role to play in engaging learners with the tools that matter in a culture. So let's begin by identifying, quite broadly, what I mean by cultural tools in the context of learning in school.

## What is to be learnt?

Academic success is usually evidence of the mastery of two aspects of learning. First is the grasp of an area of knowledge and second is the capacity to be in control of one's own learning. Let's start with the cultural tools that comprise an area of knowledge. The Chicago-based science educator and doctoral supervisor of Lee Shulman, Joseph Schwab, made the useful distinction between what he termed the substantive knowledge and syntactic knowledge that constitute what is sometimes called domain specific knowledge such as biology or physics (Schwab 1978). To summarise Schwab's argument, the former is made up of the concepts and their relation to each other in the way which matches how the subject is currently commonly understood; while the latter is best seen as the ways of thinking and representing that are expected of experts in the subject.

We can then characterise substantive knowledge as the key concepts in a subject and how they are linked to the system of meanings that comprise the subject. In history key concepts would include sovereignty, nationhood and empire: what Bruner suggested were the concepts without which you couldn't operate in a subject (Bruner 1960). Syntactic knowledge, again in history, may include inference, causality and evidence-based argument. This joint emphasis on concepts and ways of demonstrating the validity of one's arguments runs across all the subjects in school curricula. Of course content and form are intertwined. Lack of attention to syntactic knowledge in, for example, chemistry classes can lead to difficulties for learners when trying to represent scientific knowledge and construct their own understandings of it.

The second aspect of learning to be mastered, when aiming at academic success, is being an effective learner. Learning to learn is sometimes called metacognition, the process of understanding one's own understandings in order to be able to regulate one's actions as a learner; but is perhaps more usefully thought of in terms of learning strategies. One set of learning strategies which were firmly based in the early work of Flavell on metacognition, were put together and trialled with teachers by Nisbet and Shucksmith (Nisbet and Shucksmith 1986).

In summary these strategies are:

- asking questions: defining hypotheses, relating to previous work etc.
- planning: deciding on tactics and timetables, identifying what materials and skills are needed
- monitoring: making continuous attempts to match progress to initial questions or purposes
- checking: assessing preliminary results and performance
- revising; in the light of evidence
- self-testing final assessment of results and performance.

Over the last 30 years I have worked with teachers in primary and secondary schools who have helped their students to use these strategies in subjects ranging from primary school science to sixth form religious education and have observed how learning has flourished when students recognise how to use them to shape their own pathways through classroom tasks.

More latterly this approach has been strengthened by the idea of split-screen thinking. This simple, but powerful, idea has been developed by Claxton (Claxton 2007). He uses the metaphor to emphasise the need to keep a dual focus on the curriculum and on developing students' dispositions as learners. For him 'disposition' is an ability that one may be disposed to make use of. This definition takes us straight to the kinds of knowledge practices, such as student questioning, that are permitted in classrooms and the extent to which the learner's agency or sense of purpose can be exercised. Claxton explains the split-screen as follows.

> On one 'screen' inside their heads teachers are thinking about how to help students grasp the content. On the other, at the same time, they are thinking about how to help students develop their learning capacity.
> *(Claxton 2007: 125)*

Several of the teachers I have worked with in the last few years have not only used split-screen thinking themselves, but have helped their students to use the technique. For example, in one school, students discussed the learning strategies distilled by Nisbet and Shucksmith and teased out what the strategies meant for their own work in geography. They then kept reflective diaries about how they worked with the strategies and periodically discussed their success in using them, also pointing to how the routines and expectations of the school sometimes frustrated their efforts. They all claimed to feel more in control as learners, and better able to tackle the memorising and procedural aspects of classroom tasks as well as more open-ended problem-solving activities.

These findings are not surprising. Zimmerman, for example, has long argued that self-regulation in academic work of this kind can be taught and is beneficial (Zimmerman 2002). In a comprehensive overview of research on self-regulated learners (Zimmerman 2008) he was able to point to strong evidence of links between receiving guidance in self-regulation in school work and motivation for that work as well as improved learning outcomes.

Approaches to self-regulation all have their roots in metacognition research and involve strategies such as goal setting and self-monitoring. The over-arching definition of self-regulated learning that Zimmerman offers makes it clear that one cannot reasonably expect learning to occur without it: '[It is] the degree to which students are metacognitively, motivationally, and behaviorally active participants in their own learning processes.' (Zimmerman 2008: 167 ).

Although Zimmerman is at pains to explain that a self-regulating learner is also a social learner and not isolated from feedback from others, there is, in this strand of research, perhaps an overly strong emphasis on skilling up the learners and their teachers and perhaps too little on what kind of learning environment allows both learners to increase their agentic control over their own actions and learners and teachers to encourage this.

Claxton appears to share similar concerns and as a way forward suggests that teachers also need to attend more broadly to the knowledge practices or 'epistemic culture' they offer students. These cultures or environments may be: prohibiting, affording, inviting or potentiating. Arguing that even inviting students to operate as engaged learners is not enough, the practices of the classroom should simply expect students to learn through being challenged in 'potentiating' environments that stretch the learner.

> Only the fourth kind of epistemic culture, potentiating milieux, makes the exercise of learning muscles both appealing and challenging. In a potentiating environment, there are plenty of hard, interesting things to do, and it is accepted as normal that everyone regularly gets confused, frustrated and stuck.
>
> *(Claxton 2007: 125)*

As we shall see the themes of task demand and the ambiguity and risk involved in learning, together with ways of helping students manage these challenges and learn will weave their way through this chapter.

## The zone of proximal development in Vygotsky's work

My parallel focus, on what is to be learnt and how it is to be learnt, connects strongly with the way Vygotsky described how children learn to use powerful concepts as they engage with and act on the world. Helping learners to master and use the best knowledge available was central to Vygotsky's educational psychology (Vygotsky 1997). But he did not separate the acquisition and use of what he called scientific or publicly recognised concepts from changes in what he called higher mental functioning, such as the use of memory, perception and so on.

The zone of proximal development (ZPD) is probably the construct most widely associated with Vygotsky, but all too often, as Chaiklin has argued (Chaiklin 2003) the term is used to describe a zone of learning, with little or no attention to the developments in mental functioning that may also occur. In 2003 Chaiklin revisited the problem outlined by Bruner in 1966; but this time the intention was to bring development back into the picture after decades of a focus on concepts and curricula.

> If instruction is not viewed as an end in itself, then a theory about the relationship between specific subject-matter instruction and its consequences for psychological development is also needed. This last problem was the main tension against which Vygotsky developed his well-known concept of 'zone of proximal development', where the zone was meant to focus attention on the relation between instruction and development, while being relevant to many of these other problems.
> 
> *(Chaiklin 2003: 39)*

Chaiklin is arguing that, because the ZPD has too readily been interpreted as a zone of proximal learning, it has been used to pursue a relatively narrow focus on helping children move from the limitations of everyday understandings to acquiring and using more powerful concepts. Of course this deployment of the ZPD chimes perfectly with emphases, over the last few decades at least, on children's high performance on international tests of their subject matter knowledge.

Chaiklin's point is that this use of the ZPD as a concept to guide teaching is too limited and has resulted from an over-simplification of Vygotsky's theory of development. Chaiklin goes on to remind us of Vygotsky's thesis that there is a structural inter-relationship between higher mental functions such as perception and memory and how one uses and refines concepts when engaging with the world. Chaiklin's argument is a detailed one and worth pursuing, not least because it calls attention to learners as thinkers who use the best resources available to them to organise their encounters with the material world.

Chaiklin's challenge has yet to be addressed overtly in education, perhaps because the Vygotskian theory of development Chaiklin describes is based on the idea of stages of childhood, which on first reading links it too closely with Piaget's work; and perhaps because the learning zone notion of the ZPD accords too strongly with the priorities of an educational world preoccupied with children's performance against curricular targets.

A dual emphasis on learning strategies and self-regulation, alongside the substantive and syntactic knowledge of curricula, does not coincide directly with Vygotsky's interest in the unity of personal mental processes and publicly valued knowledge; but his concerns do direct our attention to students' development as learners within particular material conditions. Chaiklin describes Vygotsky's view of the unity between the personal and the public in the following way.

> [V]ygotsky [1982]... realize(s) his goal of 'understanding development as a process that is characterized by a unity of material and mental *aspects, a unity of the social and the personal during the child's ascent up the stages of* development' (p. 190). These two unities (material/mental and social/personal) are alternative ways of expressing the same idea, and they are both unities because the child's psychological structure (i.e., the mental, the personal) is always reflecting a relation to the social and material.
>
> *(Chaiklin 2003: 46–7)*

The swings between an overemphasis on the developing child, criticised by Bruner, and an overemphasis on curriculum delivery, implicitly criticised by Chaiklin, have bedevilled systems of schooling ever since these systems have become matters of policy concern. The argument in this chapter is that the dialectic nature of the relationship between learners' mental processing and the knowledge they encounter needs to be recognised, so that processes of learning and the various roles to be taken by teachers can be understood. The argument I shall make will owe a great deal to Vygotsky, but will be grounded in the day–to-day life of planning lessons and supporting students as they engage with tasks in them and learn.

## My life is measured out in classroom tasks

With apologies to T. S. Eliot and J.A. Prufrock, this statement would probably be true for both teachers and students. Doyle's seminal research programme in US classrooms in the 1970s and 80s showed us beyond doubt that teachers used classroom tasks to place order on the school day. Tasks, unsurprisingly, were therefore sites of negotiation between teachers and students, where students frequently aimed at bidding down the demands in tasks and teachers often acquiesced in order to prevent ruptures in their careful orchestration of pupils and tasks over the school day (Doyle 1983, 1986).

Doyle has explained the features of tasks that his research examined in a way that reflects Schwab's substantive and syntactic distinction, and also points towards Vygotsky's concern with the development of higher mental functions such as memory.

> This task perspective can be summarized in two basic propositions: (1) Students' academic work in school is defined by the academic tasks that are embedded in the content they encounter on a daily basis. Tasks regulate the

> selection of information and the choice of strategies for processing that information. Thus, 'changing a subject's [i.e. person's] task changes the kind of event the subject experiences' (Jenkins 1977: 425). (2) Students will learn what a task leads them to do, that is, they will acquire information and operations that are necessary to accomplish the tasks they encounter (see Frase 1972, 1975). In other words, accomplishing a task has two consequences. First, a person will acquire information – facts, concepts, principles, solutions – involved in the particular task that is accomplished. Second, a person will practice operations – memorising, classifying, inferring, analysing – used to obtain or produce the information demanded by the task.
> *(Doyle 1983: 162)*

Doyle's arguments in this programme of classroom studies were of course dealing with the debates of the day. For example, one point that he pursued quite strongly was that direct instruction which focuses only on the skills needed to accomplish a task will not have any long-term effect unless learners are also helped to fit what they learn in that task into wider systems of inference and are able to recognise the relevance of those skills for other tasks.

> Available research suggests that direct instruction that concentrates on specific operations for accomplishing a task will produce immediate effects, but it is not likely to engender the higher level knowledge structures or strategies required for the flexible use of these operations.
> *(Doyle 1983: 175)*

According to this argument, indirect instruction needs to be added to the teacher's tool box. It will then, Doyle suggests, promote understanding. It also needs to be both open-ended and embedded within a knowledge domain. He, in addition, emphasises that learners' prior knowledge is therefore crucial for these more open-ended yet demanding tasks; and, echoing Vygotsky, he points to the need for learners to use as well as acquire knowledge if understanding is to be achieved.

Achieving new understanding involves a reorganisation of our mental schema and our relationships with the world. Its acquisition takes the learner through moments of ambiguity and uncertainty and there is always the risk of getting it wrong. Again Doyle's analyses of classroom tasks help us to recognise this aspect of task demand. By placing different types of tasks on the orthogonal dimensions of 'ambiguity' and 'risk' he shows us that: while, for example, tasks which call for opinions might be high on ambiguity but low on risk, those which call for understanding are high on both dimensions (Doyle 1983). When high ambiguity /high risk tasks are embedded within a classroom task system which, as Doyle observes, is driven by accountability, it is little wonder that Doyle and his team were struck by the efforts that students made to negotiate and reduce task demand.

The implications for teaching for understanding from Doyle's work are considerable. Teaching repertoires should include direct instruction and the development of memory as well as domain structured open-ended tasks where instruction is indirect and knowledge is used; attention needs to be paid to how the accountability system shapes the tasks, to ensure at least some high risk high ambiguity activities in a learning sequence; and, because tasks do bring order to the school day, they are sites of negotiation, where the demands of learning for understanding may be sacrificed to the need to sustain that order.

I have certainly gained a great deal from reading this work, as have the teachers who have been Master's students and Action Research Fellows with me over the decades. However, as I have already indicated, my more recent work with colleagues in schools has pointed to the importance of emphasising a little more strongly the importance of pupil agency and self-regulation as a way of managing risk without reducing the cognitive demand in tasks that aim at developing understanding.

Hedegaard, also working with Vygotskian ideas, has recently argued that we should recognise the dialectic between what the learner brings to a potential learning opportunity and the demands they encounter in that opportunity. She proposes that, because this dialectic is central to learning, we need to ensure that we give as much attention to the demands as we do to the motives of the learners (Hedegaard 2012). The arguments presented so far in this chapter suggest that it would be wise to consider how these demands include promoting the development of the capacity to manage one's self as a learner as well as progress within a curriculum area.

Of course we need to calibrate these demands so that learners are not overwhelmed. We want them to be able to propel themselves forward, becoming increasingly competent users of the substantive and syntactic knowledge that is being offered them. Student agency is, I suggest, key to their engagement as learners and we need to orchestrate tasks to enable the growth of that agency as they move through sequences of tasks which allow them to use the powerful concepts they encounter in the curriculum. Vygotsky's view, that learning involves not simply internalisation, but also externalisation, is key to this focus on student agency.

This calibration of demand and agency calls for a view of lesson planning which is akin to creating an architecture for student learning which might warrant Claxton's 'potentiating' label. Teaching then becomes the orchestration of students' action in classroom activities within a potentiating architecture, through careful responses aimed at supporting both engagement with the knowledge in use and the development of students as learners. Let us therefore turn to some detail of the architecture and then examine the kinds of teaching responses that can help students develop as learners within it.

## An architecture to support student learning

Over the last 25 years I have used a very basic model of task sequencing as a starting point for discussing how learners are supported in their increasingly agentic engagement with the substantive and syntactic knowledge that is carried in the curriculum, including engagement with some tasks that are high in ambiguity and risk and lead to understanding. The model is based on Vygotskian notions of learning. It originates in my reworking of a Vygotskian framework for understanding the development of identity offered by Harré (Harré 1983); which I first used in analysis of student teachers' learning in teacher education partnerships between universities and schools (Edwards 1995).

Commonly referred to as the quadrant model by the teachers who have worked with it, it is shown in outline in Figure 2.1. Quadrants 1 and 4 are where knowledge is displayed: by the teacher or more expert learners in quadrant 1 as they model and instruct; and by the students in quadrant 4 when they display their knowledge in some form of summative assessment. Poor teaching is frequently characterised as a direct move from 1 to 4 (see for example Douglas Barnes' stunning critique of a similar mode of teaching – Barnes 1976). Figure 2.1 is an attempt to point to the advantages of taking time to enable learners to both acquire and use – internalise and externalise – the substantive and syntactic knowledge of the subject-based curriculum; while also developing higher order thinking and taking control over their own learning through tasks given in quadrants 2 and 3.

Quadrant 2 is where learners begin to work in highly structured ways with the domain knowledge, taking some control over it and exploring what they can do with it. In quadrant 3 that knowledge becomes a resource they can deploy and test in problem-solving activities and in doing so students begin to grasp its potential and limitations and more firmly connect it to a readjusted knowledge schema and the system of inferences that go with it.

The model is simply a potential way of structuring the events that together may promote learning and develop learners. In some cases it may make sense to start a sequence of activities with some tasks in quadrant 3 rather than quadrant 1; and one frequently moves back from 3 to 2 to deal with misconceptions that arise in 3. In brief, it is a heuristic that points to the need for us to see learning as the learners' increasing control over the subject matter while also developing as learners; and to help teachers identify: the different kinds of task demand required in each quadrant, how their roles as teachers change in each quadrant and how formative assessment can help guide students' engagement.

| 4. Demonstration of grasp of key concepts and ways of enquiring | 1. Introduction of key concepts and modelling of ways of engaging with key concepts |
| --- | --- |
| 3. More open tasks which enable learners to apply key concepts and ways of enquiring | 2. Tightly structured tasks which demand engagement with key concepts and ways of enquiring |

**Figure 2.1** A model of task sequencing to promote learning

Let us work through the sequence from quadrant 1 to begin to identify what teachers and learners do in each and in particular how split-screen thinking helps. The introduction of key concepts and ways of knowing in quadrant 1 will of course include revisiting what is already known to build what Edwards (D) and Mercer have called 'common knowledge' (Edwards and Mercer 1987) as a platform for introducing what next needs to be known. Each teacher will have a preferred way of engaging the curiosity of learners at this stage in the sequence, but the intention is almost always to help the learner recognise a gap in their knowledge that can be filled in a particular way: to identify a learning need. Some teachers like to focus on developing a strong understanding of the inadequacy of previous knowledge, for example, how measuring a perimeter does not lead immediately to understanding area. But frequently this is the point when the teacher models how the gap might be addressed. We should not underestimate the importance of imitation in learning. Vygotsky certainly didn't, seeing it as part of the process of learning from others (Vygotsky 1998), a process which emphasised that instruction needs to be in advance of development (Vygotsky 1978). Activity in quadrant 1 therefore frequently involves a conversation between the teacher and the whole class, in part to demonstrate the use of the substantive and syntactic knowledge; in part to diagnose how the learners are interpreting the new knowledge; and in part to induct the learners into using the language and other forms of representation in which the knowledge is carried. This should not be seen as teacher performance and it is not simply curriculum delivery. It is an exemplification of what Bruner called the 'courteous conversation' (Bruner 1996) that leads learners towards mastery of the knowledge that matters in a subject.

The move to quadrant 2 activities ideally occurs when the teacher has made the assessment that the learners have started to make connections between what they already knew and what is being introduced. Tasks in this quadrant may be individual, paired or group, or a mixture of these, and are highly structured so that learners have little leeway in how they undertake them. The intention is that they work with the substantive and syntactic knowledge they met in the first quadrant. At the same time the tasks also make demands on them as thinkers. The students should be expected to organise how they will respond to the task demands: how they will scope the tasks, identify how long they will take, what resources they will need when and so on. The teacher is very active at this stage in the sequence. Her role is to give formative feedback on both the use of knowledge and the organisation of learning, carrying out assessment that is 'for' learning and not 'of' learning. The final formative assessment of tasks at this stage in the sequence may be best done by the students themselves, through self-assessments against criteria which attend to both the grasp of knowledge revealed and the strategies employed.

Fairly recently in England teachers received strong guidance on what was called the three part lesson: introduction, activity and plenary. For many of the teachers I was working with at the time, quadrants 1, 2, and 4 seemed to match with the best examples of this three stage process. It was certainly felt to be an improvement on the 1 direct to 4 sequence. However, over time its limitations in relation to promoting understanding became clear and I found a renewed interest in the demands of quadrant 3.

Quadrant 3 is perhaps the most challenging stage in the sequence for both learners and teachers. It is the point when learners move into open-ended problem-solving activities, confronting the twin terrors of ambiguity and risk, as they take control of the knowledge they have just begun to grasp and use it to solve problems or tackle complex tasks. The role of the teacher changes yet again. In this stage most of the effort goes into planning the task, identifying at least some of the resources that might be used to ensure engagement with the focal knowledge and ensuring that the students are able to use the strategies that will help them pursue rather than retreat from the demands of the task. The teachers I have worked with have all found this the most personally transformative stage. They have given up completely their roles as curriculum deliverers and instead are positioned as knowledgeable resources who respond to students' questions, only intervening if learners are experiencing debilitating difficulty. Year after year I am told that activities in this quadrant have 'made me completely change how I think about teaching' or 'I have had to resposition myself as a teacher' or 'there is a lot of preparation, but actually you have more time to do some good one-to-one teaching'.

Just one example might help here. John and Joe (not their true names) were teachers of religious education in a relatively high performing city school and undertaking several cycles of action research together. Their students got good GCSE and 'A' level results, but John and Joe felt that the students were failing to get a deep conceptual understanding of key concepts and certainly could become more effective self-motivated, independent learners. They decided to use a Year 9 curriculum unit as the basis of their action research study developing and evaluating quadrant 3 activities.

They set their students big and demanding questions such as: can Buddhists, who follow ahimsa, fight in war? Is there any justification for the Hindu caste system? The students were able to choose the question to pursue over the next few weeks and there was a strong emphasis on self-regulation including a requirement that they made plans and regularly evaluated their progress against the plans and also they recognised the learning strategies they were using and evaluated how well they were doing so. John and Joe acted as learning resources alongside other sources, including the internet, and gave one-to-one support where it was needed. Some students thrived and enjoyed the new freedom; while some were so unused to this level of responsibility for their own learning that they struggled at times. Nonetheless the learning outcomes for the unit were higher than in previous years and John and Joe have since worked hard to convince colleagues of the value of this approach.

This kind of teaching does require high levels of teacher subject knowledge, and as John and Joe reflected, it is much easier if other classes in the school are run on similar lines: the transition to a way of working which emphasised student agency and control of themselves as learners was difficult for some pupils.

Quadrant 4 can be seen as the end of the cycle, where assessment shifts from being for learning, to more summative notions of assessing learning and giving grades for the display of new-found understandings. However, several of the teachers who have used this framework have also seen quadrant 4 as the jumping off point for a new cycle and the basis for teacher-led activities in quadrant 1 and not simply a final assessment point.

The model in Figure 2.1 is simply a heuristic to link a Vygotskian emphasis on internalisation and externalisation with the demands of mastery of a subject alongside the development of the mental functions that help students develop as learners. It is not a blueprint. For example, several years ago the PhD produced by Rosa Gunnarsdottir at the University of Leeds (2001) provided a rationale for a very successful curriculum innovation in Iceland, where students in both primary and secondary schools undertook creative problem-solving using the skills of design, craft and technology. According to Gunnarsdottir's analysis these students started in quadrant 3 with teachers responding with quadrant 1 and 2 interventions if they appeared to be needed. More recently Prabhat Rai's DPhil study of pedagogy in a Digantar School in rural Rajasthan has drawn implicitly on this model to show how knowledge from home and school comes into play in quadrants 2 and 3 (Rai 2014).

Another Oxford DPhil student, Jessica Chan, is using the four quadrants in her critical analysis of the use of group work in Hong Kong secondary schools. By holding the model shown in Figure 2.1 against her evidence of how group work is put into operation by four teachers in two schools, Chan is able to tease out the pedagogic contradictions and compromises that are being enacted as teachers try to apply responsive, student-centred group work in a climate of high stakes testing, where students and their parents have not been helped to recognise the pedagogic benefits of what I am calling here quadrant 2 and 3 experiences (Chan, work in progress).

Chan's findings take us back to Doyle's point about the extent to which an accountability system drives a task system. I have only begun to point to how the teacher's role and the use of assessment changes over the course of the sequence. Doyle reminds us that students need to be expected to accomplish tasks and to be assessed, otherwise they may not engage at all (Doyle 1983) and task accomplishment is built into quadrants 2, 3 and 4. I have, however, been suggesting that in quadrants 2 and 3 student sense-making is perhaps best steered and supported by on-going formative feedback that encourages the metacognitive aspects of learning as well as knowledge acquisition and use. I am also suggesting that if the criteria for both aspects are clear, students' agency is enhanced by their self-assessment of their achievements.

## The importance of safety

If teaching is difficult, so is learning. One big advantage of the model in Figure 2.1 is that quadrants 2 and 3, although challenging in different ways, are also relatively safe places, where mistakes can be made, misunderstandings revealed and risks taken. I have focused on the cognitive and metacognitive features of the sequence; but would like to move towards a conclusion by briefly pointing to the affective and more emotional aspects of learning and how the semi-private or formative stages in the model provide what one teacher recently described as places of safety.

Ellie and Enid (again not their true names) have, like John and Joe, been working with me as Action Research Fellows. Their research has involved the quadrants and split-screen thinking, but they have gone one step further. They became intrigued by how helping students be in control of their own learning led their students to discuss their fears about performance in dance and drama and about speaking a foreign language or completing a timed translation. Ellie and Enid began to listen more carefully than before to what the students were saying about the fears which were inhibiting their learning. The more Ellie and Enid adjusted their responses to encourage the students to articulate their worries about academic work and jointly find solutions that helped them overcome them, the more they became convinced that the metacognitive awareness they were promoting was helping them to respond more sensitively and therefore more effectively to their students.

They now consistently report that their use of language has changed to allow them to take seriously the affective aspects of a learner perspective; that student achievement is soaring as students now recognise how to use resources such as revision strategies to help them control what they had previously seen as beyond their control; that there is greater social cohesion in their classes as all students of every ability and background now reflectively self-evaluate what they do and consider their impact on others; that the students are self-organising to a large extent; and that teaching is therefore far less tiring than it has ever been.

These are all small changes, and each example I have given has indicated that there also needs to be a systemic response in schools, at the very least to make the transitions between lessons easier for students. But it is more than that. The students who have thrived with John, Joe, Ellie and Enid and in the research sites examined by Gunnarsdottir, Rai and Chan are students who could be leaving school with a strong sense of personal agency and an enthusiastic engagement with the knowledge practices which will propel them forward as learners. But certainly, Ellie and Enid and Chan report that quite frequently the ways that learners are positioned in schools frustrate students and teachers, perhaps making a concerted focus on creating potentiating environments a good investment.

## Concluding points

I started this chapter by posing the question, what kinds of learners do we need for what kind of society, and by analogy, what kinds of teachers do we need to nurture them? I have tried to answer these questions by suggesting that those of us involved in education should aim at producing learners who relish ambiguity and risk and can work with and on new knowledge. They can do this because they have mastered the tools of self-regulation which, in turn, dispose them towards scoping the demands in tasks and organising their responses to them. I have also attempted to sustain a dual focus on what is to be learnt and how children and young people develop as learners, emphasising that the ZPD should not simply be seen as a zone of learning in which new concepts are grasped.

I have at the same time argued that a focus on student self-regulation is not simply a matter of acquiring the skills to organise oneself; students also need to find themselves in learning environments that require them to do so. The arguments advanced here therefore suggest that teachers need to create this environment: through helping students identify learning needs; through modelling expertise in a domain; through being aware of the demands in the tasks they set; through the differentiated responses they give learners as they formatively assess them; through positioning students as agentically in control of their own learning; and through, at times, positioning themselves as resources to support that learning. Love of a subject certainly helps if these efforts to engage and support learners are to be accomplished, but it is certainly not enough.

## References

Barnes, D. (1976) *From Communication to Curriculum*. Harmondsworth: Penguin.
Bruner, J. (1960) *The Process of Education*. Cambridge, MA: Harvard University Press.
Bruner, J. (1966) *Towards a Theory of Instruction*. Cambridge, MA: Harvard University Press.
Bruner, J. (1996) *The Culture of Education*. Cambridge, MA: Harvard University Press.
Chaiklin, S. (2003) The zone of proximal development in Vygotsky's analyses of learning and instruction. In A Kozulin, B. Gindis, V. Ageyev and S. M. Miller (eds) *Vygotsky's Educational Theory in a Cultural Context*. Cambridge: Cambridge University Press.
Chan, J. (work in progress). Teachers' understandings of the purposes of group work and their relationship with practice. DPhil, Oxford University Department of Education.
Claxton, G. (2007) Expanding young people's capacity to learn, *British Journal of Educational Studies*, 55(2): 115–34.
Doyle, W. (1983) Academic work, *Review of Educational Research*, 53(2): 159–99
Doyle, W. (1986) Classroom organization and management. In M. C. Wittrock (ed.) *Hndbook of Research on Teaching 3*, New York: Macmillan, pp. 392–431.
Edwards, A. (1995) Teacher education: partnerships in pedagogy? *Teaching and Teacher Education*, 11(6): 265–79.
Edwards, D. and Mercer, N. (1987) *Common Knowledge: The development of understanding in the classroom*. London: Routledge.
Frase, L . T. (1972) Maintenance and control in the acquisition of knowledge from written materials. In J. B. Carroll and R. O. Freedle (eds) *Language Comprehension and the Acquisition of Knowledge*. Washington, DC: Winston.
Frase, L . T. (1975) Prose processing. In G. H. Bower (ed.) *The Psychology of Learning and Motivation Vol. 9*. New York: Academic Press.
Gunnarsdottir, R. (2001) *Innovation Education: Defining the phenomenon*. Doctoral Thesis, University of Leeds.
Harré, R. (1983) *Personal Being*. Oxford: Blackwell.
Hedegaard, M. (2012) The dynamic aspects in children's learning and development. In M. Hedegaard., A. Edwards and M. Fleer, (eds) *Motives, Emotions and Values in the Development of Children and Young People*. Cambridge: Cambridge University Press, pp. 9–27.

Jenkins, J. J. (1977) Remember that old theory of memory? Well, forget it! In R. Shaw and J. Bransford (eds) *Perceiving, Acting, and Knowing: Toward an ecological psychology*. Hillsdale, J: Lawrence Erlbaum Associates.

Nisbet, J. and Shucksmith, J. (1986) *What are learning strategies?* London: RKP.

Rai, P. (2014) Building common knowledge: a cultural-historical analysis of pedagogical practices in a rural primary school in Rajasthan. DPhil thesis, University of Oxford.

Schwab, J. (1978) *Science, Curriculum and Liberal Education: Selected essays, Joseph Schwab* (eds I. Westbury and N. Wilkof). Chicago: University of Chicago Press.

Vygotsky, L. S. (1978) (eds), M. Cole, V. John-Steiner, S. Scribner, and E. Souberman. *Mind In Society: Yhe development of higher psychological processes*. New York: Cambridge University Press.

Vygotsky, L. S. (1982) Teaching and development in the preschool age. In Om Barnets (ed.) *Psykiske Udvikling: en artikelsamling*. Copenhagen: Nyt Nordisk Forlag Arnold Busk, pp. 89–104.

Vygotsky, L. S. (1997) *Educational Psychology*. Boca Raton, FL: St Lucie Press.

Vygotsky, L. S. (1998) *The Collected Work of L S Vygotsky. Vol. 5 Child Psychology*. New York: Plenum Press.

Zimmerman, B. J. (2002) Becoming a self-regulated earner: an overview, *Theory Into Practice*, 41(2): 64–70.

Yimmerman, B. J. (2008) Investigating self-regulation and motivation: historical background, methodological developments, and future prospects, *American Educational Research Journal*, 45(1): 166–83.

# 3
# POLICY PERSPECTIVES ON TASK DESIGN

## Classroom learning and the national curriculum

*Mark Chater*

**Introduction**

Why should the political context of task design matter to a teacher? This chapter critically examines the discourses and structures that thread between classroom learning and national policy. Using the English educational system as a case study and warning, the chapter shows how neo-liberal policy approaches have given contradictory messages to a national system by a strategy of marketisation and centralisation with a discourse of collaboration and autonomy. A teacher's power to devise and organise learning has always been a political issue. This is particularly the case when centralised power leads to high levels of prescription, and when discourses of freedom, professional autonomy and rigour are dominant. Learning is a battleground between ideological forces, whose weapons are compulsion and rhetoric.

The chapter will first survey the relationship between the legally compulsory curriculum in England and the school-based acts of task design. Tracing the models of the national curriculum since 1988, and with particular reference to the design and implementation of the 2007 secondary curriculum, it will suggest how national curriculum incoherence has created a flawed context for lesson design, and propose the notion that every curriculum design casts a pedagogical shadow. Some international comparisons will be introduced to show that this pattern is repeated globally under neo-liberalism.

Next the chapter will examine the discourses that have characterised the reform of curriculum and teaching since 2010, with particular reference to power words such as curriculum, pedagogy, prescription, professional autonomy and knowledge. The examination will expose some contradictory and deceptive traits in the discourse, particularly in its assumptions about trusting professionals and the nature of freedom.

Because it is nested in political structures and carried by political discourses, task design may be said to be a political issue. Educationalists have long believed this and argued it; politicians have tended to deny it; parents and governors have long been dubious about it; many teachers in service once believed it, but most forget it. Even those teachers who abjure the belief, and become in their own eyes detached technicians of knowledge and skill, are operating in a power context; for them, part of the power transaction is a willed naiveté and a pretended innocence. None of this is honest; none of it is helpful in the search for excellence; and above all, it is a massive waste of teachers' and learners' energy.

Between culture, community and individual, teaching is a negotiation, always finding new adjustments, fresh accommodations; a 'complex pursuit of fitting a culture to the needs of its members and of fitting its members and their ways of knowing to the needs of the culture.' (Bruner 1996: 43). As a general rule, the relationship between task design and curriculum design is problematic in the same way that the relationship between curriculum and pedagogy is problematic. Neo-liberalism has forced education systems to place curriculum design into a context in which global economic competitiveness is the first and only priority. What follows is the enforcement of certain types of knowledge content as *a priori* important, the privileging of certain approaches to pedagogy as more effective, and the policing of this through testing, inter-school competition, inspection and marketisation (Hursh 2007). In pursuing this neo-liberal agenda, governments that speak loudly about closing the rich–poor attainment gap and using education as a social equaliser have gone at least as far as more traditional governments, if not further, as the examples of the Obama administration in the USA (Sanchez 2010) and the coalition government in the UK (Pring 2013) show us. This has continued despite evidence that the project to concentrate centralised power in education systems is not effective in its own terms because it performs no better at raising standards and narrowing the attainment gap (Ravitch 2010), is oppressive in the way it forces change on schools, and is theoretically weak in comparison with liberal and radical alternatives (Torres 2009).

The extent of neo-liberal influence in teachers' thinking about their own role as designers of learning may be evaluated by setting out its main, unspoken assumptions, for example:

- That there must be a national curriculum so that central government can determine consistently what is taught in schools.
- That the national curriculum must be organised by subjects and must set down subject content so that teachers can deliver it.
- That curriculum knowledge is fixed and rational, coming down to us from our past as a heritage that we must transfer to the young.
- That 'in the beginning was the curriculum': that tabulation of knowledge is the first task, followed by the selection of teaching methods and task design.
- That, while this central determination is important, freedom from excessive forms of central prescriptiveness is also important.

- That being knowledgeable, skilled and qualified makes all young people more successful and more socially and economically mobile.
- That schools, teachers and students will do better when they are placed in competition with each other.

If it seems startling to claim that all these assumptions are questionable, and that more profitable, sustainable and democratic assumptions can be brought into play, this is evidence of how strong a grip the neo-liberal project has on an education system. Yet the world dominated by the neo-liberal agenda is not the world young people will inherit, and the yawning gap between the two is becoming more extreme and damaging. By way of illustration, this critique of educational assumptions is offered by David Orr, the writer and pioneer on environment, education and politics:

> We have fragmented the world into bits and pieces called disciplines and subdisciplines, hermetically sealed from other such disciplines. As a result, after 12 or 16 or 20 years of education, most students graduate without any broad, integrated sense of the unity of things. The consequences for their personhood and the planet are large. For example, we routinely produce economists who lack the most rudimentary understanding of ecology or thermodynamics. This explains why our national accounting systems do not subtract the costs of biotic impoverishment, soil erosion, poisons in our air and water, and resource depletion from gross national product.
> 
> *(Orr 2004: 11)*

Arguing that education needs to be redesigned to fit a post-industrial age in which our way of treating the planet must change if we are to survive, he poses this challenge to curriculum designers:

> Those now being educated will have to do what we, the present generation, have been unable or unwilling to do…They must learn how to use energy and materials with great efficiency…rebuild the economy in order to eliminate waste and pollution…begin the great work of repairing, as much as possible, the damage done to the earth in the past 200 years. And they must do all of this while they reduce worsening social and racial inequalities. No generation has ever faced a more daunting agenda. For the most part, however, we are educating the young as if there were no planetary emergency.
> 
> *(Orr ibid.: 26–7)*

Set against this backdrop, a crisis in task design is being triggered by the wider crisis in the relevance and justice of curriculum and pedagogical policy. The crisis must come in order to resolve contradictions in the political backdrop of the teacher's task. This chapter is a call to teachers to take curriculum design as a moral and political issue of supreme importance to them and their young learners, and treat it as something of daily importance to their work.

## Every curriculum design casts a pedagogical shadow

The example of the national curriculum in England is a rich case study of the crisis in neo-liberal curriculum policy-making. Much can be learnt from its 25-year historical development, which can be characterised as a movement from curriculum as prescribed knowledge to curriculum as social engineering, and back again. The 1988 Education Reform Act established for the first time a national curriculum as a framework to be used by all maintained schools to ensure that teaching and learning was balanced and consistent. It set out the subjects to be taught, and in the subsequent first version of the curriculum, defined the knowledge, skills and understanding required in each subject. A scale of attainment targets was developed to support teacher assessment. The Act created key stages and provided, for each subject in each stage, programmes of study. It created two tiers in the curriculum, the 'core' subjects of English, mathematics and science and the 'foundation subjects' of art, geography, history, music, physical education and technology, with modern foreign languages from age 11. These tiers have had a profound influence on the structure of learning in every school. Schools were also required to teach religious education, though it sat outside the national curriculum, being determined either by local authority structures (for community schools) or by religious authorities (for faith-based schools).

In addition, a number of subjects such as personal, social and health education, and cross-curricular themes or generic skills were in time added. Within the framework of the national curriculum, schools were, and technically continue to be, free to plan and organise teaching and learning in the way that best meets the needs of their pupils. The original programmes of study were developed by subject-based working groups, comprising experts from a wide variety of educational backgrounds and which drew on evidence and expertise from throughout the education system.

What is most noteworthy now about those arrangements is, first, that the idea of a national curriculum was a highly contested concept, and still is for some (Brighouse 2011; Pring 2004, 163ff). Its critics have usually argued against it on grounds of professional autonomy, a concept to which we will return in the next section. It is also noteworthy that the normative uses of 'curriculum', 'national curriculum' and 'school curriculum' have become blurred and inter-changeable. It is quite common for the media, civil servants and ministers to mistake these phrases for each other, and for Heads and teachers to assume that the curriculum is the national curriculum. In early 2013 a short film on the landing page of the Department for Education, since withdrawn, made this mistake.

The question of whether or not we should have a national curriculum has never quite disappeared, but has often been eclipsed by the question of what should be in it. The question of how the curriculum is designed has grown in perceived importance. That the makers of the first national curriculum chose, without a moment's hesitation, to construct it around a range of subjects originating from the late-nineteenth century, and to give each of those subjects a discrete programme, is more noteworthy and questionable now than in 1988. The hidden significance of that choice is exposed by Michael Reiss and John White, who point out how the designers 'take for granted a dozen or so discrete subjects. It is *their* requirements that get filled out.' (Reiss and White 2013: 1). Where there were aims, they were 'tacked on to a structure already in place. Crucially, they do not *generate* that structure.' (Ibid.). The current government fails to note that some other national curriculum designs use a strong set of aims and design content around broad areas of learning, for example the Scottish curriculum for excellence (Education Scotland 2012). The 2012 international review of curriculum and assessment frameworks managed by the National Foundation for Educational Research compared England with over 20 other jurisdictions in economically successful states in Europe, America and Asia, and revealed the extent to which England has neglected key elements of successful curriculum policy such as principles, values, competences and cross-curricular links (NFER 2012). Instead, the recent story of the English curriculum has tended to be more interested in selecting exemplars from those models that focus mainly or solely on knowledge and high levels of prescription in discrete subjects, even detailing teaching strategies, such as Singapore (DfE 2011c) and the core knowledge programme of E. D. Hirsch in the USA (Hirsch 2012).

In 1988, the major point of controversy was in the size and prescriptiveness of the programmes of study. The first version provoked fierce criticism and incredulity because of its size, inflexibility and long lists of content as well as its arbitrary range of subjects (Brighouse, 2005). A review was undertaken by Sir Ron Dearing in 1993 in response to teachers' complaints. The revised curriculum based on this review was introduced in 1995. Following the election of a Labour government, in 1999 a further review was conducted by the then Qualifications and Curriculum Authority (QCA). As well as further reducing the amount of prescribed content, the 1999 reforms introduced an overt statement of aims and purposes. This was in response to a growing number of requests from teachers for a fuller explanation of what the national curriculum stood for. In addition to the subjects specified originally, the 1999 version also included citizenship as a statutory foundation subject for the first time.

Versions of the national curriculum have sometimes included themes with the intention of promoting coherence and enhancement. The first national curriculum included guidance on cross-curricular themes, skills and dimensions to support schools in developing a coherent curriculum. The Dearing review in 1993 did not mention these elements. The 1999 version referred to such requirements as 'learning across the curriculum', including: promoting spiritual, moral, social and cultural development, promoting personal, social and health education, key skills, thinking skills, financial capability, enterprise and entrepreneurial skills, work-related learning and education for sustainable development. Much thinking and development of these elements flourished in schools during the next ten years. The 2007 version included a set of generic skills (the personal, learning and thinking skills) and eight cross-curricular dimensions.

Curriculum content and design have always been political issues in a functional sense. Public pressure groups often exert influence to have their cause included in the content of the curriculum, be it an aspect of child safety, an approach to language teaching, an outdoor experience or a particular skill or value. Curriculum writers can only respond at the cost of having very lengthy documents, considered unwieldy and prescriptive. On the other hand, reducing content to a bare minimum incurs the disappointment of many pressure groups and may lead to their cause disappearing from some or most schools. This dichotomy has led to a fragmentary approach to curriculum design, in which the details of content were built up without a sense of the overall coherence or purpose, like a piece-by-piece mosaic with no overall picture. The recurrent design fault has encouraged teachers to use curriculum documents more for their detail than for their vision.

A more profound political issue has been the impact of successive national curriculums on teacher professionalism. The growth of 'deliverology', a term used with seriousness by leading school improvement expert Michael Barber and with something close to despair by leading educational philosopher Richard Pring (Pring 2013: 30), denotes the long process by which teachers have lost control of the curriculum both politically and intellectually, so that they now tend to teach what is required rather than what their judgement tells them is appropriate. At the same time, a growing discourse of autonomy has encouraged many teachers to innovate pedagogically without due reference to research. For example, the rapid spread of learning styles has consumed many teachers' time and intellectual engagement, monopolising their approach to the design of learning. The emerging realisation that some ideas are 'flashy nonsense' or 'cod neuroscience' (Beadle 2011: 51) is tempered with awareness that they are 'immensely seductive' and 'virulent in schools' (ibid).

The version of the national curriculum (DfE 2011a) dating from 2007 to 2014, in common with the discarded 2009–10 proposals for a primary curriculum, paid closer political attention to curriculum design than any previous curriculum. It did so with specific social goals in mind, principally as a way of ensuring that key contemporary government priorities such as narrowing the rich–poor attainment gap, Every Child Matters and financial capability could be embedded at the heart of teachers' planning, rather than added on afterwards. The invention of a curriculum consciously designed as a means to strategic social or economic goals was new. Up until 2007, such challenges were usually addressed through other methods, such as behaviour management, teaching and learning approaches and staff accountability. Yet there was inspection evidence that the curriculum could be either an aid or an impediment to strategic goals (Ofsted 2009a).

The 2007 design included aims that identified desired outcomes for children more specifically and concretely than any previous versions. The aims in the threefold phrase, 'successful learners, confident individuals and responsible citizens' (DfE 2011a) were underpinned by non-statutory discursive illustrations of what was meant, and by text on how each subject contributed to these aims. The curriculum included the traditional range of subjects, but these were designed in such a way as to avoid being lists of content. Key concepts for each subject attempted to represent the hard core of archetypal ideas in each discipline, while skills and particularly the personal, learning and thinking skills (known as PLTS) gave teachers an opportunity to design learning around notions of skill and aptitude. Lastly, the non-statutory curriculum dimensions, such as enterprise, technology and creativity, added a feature enabling schools to plan across traditional subjects. These features have now been deleted from the DfE website, leaving only subjects.

Not only did the 2007 curriculum have a conscious design: it had an implied set of pedagogical principles, which included an aspiration to inspire young people with a lifelong love of learning, to trust schools and teachers with a variety of design approaches and to encourage a reduction of subject isolation in favour of overall school and community priorities. The model had weaknesses: its design was not as radical as its rhetoric, and the key concepts were inconsistent in their density and rigour.

Implementation in schools was supported and monitored by the then QCA. The implementation reports have been suppressed following the QCA's closure. Schools responded enthusiastically to the new flexibility, but never quite escaped from 'deliverology'. They continued to use concepts and content as check lists, under-emphasised the importance of the aims, took up the PLTS with alacrity but in mechanistic ways and were conservative and repetitive in the ways they allowed inter-subject collaboration. Stirred up by the new discourse of flexibility, teachers heard the word 'freedom' and began to polarise their thinking between traditional knowledge-based curriculum design (bad) and aims-led or skills-driven design (good). Newer curriculum models appeared on the market, notably the Royal Society of the Arts' 'Opening Minds' curriculum (RSA 2012), with attendant pedagogical messages that emphasised the centrality of learning as an active engagement (Claxton 2005).

Up until 2010, successive curriculum versions had moved from higher towards lower levels of content prescriptiveness. Reviews were conducted at different times, and often to different agendas, from other initiatives such as qualification development and approval. Whilst a discourse of trusting teachers and reducing state prescriptiveness gained dominance in curriculum statements, the same was not true of testing, national strategy definitions of good practice, community cohesion and other duties on schools. For example, the national strategies for literacy, numeracy and general teaching and lesson design, while never statutory, became hegemonic definitions of good practice from the late 1990s until their closure in 2011. Evidence of the scale of their prescriptiveness can be seen in what remains of the materials online (National Strategies 2011). The government's message to teachers was ambivalent: curriculum and pedagogy were seen as different entities, apparently with no relation. It seemed that teachers were being trusted increasingly on the curriculum, though within specific limits, whilst being told in detail how they should teach it. The discordance between a discourse of curriculum flexibility and a reality of pedagogical prescription has generated tension and incoherence in the system.

Ofsted's impact evaluation of the 2007–14 secondary curriculum suggested that coherent whole school curriculum planning was a significant factor in determining successful implementation. Inspectors (Ofsted 2009b) identified vision, coherent whole-school work and systematic monitoring of the whole as key elements of success: the corollary being that less successful schools were the ones where teachers had continued using national curriculum documents as direct check lists for content in task design.

The curriculum's high-water mark had come: no longer seen as merely an inert body of content, its capacity to shape teachers' work for good or ill, thereby influencing outcomes for children, was established. Curriculum design was more than lesson planning, more than subjects, more than the national curriculum and more than qualifications (Male and Waters 2012: 9). Its advocates began not with a statement about what knowledge should be taught, but with the question of what young people need (Ibid.: 23ff.). Internationally there is a high level of consistency in identifying the skills, aptitudes or competencies that young people need (Male and Waters 2012: 25ff.).

The introduction of overarching social and economic goals into curriculum design was seen as a triumph of centre-left politics, (Margo *et al.* 2008) and a disaster for libertarians of the left (Postman 1995) and right (Furedi 2009).

The libertarian right set the terms for the next curriculum development. In arguing that education should be about cultivating children's cultural capital and understanding 'humanity's intellectual and cultural legacy', Furedi (2009: 61) introduced a note of pessimism and loss. His analysis of the task of schools was characterised by narratives of devaluing, erosion, dumbing-down, loss of clarity and loss of authority. His prescription was of reclaiming, returning, restoring and reviving. Think tanks of the right prepared the way for a radical restoration, arguing that the curriculum had become overloaded with 'fashionable causes' and that the 'importance of knowledge' had been lost as a value (Whelan 2007: 1). By rolling back the state's prescriptive power, the right proposed to revive innovation and excellence in teaching:

> …we have developed a 'tight, loose, tight' framework for English education: clear vision from the centre (first 'tight'); autonomy for schools to achieve that vision as they see fit ('loose'); and strong accountability so the vision can be transparently achieved (second 'tight').
>
> *(Freedman 2008: 7)*

The tight, loose, tight formula built on pre-2010 intentions to be less prescriptive, and in practice went much further. The next section will discuss the coalition government's changes to the curriculum and their implications for task design.

Looking back at curriculum development in the late-twentieth, early-twenty-first centuries, a number of perennial themes emerge which have long-term influence on teachers and pose challenges for the way they plan learning experiences for pupils:

- The case for having a national curriculum depends to some extent on minimising its prescriptiveness. How can this be reconciled with any government's legitimate desire to use all instruments at its disposal to work towards its desired goals?
- Popular polarisations, for example between a 'knowledge-based', 'aims-led' and 'skills-driven' curriculum, are misleading. How can teachers be helped to see the curriculum as both, and to use it flexibly?
- Most teachers would agree that learning in schools should be compelling and enjoyable in itself, not overshadowed or determined by national tests or examinations. How can government and teachers collaborate to produce a curriculum model that has the robustness and coherence to make sense in itself and integrate well with qualifications?
- In each subject, there are some pupils who are generalists and some who are or will become specialists. For example, we teach science to all children because we want all citizens to be scientifically literate, and to some children because they have the aptitude and interest to become potential Nobel prize-winners. How can the curriculum be designed to meet the needs of both groups? How can the definitions of attainment encompass the achievements of both groups, while still being clear and credible, providing a rigorous and flexible structure for teaching and learning?

Curriculum design has come into the foreground as a political issue affecting the design of learning. Influenced by innovations in the science of learning, in learning technology and from inspection evidence, the 2007 secondary curriculum took some steps in the direction of a design that intentionally influenced pedagogy. Every curriculum design, we now see, casts a pedagogical shadow. Previous curriculum versions certainly had an implied pedagogy with a hidden influence on teachers. Now the influence is more explicit. However, all this must next be considered in the light of the 2010 coalition government's discourses and curriculum proposals.

## The monkey in the museum: curriculum and pedagogical mayhem

The politics of task design took a new turn with the creation of a coalition government in 2010. At the time of writing, the government's hypothesis on the public sector generally, and schools in particular, is that less intervention and more freedom will lead to innovation and promote excellence (Freedman 2008: 7). But is this freedom from – an essentially reactive and restrictive freedom – or freedom to? The discourse points strongly in the direction of the former sense.

> Conservatives have always believed that if you trust people, they will tend to do the right thing. That if you give people more responsibility, they will behave more responsibly. That if you give people more power and control

over their lives, they will make better decisions than those the state would make on their behalf.

*(Conservative Party 2007: 3)*

The same document calls for a post-bureaucratic age in which professionals will be liberated from the top-down, stifling impositions of the state. The promise of liberation was much repeated in the media and key speeches, notably that of Nick Gibb, when a minister, to the Reform think thank:

> We're going to place greater trust in professionals to give teachers more freedom to decide how to teach. And we're going to reduce bureaucracy so that schools can get on with their core business.
>
> *(Gibb 2010)*

This is a good articulation of 'freedom from'. It says nothing about how such freedom could be used as a platform for particular types of learning. On the strength of this principled position came a more specific promise:

> We will enact radical reform of our curriculum and qualifications structure. We will ... seek to dismantle the power of a centralised bureaucracy which has failed to create a system where dispersed power encourages innovation and drives excellence.
>
> *(Gove 2009b)*

> We will promote the reform of schools in order to ensure that ... all schools have greater freedom over the curriculum; and that all schools are held properly to account.
>
> *(Cabinet Office 2010: 28)*

And a programme to apply an absolute distinction between curriculum and pedagogy:

> [The country requires] a national curriculum that sets out broad goals to be reached by the age of 16. The curriculum would set out a framework of the core subjects and would include no further instruction as to what aspects of those subjects should be taught or how subjects should be taught...
>
> *(Gove 2009b)*

As Secretary of State, Michael Gove instigated a curriculum review every bit as radical as promised, starting with a diagnosis which painted the schooling system as being in crisis. He diagnosed a curriculum that was too big, complex and unclear as to what was and was not statutory; and he saw this as part of a wider disfunction, a lack of coherence whereby the elements of curriculum, pedagogy, assessment and testing were not constructed together. Frequent curriculum and qualification changes compounded the problem. The solution was a more minimalist model, better informed by research and particularly by international comparisons (Oates 2010: 1–2). Although independently published, this report had a foreword by Michael Gove as Secretary of State, and was the basis of the subsequent curriculum proposals.

The proposed programmes of study for the curriculum (DfE 2013) are indicators of the direction of travel. They take a mainly knowledge-based approach to curriculum design. Michael Gove had already endorsed the idea: justified as a desire to be less prescriptive, his apparent preference is for a curriculum that simply lists the knowledge to be taught: 'I just think there should be facts'. (BBC 2011) In the USA, the Hirsch-inspired core knowledge programme constructs a curriculum from the same basic building blocks (Hirsch 2012). The definition of learning as knowledge, and furthermore knowledge of the past, is reinforced by erstwhile minister Nick Gibb: 'I believe very strongly that education is about the transfer of knowledge from one generation to the next. Knowledge is the basic building block for a successful life.' (Gibb 2010).

How have these premises been translated into the new curriculum for 2014 onwards? The most obvious feature is that discrete, subject-based programmes of study remain, and have far less to do with each other than in previous versions. Indeed, schools must publish their curriculum by subject (DfE 2013). Each subject has between three and seven distinct aims. For English, mathematics and science, the level of statutory specification is higher, and the length greater, than in former programmes. Taking two typical examples from the English programme of study, the pedagogy of reading is prescribed through phonic knowledge (DfE 2013) and two statutory appendices give a further 31 pages of spelling, vocabulary, grammar and punctuation in a way comparable to the erstwhile non-statutory National Strategies. The proposed definition of progress is that 'by the end of each key stage, pupils are expected to know, apply and understand the matters, skills and processes specified in the relevant programme of study' (DfE 2013). This is consistent with the expert panel's call for coherence and for a simplified progression model formed of 'statements of specific learning outcomes related to essential knowledge.' (DfE 2011: 43).

There are several reasons for warning that this approach to curriculum making should be troublesome for any teacher who values professional autonomy over task design and engagement with rigorous learning.

First, the claimed radical shift in favour of small government and teacher autonomy – the 'loose' of tight-loose-tight – has not only not materialised: the prescription is far higher than in 2007, and returns to 1988 levels. The curriculum–pedagogy distinction, by which Mr Gove claimed he would lay down knowledge and let teachers decide how to teach it, has been belied by the position on reading and by the design of some other subjects such as history. Providers of primary initial teacher education have been told they must use only synthetic phonics in training primary teachers to teach reading. Other methods must not be referred to.

Next, the implied epistemology is questionable. While the aims in most subjects give a balance of knowledge, understanding and skills, the model of progression used repeatedly (DfE 2011b; DfE 2013) is of content coverage. More than its predecessors, this curriculum is driven by knowledge, and this establishes an epistemological framework which teachers will be unable to question.

Jerome Bruner warned against reducing pedagogy to information-giving. He believed that it not only fell short of the aims of education but disfigured the human self at the heart of learning, disabling people from dealing with ambiguity, layered meanings, metaphors and complexity. A pedagogy based on knowledge alone was 'a monkey in the British Museum, beating out the problem by a bone-crushing algorithm or taking a flyer on a risky heuristic.' (Bruner 1990: 5). This simian image is a graphic statement of curricular and pedagogical mayhem: it describes behaviourally the reduction of all questions of human existence to matters of measurement alternating with ill-informed, undisciplined personal interpretation: it characterises the lives of those individuals who have not dared to go beyond knowledge. We might add that it characterises the minds of ministers when let loose in the museum of the curriculum, alternately thumping themselves and others with a claimed fact, then leaping into the air on a wild surmise of policy by hunch.

Both these factors should cause alarm as they are forms of cultural censorship. Pierre Bourdieu, the philosopher of cultural capital, analysed the way in which censorship determines 'the very structure of the field in which the discourse is produced and circulates' (Bourdieu, 1991: 137), showing how the structure makes some discourses possible and others illegitimate. Union leader Mary Bousted, writing in the *TES*, commented that 'the weight of subject content and its sequencing can only lead to teachers ... transmitting information' (Bousted 2012: 44). Teachers' professional choices about teaching and learning strategies will be severely reduced. Bousted also predicts that a broad and balanced curriculum is endangered, and will become a 'forlorn memory' for all primary teachers (ibid.: 45).

If it is true that every curriculum design casts a pedagogical shadow, Mr Gove is striving to deny it. If between curriculum and pedagogy there is an invisible, but strong connection, it is one utterly denied (in public) by current ministers and ignored by their preferred curriculum design. Designing a curriculum around pupil outcomes – as in 2007 and 2010 – encourages pedagogy and planning that thinks about ECM outcomes, coherence and meaning in learning. Many teachers are worried that designing a curriculum around knowledge alone will tend to produce 'delivery' teachers whose pedagogical default style is invariant content coverage. It takes a rare teacher to transform such a curriculum – which is really a syllabus – into learning experiences that absorb the learner and vivify the subject. This is as difficult as turning flat cola into sparkling champagne.

We look at Mr Gove's promise of freedom from prescription, then at his proposed curriculum, and back again. We try to believe his claim that the proposed curriculum is non-prescriptive, an objective and essentially apolitical array of 'facts' with no pedagogical strings attached. Then we hear Mr Gove's declared admiration for a particular practice, in a party conference speech:

> 'What Sir Michael [Wilshaw, then Head of Mossbourne Academy, Hackney] does is deliver what every sensible parent knows is needed in our schools... He teaches traditional subjects in a rigorous way and when the bureaucrats try to insert the latest fashionable nonsense into the curriculum he tells them where to get off... Why isn't every state school like that? It's my job to make sure they are.'
>
> (Gove 2009a).

This moment of candour helps us to understand Mr Gove's programme more intimately, perhaps, than he intended. After all and clearly he does recognise that every curriculum design casts a pedagogical shadow; he intends his shadow to be a traditionalist one, featuring content coverage, heritage transmission, teacher talk, pupil passivity. He does after all have pedagogical views, and feels that teachers would benefit from knowing them. His pedagogy will have no truck with the new neuroscience of learning, nor with group work, learning outside the classroom or the Every Child Matters outcomes. He has discarded tight-loose-tight for an even closer-fitting garment. Is this freedom, or a new form of compulsion? Is it an hypothesis about schools' freedom, or an experiment in which the scientist already knows the answer? Is it a radical dismantling and dispersal of power, or a *coup d'etat* against the ideals of teaching and learning?

We must also consider a class factor at work in the proposed curriculum design. Content-led teaching favours teachers and learners in privileged environments, where pupils have already tasted the rewards of conformity. In such schools, the design of learning demands less skill and effort from a teacher to interest and motivate learners. Correspondingly in more challenging schools a flat, content-led design will either create more planning challenges for teachers, or become a deficit that is passed on to the learners, whose progress will suffer as a result. We see this agenda reflected in another moment of candour, this time from Nick Gibb's speech to Reform:

> 'The facts, dates and narrative of our history in fact join us all together. The rich language of Shakespeare should be the common property of us all. The great figures of literature that still populate the conversations of all those who regard themselves as well-educated should be known to all.'
>
> (Gibb 2010)

Whose history? The common property of whom? Despite a stately nod at egalitarian sensibilities, Mr Gibb's main purpose is a furtive lunge at the elitist pleasure button. The phrase 'those who regard themselves as well-educated' speaks loudly in accents of self-regard. The hallmark of those who so regard themselves is a knowledge of literature, rather than, say, technology, science, spirituality or the arts: a hand-me-down definition of education heard at a thousand dinner parties.

Teachers must now contemplate the probable advent of a curriculum composed of knowledge, posing as facts, with high levels of prescription and a discourse of neutrality in regard to pedagogy accompanied by a clear directive towards those pedagogies that are favoured. The following questions, amongst others, will be daily companions for teachers engaged in creating learning:

- How do I understand my curriculum document? Do I have a strong enough subject pedagogical understanding to turn a list of 'facts' into a coherent sequence of meaningful learning experiences, leading to engagement, enjoyment and success?
- Even though composed of 'knowledge', does my design of learning offer to young people questions, sustained enquiries, projects, the opportunity to change things? Or does my offer to young people preclude debate?
- How can I use a knowledge-based curriculum with integrity, in ways that offer equally strong learning opportunities to all my pupils?
- Am I able to carry out these tasks in ways that will inform and inspire my younger colleagues entering the profession?

## Curriculum crisis and its possible outcomes

There is now the possibility that the notion of a national curriculum will enter a crisis from which it will not recover. Critiques of the concept have returned in greater force, focusing on the limitations of statist solutions (Facer 2011) and the outmoded construction of knowledge (Gerver 2010). Mr Gove, having seized the curricular ship's wheel from the quangocrats, seems zealously intent on steering into shallow rocky water. What will be left of the curriculum, once it has hit the rocks of centralised control or ground itself irrevocably into the shallows of facts, is not much: it will have to be abandoned, and will be left there, a vast, useless and decaying hulk, for all to see.

Meanwhile, teachers who have become politically and culturally accustomed to a delivery and compliance relationship with national documents will need to review the relationship between their chosen pedagogy and the curriculum. A dialectical relationship, in which consideration of pedagogy and the classroom is extended to embrace institutional and political forces (Di Leo and Jacobs 2004) would be a fruitful substitute for compliance. A renewal of reciprocal collegiality with other teachers, enabling collaborative participation in design, will be a crucial hallmark of success (Littleton et al. 2012) and could lead to interpretive habits of mind, overcoming research–practice dualisms (Pring et al. 2009). Better structural and intellectual links between schools and universities (Tripp 2012) will be a highly necessary element of recovery in the art of designing learning. Above all, teachers need to engage vigorously in a re-drawing of the defining boundaries between pedagogy and curriculum, grounded in shared pedagogical subject knowledge, curriculum knowledge and principles and aims (Alexander 2010), allowing these new understandings to become the key to task design.

The system cannot go back to pre-1988 and should not listen to the siren voices of teacher nostalgia for a supposed absolute of professional freedom. Instead what teachers are now challenged to grapple with is a crisis in the use of state power over classrooms, a catalyst for fresh thinking and practice and a changed relationship between themselves and the way knowledge is defined. These final questions offer specific focuses for considering the changed relationship:

- Instead of curriculum, then pedagogy, then task design, what if we thought of pedagogy shaping curriculum, and task design re-shaping pedagogy?
- Instead of curriculum as heritage and knowledge of the past, what if we thought of it as a shaping of the future we want – ecological, economic, cultural, physical?
- Instead of a discourse of freedom from, supposing we spoke of freedom to?
- Supposing questions, enquiries, projects and the insights they brought were recognised as a form, perhaps the highest form, of knowledge – as wisdom?
- Instead of thinking about the design of learning as solo delivery, supposing we considered it as collaborative construction?
- Could we raise a generation of teachers who were able to work and think in this way? Could they do so even when curriculum documents cast a shadow in the opposite direction?

## References

Alexander, R. (ed.) (2010) *Children, Their World, Their Education: Final report and recommendations of the Cambridge Primary Review.* Abingdon: Routledge.
BBC (2011) 'Gove stresses "facts" in school curriculum revamp', London: BBC, Radio 4 Today Programme, 20 January 2011, www.bbc.co.uk/news/education-12227491, accessed 2 January 2013.
Beadle, P. (2011) *Bad Education.* Carmarthen: Crown House Publishing.
Bourdieu, P. (1991) 'Censorship and the imposition of form', in John B. Thompson (ed.) *Language and Symbolic Power*, Cambridge, MA: Harvard Press.
Bousted, M. (2012) 'Teachers, prepare to be straitjacketed', in *Times Educational Supplement*, 6 July 2012, pp. 44–5.
Brighouse, T. (2005) *Accidents can Happen.* London: Qualifications and Curriculum Authority.
Brighouse, T. (2011) *Decline and Fall: Are state schools and universities on the point of collapse?* First annual lecture to the Oxford Education Society, Oxford: Department of Education.
Bruner, J. (1990) *Acts of Meaning.* The Jerusalem-Harvard Lectures. Cambridge, MA: Harvard University Press.
Bruner, J. (1996) *The Culture of Education.* Cambridge, MA: Harvard University Press.
Cabinet Office (2010) *The Coalition: Our programme for government.* London: Cabinet Office.
Claxton, G. (2005) *Learning to Learn: A key goal in a 21st century curriculum.* London: Qualifications and Curriculum Authority.
Conservative Party (2007) *Raising the Bar, Closing the Gap: A policy green paper.* London: Conservatives.
Department for Education (2011a) *National Curriculum.* London: DfE, www.education.gov.uk/schools/teachingandlearning/curriculum, accessed 2 January 2013.
Department for Education (2011b) *Framework for the National Curriculum: A report by the expert panel for the national curriculum review.* London: DfE, www.education.gov.uk/publications/standard/publicationDetail/Page1/DFE-00135-2011, accessed 2 January 2013.
Department for Education (2011c) Review of the National Curriculum in England: what can we learn from the English, mathematics and science curricula of high-performing

jurisdictions? London: DfE, www.gov.uk/government/publications/review-of-the-national-curriculum-in-england-what-can-we-learn-from-the-english-mathematics-and-science-curricula-of-high-performing-jurisdictions, accessed 17 August 2013.

Department for Education (2013) *The National Curriculum for September 2014*. London: DfE, www.gov.uk/government/collections/national-curriculum#programmes-of-study-by-subject, accessed 18 January 2014.

Di Leo, J. and Jacobs, W. (2004) *If Classrooms Matter: Progressive visions of educational environments*. London: Routledge.

Education Scotland (2012) *Curriculum for Excellence*. Livingston: Education Scotland, www.educationscotland.gov.uk/thecurriculum/whatiscurriculumforexcellence/index.asp, accessed 17 August 2013.

Facer, K. (2011) *Local Curriculum or National Curriculum: Which best serves social justice?* London: Royal Society for the Arts, www.thersa.org/action-research-centre/education/practical-projects/area-based-curriculum, accessed 2 January 2013.

Freedman, S. (2008) *Helping Schools Succeed: A framework for English education*. London: Policy Exchange, www.policyexchange.org.uk/publications/category/item/helping-schools-succeed-a-framework-for-english-education , accessed 2 January 2013.

Furedi, F. (2009) *Wasted: Why education isn't educating*. London: Continuum.

Gerver, R. (2010) *Creating Tomorrow's Schools Today*. London: Continuum.

Gibb, N. (2010) *Speech to Reform*. London: Department for Education, www.education.gov.uk/inthenews/speeches/a0061473/nick-gibb-to-the-reform-conference, accessed 2 January 2013.

Gove, M. (2009a) *Speech to Conservative Party Conference*. London: Conservatives, www.conservatives.com/News/Speeches/2009/10/Michael_Gove_Failing_schools_need_new_leadership.aspx, accessed 2 January 2013.

Gove, M. (2009b) *Speech in House of Commons Queen's Speech Debate on Education and Health*, 19 November 2009. London: BBC, http://news.bbc.co.uk/democracylive/hi/house_of_commons/newsid_8366000/8366972.stm, accessed 2 January 2013.

Hirsch, E. (2012), *Core Knowledge*, www.coreknowledge.org/about-the-curriculum, accessed 2 January 2012.

Hursh, D. (2007) 'Assessing No Child Left Behind and the rise of neoliberal education policies', in *American Educational Research Journal* 44: 3, pp. 493–518, http://aer.sagepub.com/content/44/3/493.abstract, accessed 17 August 2013.

International Review of Curriculum and Assessment Frameworks (2012), *Curriculum Structure and Organisation*, Slough: National Foundation for Educational Research, http://webarchive.nationalarchives.gov.uk/20130220111733/http://inca.org.uk/documents/Table8.pdf, accessed 17 August 2013.

Littleton, K., Scanlon, E. and Sharples, M. (eds) (2012) *Orchestrating Inquiry Learning*. Abingdon and NY: Routledge.

Male, B. and Waters, M. (2012) *The Secondary Curriculum Design Handbook: Preparing young people for their futures*. London: Continuum.

Margo, J., Benton, M., Withers, K., Sodha, S. and Tough, S. (2008) *Those Who Can?* London: IPPR.

National Strategies (2011) webarchive.nationalarchives.gov.uk/20110113104120/http:/nationalstrategies.standards.dcsf.gov.uk/, accessed 2 January 2013.

Oates, T. (2010) *Could Do Better: Using international comparisons to refine the National Curriculum in England*. Cambridge: University of Cambridge.

Ofsted (2009a) *Twelve Outstanding Schools: Excelling against the odds*. London: Ofsted, www.ofsted.gov.uk/resources/twelve-outstanding-secondary-schools-excelling-against-odds, accessed 2 January 2013.

Ofsted (2009b) *Planning for Change: The impact of the new Key Stage 3 curriculum*. London: Ofsted, www.ofsted.gov.uk/resources/planning-for-change-impact-of-new-key-stage-3-curriculum, accessed 2 January 2013.

Orr, D. (2004) *Earth in Mind: On education, environment and the human prospect*. Washington DC: Island Press.

Postman, N. (1995) *The End of Education: Redefining the value of the school*. New York: Vintage Books.

Pring, R. (2004) *Philosophy of Education: Aims, theory, common sense and research*. London and New York: Continuum.

Pring, R., Hayward, G., Hodgson, A., Johnson, J., Keep, E., Oancea, A., Rees, G., Spours, K. and Wilde, S. (2009) *Education for All: The future of education and training for 14–19 year olds*. London and New York: Routledge.

Pring, R. (2013) *The Life and Death of Secondary Education for All*. Abingdon: Routledge.

Ravitch, D. (2010) *The Death and Life of the Great American School System*. New York: Basic Books.

Reiss, M. and White, J. (2013) *An Aims-based Curriculum: The significance of human flourishing for schools*. London: Institute of Education Press.

Royal Society for the Arts (2012) *Opening Minds*. London: RSA, www.rsaopeningminds.org.uk/, accessed 2 January 2013.

Sanchez, A. (2010) 'The education shock doctrine: disaster schooling', in *International Socialist Review* 71, www.isreview.org/issue/71, accessed 17 August 2013.

Torres, C. (2009) *Education and Neoliberal Globalisation*. New York and Abingdon: Routledge.

Tripp, D. (2012) *Critical Incidents in Teaching: Developing professional judgement*. Abingdon: Routledge.

Whelan, R. (ed.) (2007) *The Corruption of the Curriculum*. London: Civitas.

# PART II
# Learning from the subjects

# 4

# THE INTERPLAY BETWEEN MATHEMATICS AND PEDAGOGY

Designing tasks for mathematics teacher education

*Gabriel J. Stylianides and Anne Watson*

## Introduction

In this chapter we use the distinction suggested by Christiansen and Walter (1986) between 'task' and 'activity'. 'Task' refers to operations undertaken within certain constraints and conditions (Leont'ev 1975) and 'activity' refers to the subsequent mathematical or pedagogical actions that emerge from interaction among the students, the teacher, the resources and the environment around the task. The teacher's work is to engineer the milieu (Chevallard 1999) in such a way that the activity is likely to be directed purposefully towards the teacher's intentions for learning.

At the school level, 'tasks' in mathematics classrooms are generally equivalent to 'mathematical tasks' and so tasks can be seen as the mediating tools for teaching and learning mathematics. At the teacher education level, which is our focus in this paper, the meaning of the term 'task' becomes more complicated. Some tasks may start as being just about engaging prospective teachers in mathematical activity ('mathematical tasks'), others may start as being about engaging them in issues of pedagogy ('pedagogical tasks'), and others may be somewhere in-between these two viewpoints. A major point we aim to make and illustrate in this paper is that, when we design tasks for use with prospective secondary teachers, even if these tasks on the surface look purely 'mathematical' or 'pedagogical', there is value during the implementation of these tasks to not limit the discussion to mathematical or pedagogical issues, respectively, but to explore with prospective teachers issues that the tasks can raise in the interplay between mathematics and pedagogy. In our experience, helping prospective teachers to explore connections between mathematics and pedagogy facilitates the development of a deeper understanding of the complexities of mathematics teaching.

The students with whom we work as teacher educators are in a continuous relationship with schools during their training in the form of an internship (see

Hagger and McIntyre 2000; Thompson this volume). Throughout their one year course they are encouraged to integrate, through problem-solving and reflective approaches, their experiences of teaching and observing in school, reading and participating in university sessions. The teacher educators who teach these sessions are the same people who visit them and observe their work in schools. Experience over time has taught us that at times during the university sessions, some prospective teachers will focus more on the mathematics and others will focus more on similar teaching situations they have experienced in school. Thus, our students' rich mathematical knowledge and recent school experiences come into play in how they react to different kinds of tasks in the university sessions. In our planning and teaching of these sessions, we take account of their background knowledge and experiences in the design and sequencing of tasks.

In our university-based work with prospective secondary mathematics teachers we use tasks as mediating tools. For example, through engaging them in mathematical tasks we promote reflection on their own mathematical activity and also on pedagogical implications of this activity. This interplay between mathematical and pedagogical issues helps to illustrate, and to give them experience of, the subject specific didactics of mathematics with its layers of increasingly general and abstract mathematical meaning explored through the use of mathematical modes of enquiry. In this paper, we make a distinction between general pedagogic issues that could apply to any subject and aspects of teaching that are specific for learning mathematics. The latter we call 'didactics' and one way in which our students encounter these ideas is by taking a pedagogical stance towards the work we do with them.

Possible pedagogical issues include the selection, modification, design, sequencing and evaluation of tasks, thus requiring two levels of engagement with mathematical tasks: firstly as a prompt to mathematical action, and secondly as examples of what they themselves might produce or use in the classroom. So, although these prospective teachers are generally strong mathematicians (with at least a bachelor's degrees in mathematics or the equivalent), they get opportunities to reflect on their own learning of mathematics and also to (explicitly or implicitly) become more insightful and articulate about the didactics of mathematics. Because we are hoping they will reflect not only on their own actions but also on the milieu that shapes those actions, our teaching aims to scaffold their shifts between different reflective perspectives, gradually introducing them to different issues that are involved in mathematics teaching and learning.

There is often a tacit assumption among publishers of school textbooks and between inexperienced teachers that the implementation of mathematical tasks chosen or designed by the teacher in a school classroom will lead to the intended student learning. This view is persistent despite extensive research that indicates that this is not a direct relationship (for example Henningsen and Stein 1997; Margolinas 2004, 2005; Stylianides and Stylianides 2008). Seemingly minor differences in the design or implementation of tasks can have significant effects on learning (for example Runesson, 2005) as can differences in aspects of milieu; we try to make prospective teachers aware of the effects of subtle differences, for example, by asking them to reflect on their own mathematical activity and on their classroom experiences. In secondary school mathematics teaching, it is particularly important to understand that tasks on their own cannot scaffold the shifts in perception and cognition required to understand abstract mathematical ideas. In the two task sequences we present below, prospective teachers are explicitly invited to consider differences in task formulation. To understand how tasks can be linked in order to support teaching, it is important to understand the nature of the transformation of knowledge from the implicit knowledge-in-action used by confident students (see Vergnaud 1982) to the knowledge which is explicitly formulated, formalised and memorised that they must handle as teachers. This thinking underpins sequences we present in our sessions.

There is significant recent interest in the multilayered roles of tasks in mathematics teacher education, including tasks that help teachers think about classroom tasks. Zaslavsky and Sullivan (2011) have coordinated the diversity of approaches to tasks for mathematics teacher education, some of the goals being pedagogic, some being about development of professional habits of mind, and some about developing didactic awareness. Watson and Mason's (2008: 207–8) overview of tasks focuses on the development of didactic awareness through engaging teachers in mathematics, thus:

- bringing aspects of mathematical knowledge to the fore in ways that promote deep understanding
- bringing aspects of mathematical thinking to the attention of teachers and providing a context for articulation of them
- developing awareness of multiple perspectives through task-centred discussion and
- focusing on didactic decisions relevant for specific topics.

In our work, in common with many examples discussed in Watson and Mason (2008), we prioritise the didactics of mathematics, namely specific modes of enquiry, reasoning and behaviour such as questioning, symbolising, representing and switching representation, generalising, abstracting and interpreting in mathematical contexts. Thus, for example, any tasks for which the immediate (or primary) engagement of prospective teachers is mathematical activity would provide not only mathematical experiences but also didactical experiences and a context for the broader pedagogical purposes outlined above (Watson and Bills 2011); this kind of task is similar to what Stylianides and Stylianides (2010: 163–5) called 'pedagogy-related mathematics tasks'. Along the same lines, tasks for which the immediate (or primary) engagement of prospective teachers is pedagogical activity would be rooted in the teaching and learning of important mathematical ideas and would generate discussion around the particular mathematical content; these types of tasks are similar to what Stylianides and Stylianides (2010: 171) called 'mathematics-related pedagogy tasks'. Our reason for these priorities is that generic pedagogic knowledge can be gained in the school-based components of the course, as can enculturation into professional habits of mind, whereas learning about subject-specific teaching has to include research-based knowledge. University teacher educators, who are more familiar with research findings and methods, provide a critical context for input and discussion about research-informed practices.

One of the tensions that arise in working with (prospective) teachers is that they often want something they can use to teach in their classrooms. We establish early on with our class of about 30 prospective secondary mathematics teachers that doing a mathematical task is a way to experience for themselves at their own level something of what their students might experience. This becomes a cultural norm of our classroom. However, our situation is not 'realistic' because the tasks and activities of our sessions are not the tasks and activities of school teaching, even if some tasks may be adaptable to the school context. The teacher education milieu is not the same as that of a school classroom; 'reality' has to be constructed through internalisation rather than immediate action. For this reason we are particularly interested in what prospective teachers identify as the key ideas of a session and how they envision using these ideas in their practice (for example possible implications of these ideas for their practice). Their direct experience in sessions has therefore to be objectified, perhaps through structuring and discussion, to make it more likely that the experience can inform their future thinking and planning. In our planning, therefore, we think about the activity that might be prompted by doing a task, and how discussion of the activity can bring new insights about learning and teaching mathematics into the public arena.

The task sequences we describe below have been carefully developed over time for particular purposes. The first sequence was designed and implemented by Stylianides and the second by Watson; each sequence was implemented during a two-hour session. We use these sequences at a time in the course when the classroom cultural norms described above are established. Consistent with what we described above about 'key ideas' and also to gain further insight for this chapter we presented a questionnaire for immediate feedback at the end of each session on the two prompts summarised in Table 4.1. Prompt 1 asked for identification of three key events during the session and to explain what made them 'key' for our students, whilst Prompt 2 required them to anticipate how the session may influence their future planning and teaching. We shall now present the intentions, actions and outcomes of each of the two sessions undertaken with one cohort of 29 prospective teachers. Note that it is necessary to use mathematical terms and to refer to mathematical concepts in order to show the didactic detail of our work. However, we have written with general readers in mind and it should be possible to follow the discussion without needing to fully understand the mathematical terms by treating them as placeholders for concepts.

## First Task Sequence

In Stylianides' session the task sequence includes a range of tasks in which prospective teachers' primary or immediate engagement shifts several times between

**TABLE 4.1** The two prompts to which prospective teachers responded at the end of the session

| | |
|---|---|
| 1 | Please describe briefly 2–3 key events in today's session and explain what made them 'key' for you.<br>(Note: Interpret the term 'event' in any way that makes sense to you. It could be, for example, a task, an activity, a question, a solution to a mathematical problem, a pedagogical issue, discussion about any of the aforementioned, etc.) |
| 2 | Please write down 2–3 ideas about your future planning and teaching arising from today's session. Explain what about the session provoked those ideas. |

mathematics and pedagogy, thereby promoting discussions on the interplay of mathematics and pedagogy. In addition to a brief introduction and conclusion, the main part of the session can be divided into four major, closely connected sections. Because of space limitations, we omit here discussion of some subsidiary (to the focus of this paper) parts of the sequence.

## *Introduction*

At the beginning of the session, Stylianides provided an overview of the session and reminded the class about key mathematical terms to be used in the session, namely, 'convex polygons', 'nonconvex or concave polygons', and 'interior and exterior angles of convex polygons'. Although, as we mentioned earlier, all our students are graduates in mathematics or mathematics-related subjects, we do not expect them to remember specific terms from school geometry.

## *Main session part 1: Mathematical work*

The mathematical task in Figure 4.1 was then presented, which asked prospective teachers to work on two statements (one about the sum of the interior angles of convex polygons and the other about the sum of the exterior angles of convex polygons) and to prove their answers for each statement in two different ways. They could take as known in their work the facts at the bottom of the slide. Note that, although the mathematical content of the task (the sum of interior and exterior angles of convex polygons) is part of the secondary school curriculum, the requirement to prove each answer *in two different ways* makes the task go beyond the school level. Indeed, the requirement for two different proofs makes the task challenging even for this group of prospective teachers and was an intentional feature of the design of the task. As we explain below, our students were unable to produce two different proofs for the sum of the exterior angles (which was expected based on prior experience) and the sample of school student work in part 2 of the main session was intended to provide insight into an important proof that prospective teachers tend not to think about, thereby initiating more mathematical work on the task.

## Sum of interior and exterior angles of convex polygons

What is the sum of:

1) The interior angles of any convex polygon with *n* sides?
2) The exterior angles (one at each vertex) of any convex polygon with *n* sides?

Prove your answer to each question in different ways.

You may take as known the following:

1) The sum of the interior angles of any triangle is 180°.
2) The sum of the angles around a single point as shown in the figure below is 360°.

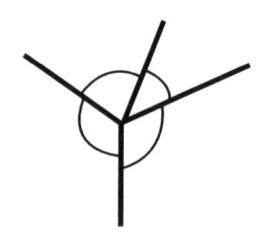

**Figure 4.1** Mathematical task about the sum of interior and exterior angles of convex polygons

The prospective teachers first worked on this mathematical task individually for a few minutes and, then, they shared ideas and strategies in their small groups of five. The small group work on the task continued until there was a whole class discussion. In the whole class discussion, different small groups presented their work on each of the two statements and the class discussed the proposed solutions.

Although the task in Figure 4.1 was a mathematical task, in the sharing and discussion of approaches to the task, a pedagogical perspective was also naturally raised. For example, when one small group presented a non-mathematically valid argument to one of the statements, Stylianides asked the class 'What might a skeptic ask/say in relation to this argument?' and introduced to the students the following idea discussed in Mason (1982): 'convince yourself – a friend – a skeptic'. This question was aimed at encouraging prospective teachers to be more critical of the proposed argument in a way that did not feel personal. Although Stylianides' comment was about their own mathematical work, some prospective teachers (drawing on their school experiences) quickly suggested the idea that they could use a similar strategy with their own students. Below are three excerpts from responses at the end of the session to the two prompts in Table 4.1:

- [Response to Prompt 1.] We saw a rule-of-thumb approach of proof: 'convince yourself, a friend, a skeptic' which was key because it showed to me that it is not enough to convince myself of something. As a teacher, I will have to explain my ideas to a class who do not always understand concepts after one hearing.
- [Response to Prompt 1.] Encouraging students to challenge the teacher and each other discussions about 'playing skeptic' and us all offering various arguments.

- [Response to Prompt 2.] I will have to approach proving an idea as if to a skeptic, and show as much information as I can to ensure that a class is fully aware of all the ideas necessary to be familiar with a concept.

Later on in the whole class discussion of the mathematical task one small group proposed a proof that did not adequately address the general case. Specifically, the figure drawn by that group did not indicate that the argument proposed would apply for any convex polygon (which is essential for an argument to meet the standard of 'proof') even though the group's description that accompanied the figure accounted for the general case. So there was a discussion in the class on how a figure could be drawn that would match the description and would also apply to the general case (see notion of 'generic example', Balacheff 1988; Mason and Pimm 1984). Similar to the previous example about convincing a skeptic, and without any prompting from the teacher educator, the prospective teachers started making connections between the mathematical issues discussed and implications of these issues in their teaching; this provides another example of the interplay between mathematical and pedagogical issues in the discussion. Below are two more excerpts from responses to Prompt 1 in the end-of-session reflection that illustrate the connections the prospective teachers made between their own mathematical work on the task and possible implications for their teaching:

- Explanation of generic or specific problem of diagrams for students. Do they understand it is to represent ANY such shape, not the specific one they see?
- The way in which we all tackled the same problems in different ways emphasised how pupils may work in different ways.

As expected, prospective teachers were not able to produce two different proofs for the second statement in the mathematical task about the sum of the exterior angles. After the analysis of student work that follows, the mathematical task will be revisited.

## *Main session part 2: Analysis of student work*

The second part of the main session of the task sequence included analysis and discussion of secondary students' work on a related mathematical task. The student work was derived from Hadas, Hershkowitz and Schwarz (2000). As background to the activity, Stylianides offered the following information to the class:

Some secondary students worked on the following task:
Measure with Cabri (a dynamic geometry software) the sum of the exterior angles of a quadrilateral. Hypothesize the sum of the exterior angles for polygons as the number of sides increases. Check your hypothesis by measuring and explain what you found.

The sample of student work that the prospective teachers were asked to try and make sense of is presented in Figure 4.2. The secondary students, whose work is described in the figure, have already explored the case of quadrilaterals and found out the sum of exterior angles is 360°. The figure presents the students' exploration of what happens to the sum of the exterior angles as they move on from the case of a quadrilateral to the case of a pentagon. The discussion of the student work not only led to more mathematical work for the prospective teachers as we explain in the next section, but presumably also helped them see how their mathematical exploration could relate to engaging secondary students in a similar task.

## Main session part 3: More mathematical work

As we mentioned earlier in the 'mathematical work' section, the prospective teachers were not able to produce two proofs for the statement about the sum of the exterior angles. This was expected and the choice of the student work in Figure 4.2 was intended to provoke further mathematical work on the task by engaging them in a proof about the task they had not produced on their own but which used an important proof method, namely, proof by mathematical induction. In more detail, implicit in the student work is the inductive step of a possible proof by mathematical induction. The prospective teachers did not think of using mathematical induction in their initial work on the mathematical task, which was

**Exploring the sum of the exterior angles of pentagons**
(the case of quadrilaterals has already been examined)

### Can you make sense of Inbal's argument?

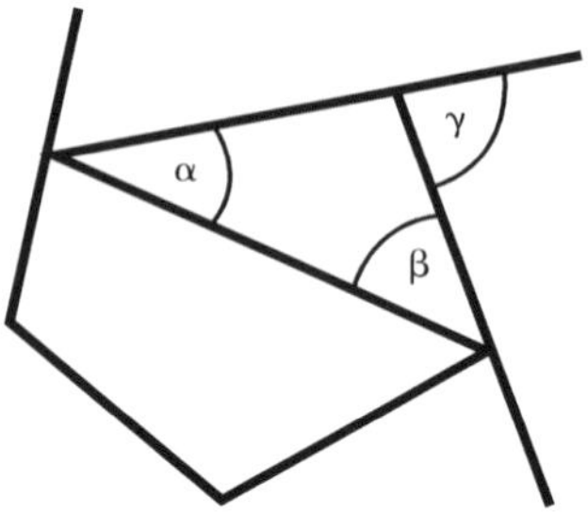

**Inbal:** If we add a triangle, it is like the sum of the angles doesn't change... I am not sure about it...

**[Inbal then drew the above figure to support her explanation].**

**Inbal:** This is what was added ($\gamma$), and this is what was reduced (Inbal is pointing to $\alpha$ and $\beta$).
**Limor:** This was outside before (pointing at $\alpha$ and $\beta$).
**Inbal:** Because this is ahh... I know why... the sum of the exterior angles... This (pointing at $\gamma$) is equal to these two (pointing at $\alpha$ and $\beta$). It is equal to both of them.

**Limor and Inbal:** Yes, yes it is true.

Figure 4.2 Analysis of student work on a related mathematical task

The interplay between mathematics and pedagogy **55**

expected given (1) that this proof method causes many difficulties to students including mathematics graduates (Dubinsky 1986, 1990; Dubinsky and Lewin 1986; Harel 2002; Knuth 2002; Movshovitz-Hadar 1993; Stylianides, Stylianides and Philippou 2007) and (2) that most of the prospective teachers would not have ever seen this proof method used in geometry.[1] So the student work motivated the group to revisit the mathematical task to produce a proof by mathematical induction, first for the sum of exterior angles of convex polygons and then for the sum of interior angles. Specifically, Stylianides provided a brief reminder of proof by mathematical induction (see Figure 4.3) and then asked them to think about the connection between their mathematical work and the work of the student in Figure 4.2:

> Use proof by mathematical induction to prove that the sum of the exterior angles of any convex polygon is 360°. How does your proof relate to Inbal's argument [see Figure 4.2]?

### Proof by mathematical induction

The simplest and most common form of **Mathematical Induction (MI)** proves that a statement holds for all natural numbers $n \geq n_0$ and consists of two steps:

1) The **base step**:

    Showing that the statement is true for $n = n_0$.

2) The **inductive step**:

    Assuming that the statement is true for $n = k$, show that the statement is true for $n = k + 1$.

**Figure 4.3** Proof by mathematical induction

Below are some excerpts from prospective teachers' responses to Prompt 1 in Table 4.1 in relation to their mathematical work in this section of the session:

- Proof by induction for geometry was another thing I had not done before. It was interesting to apply the mathematical induction knowledge to a different environment then I am used to.
- I found the proofs by mathematical induction interesting mainly because I can't remember studying this myself, so it was a new concept to me.
- Correspondence between thought processes for geometrical argument and proof by induction.
- Key because: shows how inductive type arguments are common and full induction can arise from other arguments and illustrations.

- The switch from geometric diagrammatical proofs to more rigorous proofs by induction was interesting as it made me think which would be more relevant for a certain class. While the inductive proof was certainly more mathematically sound for students to understand the mechanics involved I think it would be better to use the diagrams.

## *Main Session Part 4: Discussion of different task formulations*

After a brief summary of the activities that were covered in the session thus far, Stylianides introduced the next activity presented in Figure 4.4. Note here that Stylianides did not explicitly mention the purpose served by the particular selection of the student work in terms of initiating further mathematical work on the task. It is likely that this feature of the design of the sequence went unnoticed by the majority of the prospective teachers, thinking that the analysis of student work was merely part of the normal emphasis in the course of carefully attending to student contributions during a lesson.

The new activity asked for comparison of four different formulations of the mathematical task that the class worked on earlier (Figure 4.1) in terms of the kind of student activity each formulation would likely support in the classroom. This activity capitalised on prospective teachers' earlier mathematical and pedagogical work because they could use their experiences and insights in the discussion of the new activity.

As we will discuss in a following section, coding of responses to Prompt 2 in Table 4.1 indicates that most ideas that the prospective teachers mentioned in terms

**Four different formulations of a task**

1) What is a formula for the sum of the interior angles of any convex polygon with *n* sides? Prove your answer.

2) Is it possible to find a formula for the sum of the interior angles of any convex polygon with *n* sides? Prove your answer.

3) Use GeoGebra to measure the sum of the interior angles of convex polygons with different numbers of sides. Formulate and investigate conjectures about the sum of the interior angles of any convex polygon with *n* sides.

4) Prove that the sum of the interior angles of any convex polygon with *n* sides is given by the formula $(n-2) \times 180°$.

[Compare these formulations in terms of the kind of **student activity** they are likely to support when implemented in a classroom].

**Figure 4.4** Discussion of different task formulations

of their future planning and teaching arose from the activity in Figure 4.4. Below are some illustrative examples of responses to Prompt 2 in relation to this activity:

- Listening to how the statement of the task can be written in a number of different ways and how these can motivate students differently made me think that I will need to consider the best formulation of the task for my lesson objectives in each lesson.
- Careful consideration when I am designing a task, especially the purpose the task is aimed to achieve and to what extent is it going to achieve it.
- Discussion of different activities to offer students led me to think that we could also discuss these possible activities within the class – so students could have their preferences and justify their choices.
- I will think more carefully about how I phrase a question when asking pupils to prove something to get them to follow a specific path or try many different things.
- It is important to think about the students' thinking when designing tasks. What will the task provoke them to do? Will they understand what they have to do? Will it give them an opportunity to generalise or will it be too time consuming?
- Evaluate carefully the group that you are teaching in order to decide how to set each task.
- Continuing to think about task design and the implications of the decisions (however seemingly inconsequential) that teachers make.

It seems that the discussion of different task formulations had made explicit the important connection between what the teacher says and how mathematical action is shaped by what has been said. This could be expressed as indicating a need to plan for the move from intermental to intramental understanding, so that how the task is presented becomes internalised by learners rather than interpreted merely as direct instruction. We shall return to this possibility in the analysis of the responses to the second task sequence.

## Conclusion

The session ended with Stylianides providing a summary overview of the different activities in the session. The overview served as a reminder of the activities and did not include discussion of Stylianides' intentions for the activities in order not to influence prospective teachers' responses to the two prompts in the questionnaire that followed.

## Coding of prospective teachers' responses to the two prompts

Table 4.2 summarizes the number of times each of the activities in the main parts of the session was mentioned (directly or indirectly) in prospective teachers' responses to Prompt 1. The codes were derived from the description of the session provided above:

- mathematical work (main session parts 1 and 3)
- analysis of student work (main session part 2) and
- discussion of different task formulations (main session part 4).

Multiple coding of each event was possible, but this option was chosen in a restricted way.

**TABLE 4.2** Coding of prospective teachers' responses to Prompt 1 in the first task sequence

| Activities | Frequencies |
| --- | --- |
| Mathematical work | 31 |
| Analysis of student work | 12 |
| Discussion of different task formulations | 25 |

Table 4.3 summarises responses to Prompt 2. The coding for Prompt 2 focused on the origin of each idea from the session, considering what activity/key event from the session provoked the particular idea mentioned in each prospective teacher's response. This allowed us to use the same codes as for the coding of the responses in Prompt 1. On those occasions where it was not possible to identify the particular origin of a response or the origin related to an other event outside the main part of the session, we used the code 'Other'. Similar to the coding in Table 4.2, multiple coding of each event was possible, but this option was chosen in a restricted way.

**TABLE 4.3** Coding of prospective teachers' responses to Prompt 2 in the first task sequence

| Activity from which each idea seemed to originate | Frequencies |
| --- | --- |
| Mathematical work | 19 |
| Analysis of student work | 2 |
| Discussion of different task formulations | 28 |
| Other | 10 |

## Second task sequence

This task sequence was constructed and implemented by Watson to give teachers (including prospective teachers) experience of how particular forms of questioning can direct shifts of focus and levels of abstraction. Throughout mathematics, learning new ideas usually involves looking at existing knowledge in new ways, in particular what can be seen as a procedure at first might have to be understood as an abstract concept later on. In a Vygotskian view, without scaffolding most students might not make the ascent to a new level of thinking that takes what at first appears abstract but later becomes a concrete example for a new concept. For example, children first calculate products by multiplying; then the product itself becomes an example of a composite number, which can be factorised; then the factorisation becomes an example of a number structure; and so on. Teaching must help learners shift their perspective but new teachers often suppose this happens naturally as an outcome of completing tasks, or by being told new definitions, or by being given sophisticated methods. The aim of this session was to provide a sequence in which prospective teachers could experience and discuss how shifts of focus can be engineered.

There were nine elements to the task sequence and each had multiple purposes relating to generic pedagogy, subject specific didactics, and to specific mathematical ideas that Watson hoped the prospective teachers would encounter. The aim was to provide situations in which, at any moment, some might be focusing on mathematics, some on pedagogy and some on didactics. However, the main purpose of this sequence is to understand, through personal mathematical experience, how variation of task components and questions can shape different mathematical actions. For this reason, mathematical flow between tasks was at times interrupted for attention to be directed at the didactics. The session was not divided clearly into nine elements, but for easier reading that is how we present it. In each section the 'general pedagogic purpose' can give access to the ideas for the general reader, and it should also be possible to discern progression in the 'specific didactic purpose'.

The second task sequence, contrary to the first, is not directly related to curriculum content, and is usually novel for teachers. They start by selecting a shape made by connecting four congruent squares (tetramino). They use this shape to identify and generalise relationships between four neighbouring cells on various number grids. Generalisation becomes harder with more variables as more variations of the task are introduced. The forms of questioning also change in deliberate ways to encourage abstraction to take place.

All 29 prospective teachers responded to the same questionnaire as in the first task sequence (the two prompts in Table 4.1). Analysis was done by first collating all responses and identifying answers that appeared to be close paraphrases of each other. These were then grouped further into broader themes about mathematical tasks and didactical intentions. Here we describe what stood out for them as key events from the session (Prompt 1) and what ideas they envisioned using in their future planning and teaching (Prompt 2). A summary overview can be found in Table 4.5.

**TABLE 4.4** Structure and purpose of the second task sequence

| | **Initial mathematical work** | |
|---|---|---|
| 1 | *General pedagogic purpose* | Importance of personal choice; how group work can shorten time to generate materials/objects/data |
| | *Mathematical content* | Congruence; reflections; reasoning about completeness |
| | *Teacher educator action* | Introduce tetraminoes |
| | *Teacher activity* | With others, construct all possible tetraminoes; choose a shape and its orientation to make and use for the rest of the session |
| 2 | *General pedagogic purpose* | Share ideas about the relationships |
| | *Subject didactics purpose* | Variety generated through choice |
| | *Mathematical content* | General expressions on multiplication grids require two variables |
| | *Teacher educator action* | Give out multiplication grids up to 10x10; place the shape on the grid to 'cover' four cells |
| | *Teacher activity* | Look for relations between the four numbers covered; move shape somewhere else and repeat, etc.; work individually but talk in pairs about the relations between the four numbers under their shape; eventually see the relation is similar wherever the shape is put; they will want to generalise with two variables |

| 1 | 2 | 3 | 4 | 5 | 6 | 7 |
|---|---|---|---|---|---|---|
| 8 | 9 | 10 | 11 | 12 | 13 | 14 |
| 15 | | | 18 | 19 | 20 | 21 |
| 22 | 23 | | | 26 | 27 | 28 |
| 29 | 30 | 31 | 32 | 33 | 34 | 35 |
| 36 | 37 | 38 | 39 | 40 | 41 | 42 |
| 43 | 44 | 45 | 46 | 47 | 48 | 49 |

**Figure 4.5** Example of a tetramino on a 7 x 7 counting grid

**TABLE 4.4** Continued.

| 3 | General pedagogic purpose | Different choices about how to express generalisations |
|---|---|---|
|   | Subject didactics purpose | The choice of grid size might introduce irrelevant issues; choose a grid that instigates generalisation; people move from local generalisation to broader generalisation by being given varied examples |
|   | Mathematical content | Generalisation with one variable; variables and parameters are different kinds of generalisation |
|   | Teacher educator action | Give out 7x7 and 8x8 counting grids; encourage generalisation. Discuss difference between generalising variables and generalising parameters |
|   | Teacher activity | On 7x7, and then 8x8 counting grids when provided, repeat the search for relations between the four numbers covered (see Figure 3.5). Past experience indicates that they can be expected spontaneously to express the underlying relation symbolically for their own choice of shape and then generalise the grid size as a new variable (parameter) |

**New forms of question**

| 4 | Subject didactic purpose | Questions that scaffold abstract conceptualisation, i.e. treating 'grid/cell' combinations like a new concept |
|---|---|---|
|   | Mathematical content | Algebraic generalisation |
|   | Teacher educator action | Ask questions that treat the 'grid/cell' combination as a new concept: 'what tetraminoes on what grids will cover cells $n+9$ and $n-2$?' |
|   | Teacher activity | Reorientate their perceptions of the task to focus on 'grid/cell' combinations. Shift from generalisations to abstract 'grid/cell' combinations |

**Reflection on task effects**

| 5 | General pedagogic purpose | Value of giving time to re-run a 'memory video' of the lesson so far for themselves |
|---|---|---|
|   | Teacher educator action | Give a few minutes to make notes about what has happened for them so far |
|   | Teacher activity | Make notes on tasks and mathematics and their own activity so far to keep track |

**TABLE 4.4** Continued.

| 8 | 13 | 20 | 29 | 40 | 53 | 68 | 85 | 104 |
|---|---|---|---|---|---|---|---|---|
| 13 | 18 | 25 | 34 | 45 | 58 | 73 | 90 | 109 |
| 20 | 25 | 32 | 41 | 52 | 65 | 80 | 97 | 116 |
| 29 | 34 | 41 | 50 | 61 | 74 | 89 | 106 | 125 |
| 40 | 45 | 52 | 61 |  |  | 100 | 117 | 136 |
| 53 | 58 | 65 | 74 | 85 |  | 130 | 149 |
| 68 | 73 | 80 | 89 | 100 | 113 | 128 | 145 | 164 |
| 85 | 90 | 97 | 106 | 117 | 130 | 145 | 162 | 181 |
| 104 | 109 | 116 | 125 | 136 | 149 | 164 | 181 | 200 |

**Figure 4.6** Example of a tetramino on a two-variable grid

| 6 | *General pedagogic purpose* | A state of expertise is expected and used |
|---|---|---|
|  | *Subject didactic purpose* | Shift from one variable to two variables. Develop this in an unfamiliar direction |
|  | *Mathematical content* | Functions with two independent variables seen as values on a 2-d grid |
|  | *Teacher educator action* | Return to the multiplication grid. Give harder two-variable grids to some (see Figure 3.6 for an example) |
|  | *Teacher activity* | Continue with a new kind of grid that makes harder demands about generalisation |

**Return to initial task with higher level perceptions**

| 7 | *General pedagogic purpose* | Using questioning to scaffold thinking to a new level of abstraction |
|---|---|---|
|  | *Subject didactic purpose* | Questions introduce new levels of abstraction |
|  | *Mathematical content* | The difference between inductive reasoning from numerical examples and structural reasoning from visual images |
|  | *Teacher educator action* | Pose new questions such as: 'what size shape do I need to cover cells (m, n+1) and (m-7, n+2)?' |
|  | *Teacher activity* | Move from concrete work on grids and operations to positional, abstract, mental image; think about shapes and cells |

The interplay between mathematics and pedagogy **63**

**TABLE 4.4** Continued.

| | Reflection on whole task sequence | |
|---|---|---|
| 8 | *General pedagogic purpose* | Perceptions and generalisations depend on the variation available to learners |
| | *Subject didactic purpose* | Identify the shifts of thinking and how they were achieved through task design. Experience the power of 'backwards' questioning |
| | *Teacher educator action* | Tell them the intentions for mathematical attention at each stage of the sequence and how the task was structured to bring them about. What did they notice about variation of questions at each stage of the abstraction process? |
| | *Teacher activity* | Discuss the entire sequence of tasks using notes made previously and memory. Relate shifts in own thinking to changes in the task |
| 9 | *Teacher educator action* | Give questionnaire with the two prompts in Table 3.1. |

## *Analysis of responses to Prompt 1: key events and what made them key*

### *Gradient of difficulty mentioned in a general way*

Twenty-three prospective teachers mentioned their sense of a 'gradient of difficulty' in the tasks. Of these, eight mentioned abstraction as something achieved through the questioning, three more mentioned 'variation' as a tool for supporting generalisation. Ten mentioned the choice of numbers as important, and the remaining two remarked on the gradient but gave no more details. Five further responses commented that the first task had been harder and one said 'engagement improved dramatically with the easier [7x7 grid with single variable] task' although others thought that seeing the harder task [two-variable multiplication grid] first had been useful as giving them something to work towards. The ordering of the tasks had prompted thought about order and difficulty as intended, but it had been hoped that more of them would be specific about exactly how variation in the grids had prompted changes in levels of generality (see below). However, this would have been a new idea for them, and probably not one that is discussed with other teachers in school, and it would be sophisticated to be able to grasp this connection and also become articulate about it immediately after the experience.

### *Personal choice of examples*

Eleven prospective teachers mentioned the importance of personal choice of examples as a means of differentiation: 'allowing all to get something out of the task'. They thought variety was cognitively helpful because neighbours would then have different 'concept images' (Tall and Vinner 1981) and insight could be gained through discussion of different cases. Such comparisons between cases highlight the critical, non-obvious, features of relations. Nine further responses also mentioned personal choice of examples but emphasised affective rather than cognitive advantages: choice gave 'ownership' and hence improved engagement.

The design decision had been to show how choice could aid motivation, but without it becoming a major focus of the session. The cognitive advantage of comparing different cases in element 2 had arisen through their own discussion and was not something that had been anticipated, but will be incorporated in future use of the sequence.

## Explicit connections between task design, questioning and mathematical activity

Eight prospective teachers referred to recognising that their own mathematical approaches changed during the session in response to features of the task design, rather than the more general comments reported above; six of them mentioned the summary of intentions and that the intended effects matched their experience of doing the tasks; one said 'the pedagogical explanation was useful and related to how the lesson unfolded'. These remarks affirm the value of experiential learning for teaching. These eight also confirmed the value of explicitness in describing design decisions.

A further five responses mentioned that the questions had forced them to think backwards from abstract to concrete, to reflect on what they had been doing and construct particular cases that fitted abstract observations. Three of these mentioned the adaptations in Watson's questions; the other two described the 'backwards' questions as 'fun and increasing engagement'. We were pleased that 13 in all had made a connection between design and their own mathematical activity. The use of the word 'fun' would need further investigation because it suggests that these prospective teachers may not have recognised a shift from generalising in unknown situations to constructing examples and discussing implications. This shift may have produced a feeling of 'fun' but the mechanism by which it was brought about was cognitive rather than merely affective.

## Analysis of responses to Prompt 2: future planning and teaching

Prompt 2 in the questionnaire asked about teaching intentions and was analysed similarly.

Sixteen said they would think more about gradients of difficulty and order of tasks in future. Of these three did not elaborate further but four talked about focusing on relations and patterns; four talked of starting with a harder task so that 'there is always a higher peak'. Five students noticed that extension tasks were always more complex versions of what everyone was doing.

Fourteen mentioned the importance of controlling variation, to encourage generalisation, to be clear about purpose, and to allow students to 'use their own strategies and methods at every stage while following the structure of the lesson'. One person said that using the same resource, but slightly differently, encourages a particular way of thinking.

Fourteen prospective teachers talked about giving choice and ownership to generate variety in the classroom.

Three mentioned the importance of having 'interesting' ways to use 'algebra as generalising relationships', and one talked about how turning the task round led to seeing where a 'rule' had come from.

## Connections between questionnaire responses and task design

A main aim in the second task sequence had been for prospective teachers to experience a form of questioning that scaffolds conceptualisation at a higher level, making the 'grid-shape' partnership into a new mathematical object by asking questions that focus on the relationship rather than on particular grids or shapes separately. To a great extent this had been successful, in that they reported that something had changed for them because of the task and question construction. They mainly recognised features of the work they had been asked to do and the potential power of variation and generalisation within that work. The importance of choosing examples well and thinking about sets of examples seemed to be well understood. The personal engagement they had felt by choosing a shape made a big impression and engagement is an important issue in their teaching.

It is also heartening that some of the feedback did mention the specific abstraction processes that were intended in the design. But given that most prospective teachers had indeed changed from lower levels of conceptualisation to higher levels as the task sequence progressed, and given that it had been explained to them how

**TABLE 4.5** Coding of prospective teachers' responses to Prompts 1 and 2 in the second task sequence

| *Key features of sequence (Prompt 1)* | *Frequencies* |
| --- | --- |
| Gradient of difficulty | 23 |
| Personal choice | 20 |
| Connections between task design and mathematical activity | 13 |
| *Anticipated use (Prompt 2)* | *Frequencies* |
| Gradients of difficulty | 16 |
| Controlling variation | 14 |
| Choice and ownership | 14 |
| Interesting ways to use algebra | 3 |

these shifts of level had been engineered through questioning, why were only 13 of them articulate about this in their feedback? A plausible conjecture is that this way of thinking about tasks and cognitive challenge is new for them. Such thinking is rare in both research and professional literature. To articulate this new idea at the end of the session in which it has been first introduced is a high expectation.

## Concluding remarks

Both task sequences address the need, when doing mathematics, to generalise from mathematical experiences either by inductive reasoning or by understanding relations within a structure. In each sequence teachers learn more about the design of tasks for the classroom and also the effects of varying task presentation. Novotná and Sarrazy (2011) explain that thinking about 'didactical variability' needs to be explicit when teachers are planning and designing tasks. Looking at variations in tasks can reveal the relationship between how ideas are presented and how they are learnt, and can also avoid routinisation of mathematical activity. In the first task sequence the exploration of the issue of varying task presentation is an explicit activity, comparing different problem formulations and hypothesising about the effects of these on learning. The effects of this comparison on teachers' thinking figured strongly in the questionnaire responses. In the second task sequence variability is also experienced directly but in a slightly different form: variability is used to mathematically engineer different kinds of generalisation from which abstraction is developed. The aim in the second sequence was to notice these connections, and therefore to think in future about what generalisations need to be engineered, and how this can be done.

As mathematics teacher educators, we both have similar aims in our teaching and similar expectations of the prospective teachers' responses, but the interplay between mathematics and pedagogy was not identical in the two task sequences even though in both cases it happened in complex and multi-faceted ways

In the first sequence the interplay can be summarised as described below. The starting point of the sequence was a mathematical task that, although it related to a well-known secondary school curriculum topic, the expectations in the task in terms of producing different proofs for each of the statements made the task appropriate and challenging for the prospective teachers. Although the teacher educator did not raise pedagogical issues in the discussion of the mathematical task, the prospective teachers themselves started making such connections on their own in their contributions during the lesson and also in their responses to the questionnaire. These connections were supported by the fact that they could see the content of the task relating to the school curriculum and, also, from the fact that they were familiar with different issues of teaching and learning mathematics as a result of their school-based experiences. Although the discussion of the secondary students' work on a similar mathematical task seemed to shift the focus to pedagogy, the choice of the particular sample of student work was deliberate in order to open up more mathematical possibilities leading to a discussion of a proof by mathematical induction. The comparison of different task formulations at the end of the first task sequence capitalised on the prospective teachers' earlier mathematical and pedagogical discussions. For example, the connection between the paths they had followed in their earlier engagement with the mathematics, and the particular formulation that had prompted these paths, served as powerful empirical experiences that informed the discussion of different formulations. At the same time, their knowledge of students and their other school-based experiences provided a complementary lens both for the discussion of the different task formulations and also for the explanations they provided in the questionnaire about the importance of this activity in their own development as learners and teachers of mathematics.

In the second sequence, the interplay between mathematics and pedagogy can be summarised as described below. The mathematical work is not curriculum related and was new for the prospective teachers. The emphasis remained on their own mathematical activity until attention was deliberately drawn to elements of task design and how they have shaped that activity, which served as a link to issues of pedagogy. By staying with their own experience, connections between task features and mathematical activity were made based on immediate personal evidence. In the questionnaire there was the opportunity to focus more on pedagogical issues and articulate, for example, how their experience in the session might influence their own teaching. In their responses to the questionnaire, they overtly described and discussed how the deliberate introduction of new forms of questioning changed the mathematical activity, and how they might use these techniques in their teaching. The sequencing of tasks is central to these effects. In element 4 of the second sequence, for example, the new forms of questioning would not have a dramatic effect on changing prospective teachers' thinking if early stages had not first established a simpler form of thinking. A similar reorientation takes place later after the establishment of the 'grid/cell' generality. These shifts of attention can be replicated for classroom mathematics learners through careful task design. The underlying principle in the reorientation described above is that learners at any stage establish successive intramental understandings that are reshaped by new forms of questioning. The direct personal experience, through the tasks above, of learning mathematics and of how learning can take place, can give prospective teachers insight into how to construct pedagogic sequences for their own students.

To conclude, we have reported on two mathematics-specific task sequences that illustrate in different ways the features offered by Watson and Mason (2008: 4–6), which we summarised at the beginning of the paper. Both task sequences:

- bring aspects of mathematical knowledge to the fore in ways that promote deep understanding
- bring aspects of mathematical thinking to the attention of teachers and provide a context for articulation of them
- develop awareness of multiple perspectives through task-centred discussion and
- focus on didactic decisions relevant for specific topics.

In both sequences, prospective teachers' own learning, experience and knowledge, whether about mathematics or pedagogy, become the central reflective resource. The design of the task sequences shapes their immediate experience in the session, and also mediates interplay between past and present experience, school and university experience, and mathematics and pedagogy.

## References

Balacheff, N. (1988) A study of students' proving processes at the junior high school level. In I. Wirszup and R. Streit (eds) *Proceedings of the Second UCSMP International Conference on Mathematics Education*. Reston, VA: National Council of Teachers of Mathematics.

Chevallard, Y. (1999) L'analyse des pratiques enseignantes en théorie anthropologique du didactique. *Recherches en Didactique des Mathématiques*, 19(2): 221–66.

Christiansen, B. and Walter, G. (1986) Task and activity. In B. Christiansen, A.-G. Howson and M. Otte (eds) *Perspectives on Mathematics Education: Papers submitted by members of the Bacomet Group*. Dordrecht: D. Reidel.

Dubinsky, E. (1986) Teaching mathematical induction I. *Journal of Mathematical Behavior*, 5: 305–17.

Dubinsky, E. (1990) Teaching mathematical induction II. *Journal of Mathematical Behavior*, 8: 285–304.

Dubinsky, E. and Lewin, P. (1986) Reflective abstraction and mathematics education: the generic decomposition of induction and compactness. *Journal of Mathematical Behavior*, 5: 55–92.

Hagger, H. and McIntyre, D. (2000) What can research tell us about teacher education? *Oxford Review of Education*, 26(3–4): 483–94.

Harel, G. (2002) The Development of Mathematical Induction as a Proof Scheme: A model for DNR-based instruction. In S. Campbell and R. Zaskis (eds) *Learning and Teaching Number Theory: Research in cognition and instruction*, pp. 185–212. New Jersey: Ablex Publishing Corporation.

Henningsen, M. and Stein, M. K. (1997) Mathematical tasks and student cognition: classroom-based factors that support and inhibit high-level mathematical thinking and reasoning. *Journal for Research in Mathematics Education*, 28: 524–49.

Knuth, E. J. (2002). Secondary school mathematics teachers' conceptions of proof. *Journal for Research in Mathematics Education*, 33: 379–405.

Leont'ev, A. (1975) *Dieyatelinocti, Soznaine, Ilichynosti* [*Activity, Consciousness, Personality*]. Moskva: Politizdat.

Margolinas, C. (2004) *Points de vue de l'élève et du professeur: Essai de développement de la théorie des situations didactiques*. Université de Provence. http://tel.archives-ouvertes.fr/tel-00429580/fr/

Margolinas, C. (2005) Les situations à bifurcations multiples: indices de dysfonctionnement ou de cohérence. In A. Mercier and C. Margolinas (eds) *Balises en didactique des mathématiques*, (pp. Cédérom). Grenoble La Pensée Sauvage. http://halshs.archives-ouvertes.fr/halshs-00432229/fr/

Mason, J. and Pimm, D. (1984) Generic examples: seeing the general in the particular. *Educational Studies in Mathematics*, 15: 277–89.

Mason, J. (with Burton, L. and Stacey, K.) (1982) *Thinking Mathematically*. London: Addison-Wesley.

Movshovitz-Hadar, N. (1993) The false coin problem, mathematical induction and knowledge fragility. *Journal of Mathematical Behavior*, 12: 253–68.

Novotná, J. and Sarrazy, B. (2011) Didactical variability in teacher education. In O. Zaslavsky and P. Sullivan (eds) *Constructing Knowledge for Teaching Secondary Mathematics: Tasks to enhance prospective and practicing teacher learning*, pp. 103–19. Dordrecht: Springer.

Runesson, U. (2005) Beyond discourse and interaction. Variation: a critical aspect for teaching and learning mathematics. *The Cambridge Journal of Education*, 35(1): 69–87.

Stylianides, A. J. and Stylianides, G. J. (2008) Studying the implementation of tasks in classroom settings: High-level mathematics tasks embedded in real-life contexts. *Teaching and Teacher Education*, 24(4): 859–75.

Stylianides, G. J., and Stylianides, A. J. (2010) Mathematics for teaching: a form of applied mathematics. *Teaching and Teacher Education*, 26: 161–72.

Stylianides, G. J., Stylianides, A. J. and Philippou, G. N. (2007) Preservice teachers' knowledge of proof by mathematical induction. *Journal of Mathematics Teacher Education*, 10: 145–66.

Tall, D. O. and Vinner, S. (1981) Concept image and concept definition in mathematics, with particular reference to limits and continuity, *Educational Studies in Mathematics*, 12: 151–69.

Thompson, I. (2014) Introduction to this volume.

Vergnaud, G. (1982) Cognitive and developmental psychology and research in mathematics education: some theoretical and methodological issues. *For the Learning of Mathematics*, 3(2): 31–41.

Watson, A. and Bills, L. (2011) Working mathematically on teaching mathematics: preparing graduates to teach secondary mathematics. In O. Zaslavsky and P. Sullivan (eds) *Constructing Knowledge for Teaching Secondary Mathematics: Tasks to enhance prospective and practicing teacher learning*. Dordrecht: Springer.

Watson, A. and Mason, J. (2008) Taken-as-shared: a review of what is known about mathematical tasks in teacher education. *Journal of Mathematics Teacher Education* 10: 205–15.

Zaslavsky, O. and Sullivan, P. (2011) (eds) *Constructing Knowledge for Teaching Secondary Mathematics: Tasks to enhance prospective and practicing teacher learning*. Dordrecht: Springer.

## Note

1 Typically, most students would only have met this method in algebraic/number theory contexts.

# 5

# DISCIPLINARY KNOWLEDGE

Task design in geography

*Roger Firth*

### Introduction

In geography classrooms in English secondary schools students' academic work and intellectual development is commonly defined by the learning tasks that they encounter on a routine basis, 'by the tasks they are required to accomplish with subject matter' (Doyle and Carter 1984: 130). Tasks form the basic situational structures of learning in classrooms; they organise and direct thought and action (Doyle, 1983). Accomplishing a sequence of tasks has two consequences. First, students acquire facts, concepts, principles and explanations that are part of the phenomenon called the 'school subject', in this case school geography. Second, students practice and improve their thinking and other skills necessary in completing the tasks. Tasks influence student learning by directing attention to particular aspects of content or subject knowledge and by specifying ways of processing information for meaning making, where the developmental trajectory is from common sense to subject understanding.

In terms of teaching, a fundamental responsibility of the teacher is to design learning tasks that will enable all students to achieve the intended learning. My work with teachers suggests that the design of tasks is commonly described within a wider instructional framework that is set out in terms of planning lessons, lesson sequences (curricular schemes of work) and assessing students. While recognising the significance of the individual task and its realisation in sustaining academic work and developing understanding, usually, tasks are not considered apart from this wider framework.

In designing effective instructional tasks geography teachers are likely to consider how tasks enable 'active learning' and support students' engagement with the subject matter (the 'content' of the lesson) and develop their geographical capacities (knowledge, understanding and subject specific and generic skills). Tasks determine not only the knowledge, understanding, skills and values students develop, but equally important, how they come to think about and make sense of geography. Here, constructivism has emerged as a very powerful discourse for explaining how knowledge is produced as well as how students learn. Many teachers of geography will have been introduced to some of the theoretical tenets of constructivism during their teacher preparation course and through recent government strategies to improve teaching and learning. However, the assertion of the importance of the learner and of learning, in all probability, will have been more potent than the assertion of the importance of the nature of disciplined knowledge as an object of study – if it was considered at all. With all of this, it is not to ignore the many types of constructivist theory, nor to say that teaching practices in geography are wholly constructivist, but rather, that constructivist discourses have brought important and helpful attention to the learner and the learning process at the same time as they are agnostic on the matter of knowledge.

In geography classrooms 'the learner is conceived as an active participant in the learning process rather than a receiver of knowledge' (Ford 2010: 265). Emphasis has been placed on 'the ideas that students bring with them to classrooms and how these ideas serve as building blocks from which understanding of academic content is formed' (ibid). Considerable progress has been made in developing pedagogical strategies for encouraging students to be active in their own knowledge construction in geography classrooms. 'Constructivism's great contribution… is that it has placed student understanding as the central goal of education. As such, the theory has helped educators to reorient the hierarchical structure of teaching and learning into a more horizontal one in which student constructions of knowledge play a more central role' (Stemhagen, Reich and Muth 2013: 57).

However, there is a need for a stronger conception of knowledge when thinking about student learning and task design in the subject disciplines. 'Disciplines can be understood as social fields of practice comprising both relatively formal structures of knowledge and practices, and actors who share interests and norms of knowledge production and communication' (Freebody, Maton and Martin 2008). Each discipline, so my argument goes, 'has developed norms that are applied to the question of how it is that human experience can be converted into knowledge, and how that knowledge can be appropriately disseminated' (ibid).

This chapter considers task design that takes into account the disciplined nature of knowledge: the underlying methodological and epistemic principles (norms) of a discipline that support the capacity to build knowledge over time, both in terms of the discipline and in terms of fostering and promoting the geographical understanding of students. It is grounded in the argument that the lack of clarity and precision about constructivist theories (which can refer to epistemology, psychology and pedagogy) has resulted in misunderstandings and over-simplified applications of some of its theoretical tenets with respect to teaching and learning in geography. While this issue certainly deserves attention, the focus here is with a clearer articulation of how a disciplinary-based understanding of knowledge based on how disciplinary communities produce knowledge might impact on task design.

Ball and her colleagues at the University of Michigan (mathematics education) have been struck by

> the relatively unchartered arena of mathematical knowledge necessary for teaching the subject that is not intertwined with knowledge of pedagogy, students, curriculum or other noncontent domains.
> 
> *(Ball, Thames and Phelps 2008: 402)*

Over the years I too have been struck by the absence of any consideration of the conception and nature of disciplinary knowledge (though see Firth 2007, 2011). Bringing learning and knowledge together remains a priority agenda in geography education.

While it is important to emphasise that epistemology does not address the processes of the acquisition of knowledge, it does help in our understanding of the nature of disciplinary knowledge itself: its extent and limits, the nature of evidence and the standards and criteria by which we can judge its reliability. Moreover, by doing so, this can help to show how knowledge is linked to learning, which is crucial to the development of a learning theory with a certain epistemological foundation. The stance taken here is that the epistemic nature of the discipline does have pedagogic implications. Indeed, as Morrow (2007) has emphasised in his seminal distinction between formal and epistemological access to curricula; it is also a social justice issue. The limitations of constructivism and the possibilities of a modest realist approach are discussed below.

In educational settings disciplinary knowledge has often been connected with deterministic or restrictive forms of learning. But

> a discipline embodies a productive interplay between the constraining force of knowledge development, on the one hand, and the distinctive arena for enhanced intellectual agency that each knowledge domain offers… It is this interplay… between epistemological constraint and insightful agency that is the platform on which genuine conceptual innovation and progress can be made.
> 
> *(Freebody et al. 2008: 3)*

For this reason, the insights of constructivism that put learners at the centre of the educational process should be tempered by a regard for the systematic knowledge (what Young (2008) has described as 'powerful knowledge') that emerges from the disciplines. Education, in my view, must enable young people to acquire and understand the powerful constructs and ideas of modern disciplines. As Wheelahan (2010a: 70) asserts, 'Academic disciplines provide access to the natural and social worlds, even if this access is imperfect'. These modern disciplines represent 'collective representations' and they 'are the means societies use to transcend the limits of individual experience' (Wheelahan 2010b: 94).

In this sense, this chapter questions established constructivist approaches to geography pedagogy which have failed to recognise their own limitations – in disregarding the disciplined nature of the knowledge (its epistemic nature) being taught. Geography education has become a set of tasks which are not those of geographers. What is missing from the account is any appreciation of the rules and practices that guide the construction of knowledge in the disciplinary community. Given these arguments, it is clear students will not possess sufficient resources for constructing disciplined knowledge; and it is not difficult to imagine how this might result in static/inert knowledge that a student either acquires or fails to acquire. What would be learned regarding disciplinary content is likely to be less than a suitable understanding because the resources drawn on would have less to do with the academic discipline than the existing learning context of the classroom.

In drawing attention to specific theoretical possibilities about the development of a realist pedagogy the primary concern is to explore some key issues that could help teachers' attempts to develop more balanced, practical approaches to teaching and learning in geography, based on an alternative modest realism and at the same time to move beyond the traditionalist/progressive dichotomy that has characterised debates over pedagogical reforms for so long.

To set the scene the existing situational context of teaching and learning in English secondary school classrooms is described and an overly-simplified application of constructivism is briefly highlighted. Building on recent arguments for the need to foreground disciplinarity and disciplined knowledge, the chapter then gives attention to the idea of 'disciplinary constraint'; that is the way constructivist pedagogic approaches are constrained by the structuring principles of disciplined knowledge. Examining task design in this way brings to the fore questions concerning disciplined knowledge that, it is argued, have been given little attention in the geography education literature (though see Firth 2007, 2011). The ideas presented are informed by ongoing research conducted with teachers and in particular the constructs 'disciplined judgment' (Stemhagen et al., 2013) and 'disciplined critique' (Ford 2010) which mobilise the idea of disciplinary constraint.

The focus of the discussion is the tasks themselves and not the tasks within the complex social system of the classroom. That is, the chapter is concerned with teachers' thinking and the intent of their planning and specifically: how tasks enable students to navigate between their less formally disciplined beliefs and disciplinary modes of thought. The boundaries between disciplinary knowledge (which is converted into a form known as schooled knowledge in order to provide access to students) and out-of-school knowledge (variously called 'everyday', 'lay', 'owned' or 'ethno knowledge') will vary by discipline (Bernstein 2000) with implications for how teachers make use of constructivist learning theories.

## The situational context

The ways in which teachers think about and plan tasks is a matter of professional judgement based on their own professional constructs, experiences and forms of professional development, and in particular, the existing formulation of the geography curriculum and fashions of pedagogy (over the last two decades shaped by government policy). In classroom settings in England commonly a small number of tasks are completed within the teaching and learning sequences of a lesson and they are of relatively short duration. Students sometimes work on their own, but more generally in pairs or small groups. The nature of learning tasks will normally be framed by decisions about:

1    the purpose of the lesson
2    what is to be taught (subject content)
3    the learning needs of particular students and groups of students and the desire to elicit and sustain students' attention, interest and motivation
4    the different cognitive processes involved in carrying out a task, such as listing, selecting, sequencing/ordering, ranking, comparing/contrasting, classifying, reasoning, evaluating information
5    the geographical learning to take place within tasks
6    and whether the task has a function in student assessment.

Doyle (1983) and Doyle and Carter (1984) drew attention to the way tasks organise cognition and influence learners by defining a goal and directing their attention to particular aspects of content and by specifying ways of processing information. In the kind of decision making highlighted here what is missing from the account is any consideration of the norms and practices by which geographical knowledge is constructed in disciplinary communities. In consequence, the tasks and content will present 'an opaque epistemology [to students]; where knowledge indexes the situation in which it arises and is used [and] which becomes coded and connected to the task and environment in which it is developed' (Osborne, 1996: 61). The epistemological considerations of how it is coded by the discipline (its norms and practices) and connected to the task are not thought about. And while it would be retrograde to teach students one final version of truth, they nonetheless need access to the epistemic tools that can help them make these judgements.

A number of contextual factors should be mentioned. The subject content to be covered with particular age groups is determined in England by the National Curriculum programme of study (11–14 years) or examination specification at GCSE and 'A' level (14–16 and 16–18), though how it is taught rests with the teacher. The National Curriculum programme of study is seen as being less prescriptive than the examination specifications with significantly more freedom to decide what to teach. The content-heavy examination specifications tend not only to dictate what is to be learned in each lesson but also impact on the tasks themselves; here the most important consideration may well be how much content can be covered through a particular task and time period.

Previous curriculum policy and revisions to the National Curriculum threw some doubt on the educational importance of disciplinary subjects. In 2010 the new coalition government published a Schools White Paper, *The Importance of Teaching* (DfE 2010), which introduced a new round of changes to education in England. The White Paper presented an agenda for change described by the government as 'radical reform of our schools' (DfE 2010: 4). The agenda included a further review of the national curriculum as well as the assertion of the need to allow 'schools and teachers…greater control over what is taught' (p.11). The intention of the review was to establish a curriculum that 'would be slim, clear and authoritative' (p. 42), yet with a 'tighter, more rigorous model of the knowledge which every child should expect to master' (p. 10). The new 'knowledge-based' national curriculum will be taught for the first time in September 2014. The emphasis is one in which the focus will be on the core subject knowledge that every child and young person should gain at each stage of their education.

The review has also seen the Secondary National Strategy discarded. The Strategy was introduced by the previous Labour government with the aim of transforming teaching and learning across the curriculum in the foundation subjects (including geography). The strategy was underpinned by constructivism; though at best the strategy abstracted parts of a constructivist approach from the whole. Teachers have been 'increasingly charged with engaging young people in active learning' (Drew and Mackie 2011: 451). Active learning has become a pedagogical construct widely applied in geography though conversations with teachers reveal its lack of clarity and consensus as to its meaning. Though much progress was made in developing pedagogical strategies for encouraging students to be active learners, the coalition government was critical of the centralised and prescriptive nature of the previous government's strategies to improve teaching emphasising the need to 'free teachers up from prescription, bureaucracy and central control' (DfE 2010: 40).

It is of interest that the 2012–13 Report on Schools by Her Majesty's Chief Inspector of Education, Children's Services and Skills (Ofsted 2013) emphasised some common misconceptions about what constitutes good teaching together with the statement 'inspectors do not expect to see a particular teaching style' (Ofsted 2013: 37). This may be a reference to the influence that the former National Strategy has had on teachers' approach to teaching. It is likely, however, that the 'constructivist approach' which underpinned the National Strategy and has shaped teachers' classroom practice over the last decade or so, will continue to have an influence in the future.

Within education more widely there has been increasing emphasis of the need to bring knowledge back into discussions about the school curriculum and classroom practice. The work of the British sociologist of education, Michael Young, is notable here. In *Bringing Knowledge Back In* Young's core argument is that providing students with access to knowledge is the key purpose that distinguishes education from all other activities and the knowledge acquired in schools is fundamentally more powerful than that gained from everyday life. The report by the Expert Panel (DfE 2011) for the national curriculum review took up Young's idea of 'powerful knowledge' in its deliberations on the construction and content of the new National Curriculum. In the concern to secure 'the right of all children and young people to a broad and balanced curriculum' (p. 4) it stated (as Young's work does) that perhaps the most fundamental curriculum consideration 'concerns the nature of knowledge and of learners, and crucially, the interaction between them' (p. 11). It goes on to say:

> Education can thus be seen, at its simplest, as the product of interaction between socially valued knowledge and individual development. It occurs through learner experience of both of these key elements. The school curriculum structures these processes…effective teaching 'engages with valued forms of knowledge and also equips learners for life in the broadest sense.
> *(DfE 2011: 11)*

## Constructivism and disciplinary knowledge

There is no question about the significance of the constructivist perspective on knowledge. It has served to destabilise deeply entrenched premises about its independence of the social context in which it was produced and its objectivity. There are two issues on which a more modest realist perspective and constructivism agree: (1) knowledge is not timeless, universal and independent of the social context in which it is produced; (2) knowledge is socially produced by communities of knowledge producers and these communities are characterised by struggles around power and competing interests (Wheelahan 2010a: 8). However, as Wheelahan argues, 'this is not the end of the matter' (p. 9). Constructivist arguments that knowledge is a product of social practices have led to two problematic conclusions. The first and more general is that all knowledge has equal validity. In this way the distinction between theoretical and everyday knowledge can be collapsed because both are a product of social practices. This argument, however, assumes that knowledge does not have features that are independent of these social practices; that there is no epistemologically independent basis for knowledge claims. 'In focusing on social practices, [constructivism] denies that there are epistemic relations of knowledge that must be considered in their own right and judged by the extent to which they provide access to the social and natural world' (Wheelahan 2010a: 10). The second and more specific is that knowledge is reduced to the experiences and interests of the groups whose perspective knowledge is held to represent. In this way, knowledge is conflated experientially with knowing and with knowers (Moore 2007: 28). This approach has the consistent problem of leading to relativism – which denies the possibility of objectivity in knowledge

(Moore 2007: 25). Primarily and ultimately knowledge is about power – the power of the powerful to maintain their power and privilege.

A more modest realist approach to knowledge would emphasise that relativism does not necessarily follow from a social theory of knowledge. On the contrary a social theory of knowledge can be the basis for claims to truth and objectivity by identifying the distinctive norms and practices through which they are produced. This is to emphasise the internal or epistemic relations within a discipline that are concerned with the conditions for the production of knowledge itself – and for the 'acquisition' of knowledge – within classrooms. These internal or epistemic relations have been given little attention until recently. Knowledge can be understood as emergent from the specialised collective practices of knowledge production within disciplinary/epistemic communities. Knowledge relies on a regulative or normative rather than an absolute notion of truth, an inescapable ontological realism and recognition of the fallibility of even the most reliable knowledge.

A modest approach to realism should be seen as a version of 'structural objectivity' (Daston and Galison 2007) where the structures of expert/scientific practice owe something to the schemes of intelligibility that people use to identify them as such. 'Knowledge develops on the basis of its conceptual or explanatory power, which allows experts to make choices between competing theories' (Firth 2011: 292). Such systematic knowledge develops into non-arbitrary forms that have their own necessary normative constraints. 'In this sense, constructivism is brought into a realist framework within the field of knowledge production: constructivism focused on authoritative epistemic justification' (ibid). The argument of this chapter is that curriculum designers and teachers should take this normativity into account – the development of student understanding should be a normative goal of the curriculum and pedagogy, recognising the social nature of knowledge, its fallibility and the need to revise knowledge in light of evidence.

In arguing that all knowledge is fallible but in failing to recognise that judgements about the worth of such knowledge are possible, constructivism offers no guidance or mechanism on adjudication between theories, on how one theory may be considered to be more reliable than another (Osborne 1996: 53). What is missing from the constructivist account is any understanding of the norms and practices that guide the construction of knowledge in disciplinary communities. In recognising the significance of these norms and practices it is also necessary to distinguish between disciplinary knowledge and everyday knowledge when considering task design. 'While both are theory laden and concept dependent, the former is distinguished from the latter because it represents the systematisation of knowledge that "extends and supersedes our ordinary understanding of things" and the relations between them' (Wheelahan 2010a: 84).

## The importance of the 'epistemic game'

Perkins (2006) draws our attention to the fact that disciplines are more than just concepts, theories and facts. 'They have their own characteristic *epistemes*' (p. 42).

As Perkins argues, students will probably have never heard the word episteme, but they deal with epistemes tacitly all the time. 'An episteme can be defined as a system of ideas or way of understanding that allows us to establish knowledge' (ibid). He draws attention to the work of Schwab and Bruner among others who have emphasised the importance of students understanding the syntactic structure of the disciplines they are studying. The Geographical Association (the professional association for geography teachers) highlighted the importance of procedural or syntactic knowledge during the consultation phase of the review of the national curriculum. It was presented as part of a 'knowledge framework' or typology which would be helpful in distinguishing between the different forms of geographical knowledge. What was not emphasised was the significance of syntactic knowledge; when it is omitted from teaching and learning, students will be left unsure of how knowledge is constructed within the norms of the discipline. The point is, as Perkins emphasises, the 'epistemic game' needs to be surfaced and animated; students need to know about the game and to play the game knowingly. It is a form of metacognition. If students can learn how to learn, they come to know about knowledge.

Epistemes are activity systems that activate and animate disciplinary content. In what follows, the idea of disciplinary constraint is used to illustrate ways in which teachers might think about the relationship between student knowledge constructions and the construction of powerful disciplinary knowledge and in this way introduce students to 'the epistemic game'.

The idea of disciplinary constraint as outlined by Stemhagen et al. (2013) and Ford (2010) is intended to draw attention to the relation between constructivist pedagogy and epistemology; how the epistemic nature of a discipline 'constrains the pedagogical choices open to teachers' (Stemhagen et al. 2013: 58). It is also an inducement to help teachers become more aware of their discipline: its unique approach to knowledge production and how to help students learn to employ the epistemic tools provided by the discipline. Disciplines, of course, vary in their epistemological frameworks; some will be 'more pliable… in regards to the ways in which warrants are constructed and arguments validated, while the frameworks of other disciplines are characterised as more fixed' (ibid: 60). This has implications for how subject specialist teachers should consider building a successful classroom culture that makes use of constructivism. 'The more fixed a discipline, the more attention is required by the teacher with regard to scaffolding student judgements so that they conform more closely to what is considered legitimate' (ibid: 61). What about geographical knowledge?

## Geographical knowledge

'Geography, it has become commonplace to say, spans both the natural and social sciences' (Demeritt 2005: 819). The statement illustrates how the discipline has engaged with the epistemological consequences of shifts in philosophy and sociology of knowledge and science and how geographical knowledge is differentiated. As a result of geographers' sustained engagement with these philosophical issues, 'a broad range of more or less distinct competing traditions on how best to think geographically and how most effectively to research geographical questions' (Hubbard, Kitchin, Bartley and Fuller 2005: 6) are now current in the discipline. In recognising the specialist domains and traditions of the discipline Golledge is hopeful that 'interaction between these domains might generate a new interest in an integrated science' (2002: 1).

Lack of interaction and engagement have been characteristics of the discipline, as Sheppard and Plummer (2007) have argued. In emphasising the plurality within the discipline and its ready acceptance by many geographers, notwithstanding occasional calls to monism, their concern is not its elimination or integration, but rather moving geography from a plurality of approaches to engaged pluralism. The diversity of the discipline is its strength, they emphasise, but to advance knowledge, this diversity must be the foundation for intellectual interaction. As Longino (2002) argues, knowledge about the world is more reliable when all the various approaches are placed in rigorous engagement with one another. 'A satisfactory epistemology for science [the disciplines] should not foreclose the choice of pluralism versus monism' (Longino 2002: 175).

What is evident here is that geography and geographers are differentiated from the inside out and the difference between physical geography and human geography is a distinctive characteristic. Geography is a multi-paradigmatic discipline and geographers work with different concepts of scientific knowledge and its development. Having said this, I am aware that not all geographers would agree with this representation of the discipline. Delineating exactly what the knowledge structures are in relation to geography may not be straightforward.

There is an important difference between discussions in the abstract compared with an exploration of the actual discipline. Is the nature of this structure the same for all geographers? And, significantly for education, how are teachers, teacher educators and students aware of it? There are two points. First, engagement with a discipline is both a various and specific experience. This idea is a challenge still to be taken up by geography teachers. Second, it raises a question whether there is a need for some overarching epistemological model of the disciplines for use in education, or, whether the emphasis placed here on students' engagement with the disciplinary norms and practices of knowledge production of the specific discipline (in this case geography) is sufficient.

## Disciplinary constraint

'Disciplined judgement' is the framework or tool that Stemhagen *et al.* (2013) have formulated to put disciplinary constraint into practice. It serves two purposes: the first is to orient secondary school teachers toward the discipline and its approach to knowledge. The second is to help students to employ the conceptual tools provided by the discipline arguing 'that constructivist classrooms must balance the individual judgements that students apply during the course of their work with the normalising tools of judgement as employed within the particular discipline in question' (p. 58). What these normalising tools of judgement are becomes clear when they argue 'that making the criteria of disciplinary judgement explicit will provide a crucial scaffold for students' (ibid). And as they go on to say 'disciplined judgement… describes the application of criteria that emerge from the institutional context of each discipline to judge the worth of knowledge construction' (ibid). In this way, students 'become skilled, not only at constructing knowledge, but also at evaluating it – judging its worth – in disciplined ways' (ibid). Of importance here, the implementation of this approach requires that teachers understand disciplinary knowledge in a more dynamic way, not as a static entity that students either acquire or fail to acquire. It is the contention of Stemhagen *et al.* 'that the inclusion of judgement is the fulfilment of the promise of empowerment and meaningfulness that is implicit in learner-centred constructivist pedagogy' (p. 58–9).

Of course, the idea of disciplinary constraint will only work if one can keep in mind the complexities involved in the tool of disciplined judgement. But we have to begin to consider how disciplinary concerns can modify a teacher's approach to constructivist pedagogy. And teachers will have to apply professional judgement in order to balance a number of concerns, including the need to interest and motivate students to learn, the demands of performance management judged on student achievement, as well as the desire to infuse the learning with disciplined modes of thought.

In a similar fashion to Stemhagen *et al.*, Ford (2010) also emphasises the need for 'increased theoretical specificity regarding the constructivist learning process' (p. 266). He also notes a tension in constructivist pedagogy, 'a tension between allowing students to construct their own sense of disciplinary ideas and ensuring that the sense they make is correct' (p. 265) and asks, quoting Windschitl (2002), 'if certain ideas are considered correct by experts, should students internalise those ideas instead of constructing their own? (ibid)' But whereas Stemhagen *et al.* mobilise the idea of disciplinary constraint in terms of disciplined judgement, Ford does so by the use of the idea of disciplinary critique. And while Stemhagen *et al.* are concerned with the disciplines of literacy, history and mathematics and the over-simplified application of constructivism in teacher preparation courses (secondary schools), science is used as an exemplar academic discipline by Ford for his argument.

The process of disciplinary critique is described by Ford as an implication of the way disciplinary communities generate new knowledge claims. 'Scientific and more generally all academic disciplinary knowledge is a product of public debates, emerging from communities, rather than from individuals alone' (Ford 2010: 266). Individual members of these communities play two roles – constructor and critiquer of knowledge claims. 'A knowledge claim is accorded authority by the community when critiquers judge it justified according to that field's norms' (ibid). 'This analysis highlights that the adjudication of knowledge (its justification) is driven by active disciplinary challenges – both on the level of the disciplinary community and on the level of the individual learner' (ibid). That is, coming to understand disciplined knowledge 'requires attention to and accurate interpretation of its features that justify it' (ibid). Therefore, a crucial aspect of the active learning of school subjects is challenging or questioning knowledge claims in ways that the discipline does.

> In this way, the model of disciplinary practice on the interpersonal level (between persons in a disciplinary community) can be used to highlight what the process of learning and justification on the persona level (an individual learner) must include. The reasons why one believes a knowledge claim in science (i.e. its relations to evidence) are precisely the features of the claim that provide its meaning.
>
> *(Ford 2010: 266)*

Adopting a model of disciplinary practice to inform the process of learning and justification at the level of the individual learner can help teachers to articulate the kinds of things students need to know, both generally and specifically about disciplined knowledge (in this case geography) in order to challenge nascent ideas about a geographical understanding of the world.

This approach to pedagogy 'does not assume that that students possess, in their everyday knowledge stores, sufficient resources for constructing their own understanding of disciplinary content' (ibid 276). By providing explicitly the critique resources that students lack [disciplinary norms], pedagogy can then support students to use critique to actively make appropriate sense of the content, and where 'students, rather than teachers... actively challenge their emerging understanding of content' (ibid 265). The pedagogical account being proposed 'should involve students in processes of construction and critique, to support student appropriation of a grasp of disciplinary practice' (ibid). A 'grasp of disciplinary practice' will recognise that the constructor and critiquer roles 'are not independent, because the reasoning during construction relies on an ability to anticipate critique' (ibid). And students should learn the constructor and critiquer roles authentically, so they can appropriate these forms of participation and bring disciplinary critique to bear on their learning. 'Pedagogy should involve students in critique processes, which make clear the epistemic demands of the discipline and how they are met by the methods and give rationale to the content' (ibid). 'Without critique the student would not learn to hold his or her sense-making accountable' (ibid 277). Reasons need to function epistemologically for the student.

The key to Ford's arguments is that constructivism has emphasised continuity between what he calls 'lay' knowledge (out-of-school knowledge) and disciplinary knowledge. He highlights ways in which disciplinary knowledge is distinct from out-of-school knowledge and draws implications from this for the learning process. The connection to Bernstein's (2000) later work and his typology of knowledges is clear. As is by now well known, Bernstein differentiated between two forms of discourse, horizontal and vertical, and within vertical discourse between two kinds of knowledge structure, hierarchical and horizontal. It was a way of conceptualising the underlying principles that generate forms of knowledge and how they develop over time. The concept of knowledge differentiation is a principled way of distinguishing between different forms of specialist knowledge and between school and out-of-school knowledge. Bernstein described out-of-school knowledge as horizontal discourse, where there is a direct relation between meanings and a specific material base. It is likely to be more individual, and as Ford emphasises, developed through *implicit critique*. Disciplinary knowledge is public and develops through explicit critique. Because of this, Ford emphasises, 'disciplinary knowledge is a different kind of thing than lay knowledge – and the nature of this difference implies that disciplinary critique is an important proactive aspect of learning disciplinary knowledge' (Ford 2010: 266). And further, Ford emphasises the character of the way in which knowledge is produced 'is not only important for understanding the epistemological aspect of disciplinary knowledge (how we know), but may also be important for thoroughly understanding the content itself (what we know)' (ibid). In this way, epistemic authority shifts from the teacher to the student.

Within the learning tasks students engage with in geography classrooms they should have experiences of the norms and practices of the disciplinary community. Much of this is likely to happen through productive discussion and argumentation and many instances of student–teacher and student–student interactivity. Both relativism and dogmatism need to be avoided. At one extreme everything is a matter of opinion, 'anything goes' and so there is no real point to discussion, it is undirected; at the other extreme the aim is for pre-existing truths or knowledge, and 'so discussion is restricted to apprehending and grasping the truth' (Golding 2011: 481). The disciplinary community emphasis 'takes the middle ground between 'opinions' where all answers are equally good and seeking 'correct' answers' (ibid). It seeks reasoned or reflective judgements where ideas are judged better or worse depending on the quality of reasoning supported by a respect for evidence, the significance or otherwise of established knowledge and the norms of the discipline.

## Summary

I have argued that school geography tends to ignore the nature of its own discipline and that teachers need to engage with questions about the production and nature of knowledge if they are to enable their students to make sense of how geography helps them to make sense of the world. Given all the constraints and demands on teachers' time, it is not surprising that teachers are unfamiliar with epistemic developments in the discipline. However, the call for teachers and teacher education to respond to current epistemological trends is an appropriate and indeed, a vital one (Firth 2007). The nature of subject specific teaching in schools suggests that attempts to shift teachers' thinking towards a broader realist conception of pedagogy that recognises the epistemic nature of content will not be easy and that teachers will need professional support. We therefore have to find the right approach which will allow teachers to take ownership of reform and develop their knowledge and practice over time.

The main purpose of this chapter 'has been to draw attention to some specific theoretical possibilities' (Ford 2010: 278) and how the idea of disciplinary constraint might have a potentially important influence on teachers' thinking about teaching and learning in geography. The emphasis on the way disciplinary knowledge is constructed could be an important complement to existing approaches to lesson planning and task design. The discussion has highlighted disciplined judgement and disciplinary critique as a possible starting point for teachers' consideration. While further research is needed on the subject of student critiques and judgement it does illustrate how teachers can become more epistemically aware of their discipline and its unique approach to knowledge and how students might learn to employ the epistemic tools provided by the discipline in secondary school classrooms.

'Constructivist approaches to geographical learning should balance the individual judgements that students apply during the course of their work with the normalising tools of judgement as employed within the discipline' (Stemhagen *et al.* 2013: 58). Whereas constructivism provides no well founded mechanism by which individual students might develop better constructs with which to see the world, a more modest realism and an emphasis on disciplinary constraint could do so. We do need to make a distinction between knowledge (what is taken to be known) and belief (what is personally held by the individual). As Stemhagen *et al.* (2013) argue,

> Rather than attempting to resolve this inherent tension between institution and learner; the employment of [disciplinary constraint] encourages teachers to accept this tension as both inevitable and useful. The tension is useful because it helps bring the knowledge that has been constructed – both socially and otherwise as powerful – in sharper relief for both teachers and their students.
>
> *(Stemhagen et al.: 59)*

Rather than theorise the tension away as constructivism does, to arrive at meaningful knowledge students must learn through this troublesome tension. Disciplined knowledge is distinguished from everyday knowledge because it represents the systematisation of knowledge that extends and supersedes our ordinary understanding of things and the relations between them. The tension between them invites the teacher and the student to construct an epistemic toolkit for the problems of learning and knowledge adjudication. Taking the tension seriously demands situating what is to be learned at the level of a dialogue between those involved: student–teacher–knowledge. It necessitates that we give credence to meta-criteria (norms of knowledge production), recognising that participants are all playing the same game: an epistemic game, which situates what is learned in such a way that combines elements from the specialised/disciplined view with a thoroughly local or situated view. This, moreover, points to 'knowing how to go on' which is different from what one normally understands as 'knowledge' (Smeyers 2013).

# References

Ball, L. D., Thames, M. H. and Phelps, G. (2008) Content knowledge for teaching: what makes it special? *Journal of Teacher Education*, 59(5): 389–407.

Bernstein, B. (2000) *Pedagogy, symbolic control and identity: theory, research, critique*. London: Taylor and Francis.

Daston, L. and Galison, P. (2007) *Objectivity*. New York: Zone Books.

Demeritt, D. (2005) Hybrid geographies, relational ontologies and situated knowledges, *Antipode*, 37(4): 818–23.

Department for Education (DfE) (2010) *The Importance of Teaching*. Schools White Paper 2010. Norwich: The Stationery Office.

Department for Education (DfE) (2011) *The Framework for the National Curriculum*. A Report by the Expert Panel for the National Curriculum review. Available online at: www.education.gov.uk/publications, accessed 12 February 2014.

Doyle, W. (1983) Academic work, *Review of Educational Research*, 53(2): 159–89.

Doyle, W. and Carter, K. (1984) Academic tasks in classrooms, *Curriculum Inquiry*, 14(2): 129–49.

Drew, V. and Mackie, L. (2011) Extending the constructs of active learning: implications for teachers' pedagogy and practice, *The Curriculum Journal*, 22(4): 451–67.

Firth, R. (2007) *Geography Teaching, Teachers and the Issue of Knowledge*. Nottingham: Nottingham Jubilee Press.

Firth, R. (2011) Making geography visible as an object of study in the secondary school curriculum. *The Curriculum Journal*, 22(3): 289–316.

Ford, M. J. (2010) Critique in academic disciplines and active learning of academic content. *Cambridge Review of Education*, 40(3): 265–80.

Freebody, P., Maton, K. and Martin, J. (2008) Talk, text, and knowledge in cumulative integrated learning: a response to intellectual challenge. *Australian Journal of Language and Literacy*, June 2008. Golding, C. (2011) The many faces of constructivist discussion. *Educational Philosophy and Theory*, 43(5): 467–83.

Golding, C. (2011) The Many Faces of Constructivist Discussion. *Educational Philosophy and Theory* 43(5): 467–83.

Golledge, R. (2002) The nature of geographic knowledge. *Annals of the Association of American Geographers*, 92(1): 1–14.

Hubbard, P., Kitchin, R., Bartley, B. and Fuller, D. (2005) *Thinking Geographically*, London: Continuum.

Longino, H. E. (2002) *The Fate of Knowledge*. Woodstock, Oxon: Princeton University Press.

Moore, R. (2007) *Sociology of Knowledge and Education*, London: Continuum.

Morrow, W. (2007) *Learning to Teach in South Africa*. Cape Town: HSRC Press.

Office for Standards in Education (Ofsted) (2013) *Schools 2012–2013*. Available online at: www.ofsted.gov.uk/resources/130236. [accessed 13 February 2014].

Osborne, J. (1996) Beyond constructivism. *Science Education*, 80(1): 53–82.

Perkins, D. (2006) Constructivism and troublesome knowledge. In J. H. F. Meyer and R. Land (eds) *Overcoming Barriers to Student Understanding*. London: Routledge.

Sheppard, E. and Plummer, P. (2007) Commentary: toward engaged pluralism in geographical debate. *Environment and Planning A*, 39(11): 2545–48.

Smeyers, P. (2013) Making sense of the legacy of epistemology in education and educational research. *Journal of Philosophy of Education*, 47(2): 312–21.

Stemhagen, K., Reich, G. and Muth, W. (2013) Disciplined judgment: toward a theoretical framework for a reasonably constrained constructivism. *Journal of Curriculum and Pedagogy*, 10(1): 55–72.

Wheelahan, L. (2010a) *Why Knowledge Matters in Curriculum*. London: Routledge.
Wheelahan, L. (2010b) Competency-based training, powerful knowledge and the working class. In K. Maton and R. Moore (eds) *Social Realism, Knowledge and the Sociology of Education*. London: Continuum.
Young, M. (2008) *Bringing Knowledge Back In: From social constructivism to social realism in the sociology of education*. London: Routledge.

# 6

# COMMUNICATION, CULTURE AND CONCEPTUAL LEARNING

## Task design in the English classroom

*Ian Thompson*

### Introduction

In English speaking countries, the pedagogy of English teaching, and related questions of what English is as a subject and what content English teachers should be teaching, have long been contested areas of school curriculums. English teachers can often feel under siege as they battle with the twin demands of high-stakes testing and ideologically driven political interference. Standards of grammar usage, spelling accuracy, the ability to write an extended text, the acquisition of reading skills: these are all highly politicised issues as likely to be debated on the floor of the House of Commons or on television chat shows as they are in the school staffroom. When evidence is cited as justification for literacy policy reform from educational research, as in the case of the requirement for all UK state primary schools to teach reading acquisition through systematic synthetic phonics, the contested nature of this research knowledge is often brushed aside.

Perhaps as a result of this scrutiny, English, as a secondary or high school subject, can appear to outsiders to have a split personality. On the one hand, English or literacy skills are viewed as instrumental to all curriculum understanding and attainment; on the other, English can be parodied as a soft subject concerned with aesthetics and feelings far removed from the scientific concepts that students have to understand in order to master the school curriculum. Aspects of English, through the medium of literacy across the curriculum, are seen as the responsibility of all teachers in schools; yet when school literacy standards are deemed inadequate it is the English teachers who usually get the blame. At the heart of this critique is the dichotomy between the view of literacy as a skills-based activity and literacy as a tool for making meaning of the world. The separation between product and process is critiqued in this chapter as a false one. Literacy is best viewed as social and cultural practices rather than an exercise in technical skills or competencies. At the same time, English as a subject is also about the creation and understanding of language and literary processes and products. What linguistic approaches (for example Halliday 1993), sociocultural or activity theory approaches (for example Bazerman 2012; Ellis 2007; Mercer 1995; Prior 1998), and multimodal semiotic approaches (for example Kress *et al.* 2005) to English education have in common is an understanding that English is concerned with meaning making within social and cultural environments and about students' ways of knowing and acting on the world around them. This is true about both English pedagogy and the English or literacy curriculum.

One of the challenges facing the English subject teacher educator is how to help prospective English teachers to understand the challenges that their students face in the literacy curriculum. Let me make an obvious generalisation to make the point. Prospective secondary school English teachers are articulate speakers, expert writers, avid readers, and people who like working with young people. Often they are extroverts; always they are social beings. An adolescent may be all of these things; more likely they will be some but not others. Unlike the academically successful English teacher, they may have experienced frustrations and failures within the English classroom. English teachers need to understand the diverse cultural worlds of their students and to develop pedagogical skills if they are to involve or re-engage these students in making meaning of the complex and contradictory cultural worlds of English. But they need what Schwab (1978) describes as substantive knowledge (key concepts) and syntactic knowledge (ways of knowing and representing) of the many 'subjects' of English: a variety of literary forms and narrative structures; linguistics; media, film and cultural studies. Designing tasks that engage adolescents with the subjects of English involves careful planning.

So why does the term 'task design' occur so rarely in the literature relating to the English classroom? This, I suspect, has much to do with the reluctance of many English teachers and some researchers of English teaching to be placed within a form of constructivist paradigm that appears to emphasise structure over creativity. So, for example, a very good recent book on creativity and learning ends with a warning against 'control, conformity, standardisation and compliance, so offering a model of sharing values and methods imposed from above' (McCallum 2012: 150). Whilst I would share McCallum's concerns with imposition from above and the need to foster creativity, the implication is that teachers too can stifle the transformative aspects learning through a structured approach to lesson design. Yet English teachers do design tasks that involve structuring students' engagement with aspects of language and literature and at the same time celebrate diversity and creativity. The planning of schemes or units of work involves designing tasks that both draw on students' current and developing understandings of everyday concepts such as love and loss and also introduces new concepts such as literary criticism or linguistic analysis.

I have chosen the title 'Communication, culture and conceptual learning' in order to focus on what I believe to be the central task design question for English teachers: how do students acquire the conceptual understandings that allow them to engage with and act on the cultures of literate practices? Few would argue with the view that English as a subject is concerned with the process of communication and of understanding language use in a wide variety of literary and linguistic forms. Not many would quibble with the association with the word 'culture' with the study of English, although definitions of what constitutes a culture are highly contested. In using the term 'culture' here I refer not only to the cultural understandings embedded within literate practices but also to the cultural and historical practices that shape the production, reception, and understanding of literary and non-fiction texts. The phrase 'conceptual learning' is often associated with Jerome Bruner's stress on the learner's active construction of meaning through the development of concepts based on existing knowledge. However, my reference to conceptual learning in this chapter refers to Vygotskian notions of concept development with specific reference to the secondary school student. Conceptual learning in the English classroom involves a task design focus on both the theories and practices of communicative activity: our learners need to know both why and how texts are produced or read and to be able to participate in the cultural worlds of the English classroom. As Bruner argues:

> Although meanings are 'in the mind,' they have their origins and significance in the culture in which they are created.... It is culture that provides the tools for organising and understanding our worlds in communicable ways.
> *(Bruner 1996: 3)*

Barnes' (1976) warning that orthodox curriculum theory analyses from the teacher's objectives, rather than learners' understandings and the communicative actions that create the learning environment, is apposite for English teaching. This chapter argues that task design in the English classroom often focuses on the teacher's objectives for task completion produced under the pressure of performativity (assessing what the teacher teaches and the outputs their students produce) rather than developmental demand for learners. That is not to say that objectives are not important, but rather that the objectives or goals of the task design must be focused on the learning of the students rather than curriculum delivery. The challenge for English teachers and teacher educators lies in designing demanding classroom communicative tasks that create the conditions for learning to occur through social and cultural interaction.

## A Vygotskian conception of English teaching

Burgess argues that Vygotskian theory, alongside linguistics and critical theory, can make a crucial contribution to the development of English teaching.

> Where Vygotskyan theory focuses attention is on the transformation of existing psychological functions as new resources from the culture are

internalised and appropriated. For this there must be both the interaction of the child with culture as well as culture with the child.

*(Burgess 2007: 25)*

Not only then does a Vygotskian conception of task design require the construction of classroom tasks and related activities that require students' active engagement with culture, but the students must also actively respond to their interpretation and participation in that culture. The Vygotskian theoretical focus on development through learning requires the English teacher to attend to both the work that students do as they tackle literacy tasks as cultural and communicative activities through social interaction, and also on the students' internalisation and appropriation of the psychological tools required to accomplish the activities that are embedded within the design of the curriculum task.

Vygotsky argues that social interaction plays a fundamental role in the development of mind:

> Every function in the child's cultural development appears twice: first, on the social level, and later, on the individual level; first, between people (interpsychological) and then inside the child (intrapsychological). This applies equally to voluntary attention, to logical memory, and to the formation of concepts. All the higher functions originate as actual relationships between individuals.
> *(Vygotsky 1978: 57)*

Vygotsky's methodological approach of assessing potential development departs from the conventional focusing on individual performance towards a focus on assisted process. The central questions for Vygotsky are what are children doing and how do they try to satisfy task demands? Vygotsky argues that human consciousness is achieved by the internalisation of shared social behaviour. Unlike the predominant model of children's learning that sees the function of learning as acquisition of knowledge, Vygotsky's (1987a) theory of the zone of proximal development (ZPD) stresses the importance of the educative process rather than the final outcome. The ZPD is the difference between existing and potential levels of development revealed through an analysis of how far a student is able to master a task by themselves or with help from a more knowledgeable other such as a teacher or more capable peer. As Edwards (this volume) and Chaiklin (2003) argue, Vygotsky's concept of the ZPD defines the potential development of a child rather than an abstract metaphor for learning. For Vygotsky, real learning is that which is in advance of development and is mediated through interactions with other people and through the social and cultural acquisition of sign systems. The ZPD indicates both the presence of maturing psychological functions and the possibility of meaningful interventions that stimulate conceptual development. This process of conceptual development involves co-operation and collaboration between the teacher and the learner, or between learners at different levels of development. For Vygotsky, collaboration and co-operation are 'crucial features of effective teaching'

(Daniels 2007: 311). Vygotsky (1987b) argues that learning takes place when the learning task is set at a level in advance of the student's current mental level of development. This has task design implications for the classroom teacher concerning the relationship between instruction and pupil development and the classroom environment. As Jan Derry (2008) points out:

> [a] Vygotskian approach doesn't depend simply on individuals being placed in the required environment where they discover meaning for themselves. The learning environment must be designed and cannot rely on the spontaneous response to an environment which is not constructed according to, or involves, some clearly worked out conceptual framework. For Vygotsky concepts depend for their meaning on the system of judgements (inferences) within which they are disclosed.
> *(Derry 2008: 60–61)*

Vygotsky argues that school learning introduces something fundamentally new into students' development. By giving students specific tasks of understanding scientific concepts within a designed environment, school learning introduces new concepts that stimulate their psychological development. It is within the dialectical interplay between the students' grasp of everyday spontaneous concepts and the development of their scientific conceptual understanding that learning leads development.

As Burgess points out, concepts relating to the study of English are central to: students' use of critical literacy; the ability to compare texts; the reading of a novel from another period or culture; or when writing in different genres: 'English, no less than other curriculum areas, works with students' concepts and helps to form them' (Burgess 2007: 31). The teacher's role is to design tasks and learning environments that challenge students and enable them to acquire and internalise the tools necessary for them to develop independence through conceptual learning. The key to this development is collaborative or joint activity that engages students in mediated activity. Brice-Heath reminds us of the importance of English teacher expertise in mediating students' understanding:

> To add breadth and depth to the linguistic repertoires of the young, teachers need to imagine and enable more and more valid roles through which young people gain meaningful practice with styles, genres and types of language.
> *(Brice-Heath 2007: 205)*

For this practice to be meaningful, Brice-Heath argues, English teachers have to intervene as expert mediators in their students' learning.

## The cultural historical context of English as a subject

In order to understand the development of task design in English, it is helpful to briefly trace the historical and cultural contexts of the inception and development of English as a subject. English teaching has a long history of ideological debate in Britain. In historical terms, English as an academic and university subject is a relatively new discipline that only came into existence in the nineteenth century. Yet by the 1930s in Britain and in other English speaking countries, under the influence of the Cambridge academic F. R. Leavis, the subject of English claimed an unparalleled position as a cultural arbiter of both aesthetic worth and intellectual value. The Board of Education report of 1921, known as the Newbolt Report, identified three areas for the teaching of English in schools: communication, the scientific study of language, and the celebration of an English cultural and literary tradition.

But this was a very particular form of culture: the cultural assumptions of the British elite classes reasserting their moral values after the horrors of the First World War. In contrast to Raymond Williams' (1977) notion of culture as growth, this was a culture of class value and of class belonging. Eagleton (1983) has argued persuasively that literary study was successfully appropriated by an academic elite. Eagleton argues that the victory and impact of Leavis and his followers was far reaching and complete. Above all, English was seen as a subject of literature and the critical tool of analysis was literary theory. English teachers trained in the decades after Leavis were schooled in the tradition of the civilising and enriching nature of English. Shakespeare's insights into the fatal character flaws in his tragic heroes are still deemed universal and essential reading for all adolescents (watching is more optional apparently).

However, Leavis' rejection of popular culture was fundamentally elitist and in the 1960s elements of educational research began to reject the civilising role of English and take up the view of English as personal empowerment through personal growth. This key concept of personal growth in English teaching came largely from the ideas in John Dixon's *Growth Through English* (1967). Dixon explicitly questioned the categories for writing identified by the 1921 Board of Education as well as the heritage model of Leavis:

> The skills model is only indirectly aware of such a purpose: its ideal pupils might well be copy-typists. And that is ironical, since the insistence on correct spelling, etc., is avowedly in the interests of better communication, of unimpeded sharing! A heritage model, with its stress on adult literature, turns language into a one-way process: pupils are readers, receivers of the master's voice. How, we may ask, do these private activities of writing and reading relate to the stream of public interaction through language in which we are all involved every day, teachers as much as pupils? The heritage model offers no help in answering, because it neglects the most fundamental aim of language – to promote interaction between people.
>
> *(Dixon 1967: 6)*

The central focus in this passage is on learning as an interactive or dialogic process and language is seen as central to that process. The English classroom proposed by

Dixon is one both of interaction and growth through the creation of shared experience. But there is also a form of progressive liberal idealism that came to permeate much of the child centred and student directed learning that dominated many English classrooms in the 1970s and early 80s. For example, the teacher-less process writing workshops (see Murray 1972; Graves 1994) argued against composition theories that try to structure writing and proposed that 'we should teach unfinished writing, and glory in its unfinishedness' (Murray, 1972: 12). Graves' approach also focused attention away from the finished product of writing and onto the processes young pupils need to go through as writers. Process writing theories were particularly influential in UK primary schools before the introduction of the National Literary Strategy. However, Applebee (1986), in a critique of the original concepts of process writing, argues that many projects failed because of an inadequate understanding of what writers do when they write for specific purposes. He goes on to advocate instructional support based on the idea that:

> Learning is a process of gradual internalisation of routines and procedures available to the learner from the social and cultural context in which the learning takes place.
>
> *(Applebee 1986: 108)*

From the 1970s to the present there has existed a tension between attempts to reshape the teaching of English through a return to so-called basics and traditional methods of skill-based approaches, whilst at the same time a series of government-commissioned reports have referred back to the social and language-based nature of English teaching. For example, the key message of the DES publication *A Language for Life* (DES 1975), also known as The Bullock Report, was that competence in language use comes through using language for a purpose rather than decontextualised exercises. The Bullock Report changed the three categories of Newbolt (1921) to English as skills, English as social change and English for growth (following Dixon). The Bullock Committee was set up in response to a series of Black Papers which claimed a decline in standards of literacy sufficient to damage the national economy. The Bullock Report in fact found no evidence of a decline in literacy standards and advocated the teaching of language across the curriculum, greater focus on oracy, and less prescription in areas such as grammar and spelling.

The Kingman Report (DES and WO, 1988) built on the ideas of Bullock and put forward the concept of 'Knowledge about Language' (KAL). The Kingman report recognised the diversity of uses for English and that language is socially situated. The DES publication *Report of the English Working Party 5–16* (1989) that became known as The Cox Report expanded the categories for English that Bullock identified to five areas: personal growth, cultural heritage, adult needs, cultural analysis and cross curricular views (DES 1989). Cox was one of the members of the Kingman Committee and he highlighted the central importance of speaking and listening. Like the Bullock Report, the Cox Report was initially attacked by the conservative press for a perceived lack of focus on basic skills.

The Language in the National Curriculum (LINC) training project that followed the Cox report was due to be published by HMSO in 1991 but was withdrawn by ministerial order in a move widely seen as political censorship. The approach of LINC to language owed much to the functional-systemic linguistics theorists Halliday and Hasan (for example 1989). Genre theory (for example Cope and Kalantzis 1993) which lays stress on students being explicitly taught the conventions of text genres was also influenced by the systemic functional model outlined by Halliday and Hasan (1989) which draws explicit links between the functions of language, what language is for, and the ways we make lexical and grammatical choices to achieve this.

The genre approach to teaching writing claims to empower disadvantaged groups by revealing the power structures involved in adult writing. Hodge and Kress (1988) categorise the ideological nature of genres as 'typical forms of texts which link kinds of producer, consumer, topic, medium, manner and occasion' and argue that these genres 'control the behaviour of producers of such texts, and the expectations of potential consumers' (Hodge and Kress 1988: 7). Although teaching in this theory focuses on the language features or conventions of texts in each genre, the genres themselves are viewed as social processes. For example, Kress defines a genre as 'a kind of text that derives its form from the structure of a (frequently repeated) social occasion, with its characteristic participants and their purposes' (Kress 1988: 183). Myhill (2001) argues that children who lack prior knowledge of the conventions of genre types are significantly disadvantaged in the school curriculum. Cope and Kalantzis outline the practical implications for teachers using a genre approach:

> A genre approach to literacy teaching involves being explicit about the way language works to make meaning. It means engaging students in the role of apprentice with the teacher in the role of expert on language system and function. It means an emphasis on content, on structure and on sequence in the steps that a learner goes through to become literate in a formal educational setting.
>
> *(Cope and Kalantzis 1993: 1)*

It should be pointed out that North American genre theorists (Freedman and Medway 1994; Swales 1990) view genres as more fluid than in this model and consequently criticised process writing teaching in Australia and the UK as being static and prescriptive. Likewise, Marshall hints at a 'potentially mechanistic, fact-orientated strain in genre studies' that suggests the teacher holds the knowledge that the pupil needs to learn' (Marshall 2006: 13). In fact genres in the North American model of genre theory are not simple sets of definable text conventions but specific literacy practices that act in themselves as mediators of activity (see Bazerman 1994; Russell 2010).

However, the stress in systemic functional linguistics on the dynamic and evolving nature of language is in stark contrast to the incremental attainment definitions that were published in the national curriculum (NC) that was introduced for England, Wales and Northern Ireland schools in the Education Reform Act of 1988. The NC established the concepts of key stages, programmes of study, assessment levels and attainment targets alongside the publishing of national league tables. A narrow form of genre theory was embedded in the programmes of study. There has also been an obsessive and recursive focus on grammar in English strategies from both New Labour and the coalition (Conservative and Liberal) governments of the late- twentieth and early-twenty-first centuries. This is despite research that demonstrates that the explicit teaching of grammar has either little or no effect on pupils' literacy skills (for example Andrews *et al.* 2006) or that effective grammar for learning teaching has to be contextualised (Myhill *et al.* 2012).

So how does the cultural historical context of English relate to the setting of tasks? Task design for the followers of the great tradition consisted of setting exploratory questions designed to provoke discussion and analysis of particular identified writers' genius. In extreme cases of new criticism, culture is entirely divorced from history as we are asked to celebrate the timeless and universal quality of a literary text. Yet throughout the discussion of the literature as a civilising and moral force there remains a disconcerting sense of elitism: literary high culture for the educated elite; basic skills for the masses. Task setting under the pressure of the NC and external examinations has meant guiding students through the attainment levels by means of tightly structured three part lessons. These task design assumptions and contradictions are encapsulated in the following statement from the Office for Standards in Education in the UK (Ofsted) in the 2012 document 'Moving English forward: actions to raise standards in English':

> There can be no more important subject than English in the school curriculum. English is a pre-eminent world language, it is at the heart of our culture and it is the language medium in which most of our pupils think and communicate. Literacy skills are also crucial to pupils' learning in other subjects across the curriculum.
>
> *(Ofsted 2012)*

This is the language of Newbolt revisited: for authority at least, it appears little has changed in the priorities for English teaching.

Of course for teachers, change is an everyday occurrence. Classrooms are increasingly diverse in both cultural and linguistic senses. The production and reception of texts are radically different today from even ten years ago through the impact of new literacy technologies and mediums. Yet efforts to measure what constitutes subject knowledge in English can sometimes result in checklists of teachers' knowledge of subsets of literacy skills. For example, most UK initial teacher training programmes in English conduct a subject audit of knowledge (Ellis 2009). Unsurprisingly, at the start of their training prospective secondary school English teachers with English Literature degrees worry about their understanding of grammar at sentence level whilst linguistic graduates are concerned by their lack of knowledge of key literary texts.

So what knowledge does an English teacher need to teach their subject in a way that develops the learning of their students? As a subject English is concerned with a wide range of interrelated literacy practices: the study of various text genres of literary and non-fiction texts; an understanding of the development of the English language and linguistic structures; cultural representation within literature and the media; practices of written communicative; active reading; speaking and listening.

> The high degree of imagination, information gathering, mental framing, and meaning making required for reading and writing suggests that literate processes are constantly adaptive to and constructive of situations, organising the brain for situated action.
>
> *(Bazerman 2012: 102)*

This situated activity of participation in literate processes and practices is not an isolated individual act of cognition as the learning takes place within specific cultural and historical activity settings in which social interaction plays a crucial mediating role. As Derry (2013) argues 'it is necessary to look beyond the individual and to attend to external mediation in the formation of higher mental functions' (p. 3).

So what sort of English classroom environments enable learners through mediated activity to engage in social learning as active agents? Pictures of Victorian classrooms show densely packed classrooms arranged in rows facing the authoritarian figure of the knowledgeable teacher. This is the classroom and learning environment lampooned by Dickens in his portrayal of Thomas Gradgrind's exhortations for the teaching of facts. Yet as a teacher educator I have observed English lessons where the students are arranged in rows facing a PowerPoint presentation bearing 'learning objectives' such as 'To learn how Shakespeare uses language to create meaning' or conversely 'To learn how to use a semi-colon'.

Smagorinsky (this volume) follows Newman, Griffin and Cole's (1989) metaphor of the classroom as a construction zone for conceptual development. This view of knowledge as a co-constructed activity is an important link to Vygotsky's (1987b) conception of social interpersonal learning leading intrapersonal (individual) development. Michael Gove, until recently, Secretary of State for Education in the UK, holds a very different view of education. In a recent speech, Gove championed knowledge transmission and attacked what he views as progressive educational strategies:

> All too often, we've seen an over-emphasis on group work – in practice, children chatting to each other – in the belief that is a more productive way to acquire knowledge than attending to an expert.
>
> Although, as the great Texan President Lyndon B Johnson said, 'you aren't learning anything when you're talking.'
>
> *(Gove 2013)*

This is easy for a politician to say of course, and in many ways a simple argument to refute: talk comprises of an interaction with others and can be a way of restructuring and developing thought. But the challenge in Gove's twin assault on group work and on classroom talk here is a real one. For group work is not productive if it is not designed in a way that focuses the talk on the purpose of the communicative task. Put another way, the group task design has to provide an intervention in the students' learning. In Vygotsky's (1997) terms, if 'nothing changes, then nothing has been taught' (p.104).

Anne Edwards' (this volume) heuristic of the quadrant model for task sequencing is instructive here as collaborative English tasks often start from her definition of quadrant three: open tasks that allow learners to apply key concepts to their understanding of a text though reading or creation of a text through writing. But those key concepts will have been previously introduced by the teacher through a quadrant one sequence of modelling and examples. The transformational change comes through the students developing the ability to apply their conceptual understanding of literacy to their everyday understandings. In this way, and through interaction with others, the students learn though their experience of engagement with literate practices.

In the two task design examples that follow on writing and reading I develop a Vygotskian understanding of the development of pupils' interactions with language and literature through a task design focus on collaborative learning, interactive teaching and social communication in the English classroom.

## Task design for writing

Writing can be viewed as both a social and an individual activity. When we write we do so for an audience: we are, in both the real and metaphorical senses, engaged in a dialogue with others. At the same time, writing can be viewed as the translation of inner speech or an attempt to make thought visible. As a teacher educator, an important starting point for my work with prospective English teachers in the teaching of writing has been two relatively recent books by Peter Smagorinsky, *Teaching English by Principled Practice* (2002) and *Teaching English by Design* (2008), and a much older work that came out of the influential School Councils Research Studies project of the late sixties and early seventies in the UK published under the title *The Development of Writing Abilities (11–18)* (Britton, Burgess, Martin, McLeod and Rosen 1975). Britton *et al.* remind us of the central importance of the function of the writing genre and the intended audience of the writing. Smagorinsky in the books cited and in this volume (see Chapter 11) makes a powerful case for the design and instruction of conceptual units based around: a theme such as conflict; an author or group of authors; a reading strategy; a period such as the Victorian era; a regional theme; a literary period; a literary movement such as romanticism; or a literary genre.

Cognitive theories of writing stress the individual cognitive developmental properties of students learning to write academic texts like accomplished adult writers. Collaborative writing, on the other hand, moves the assessment focus away from the finished product to an emphasis on process. As I have argued elsewhere (for example Thompson 2012a, 2012b), communicative activity plays a mediational role in the co-construction of social and cultural meaning that is involved when pupils write collaboratively. The teacher's focus in the task design of collaborative writing is on the process of composition.

In this section, I focus on the task design and sequence of a collaborative expressive writing task that would form part of a conceptual unit. By setting a collaborative writing task the teacher can create the potential for dialogical activity as students negotiate meaning through their use of the cultural tools required to negotiate a writing task. Of course simply pairing or grouping students of differing ability does not guarantee development. Rather, it is through complex processes of semiotic interaction involved in collaborative activity that pupils develop the psychological tools required to appropriate the cultural significance of language. The sequence that I present here is not supposed to be either a blueprint or a straight-jacket. Sensitivity to the nuances of the learning actually going on in the classroom and the ability to change a plan or task sequence accordingly are essential tools for good teaching.

Collaborative writing can take the form of paired or small groups writing a text together. Some tasks lend themselves naturally to pairs writing. For example a dual narrative, where students use different narrative voices to tell a single story from two contrasting perspectives. However, prospective English teachers are also encouraged to organise small groups of three working on expressive pieces of writing such as editorials or blogs where students negotiate the shared production of a text.

Task design for collaborative writing involves attending to the mediating roles and functions of the teacher and peers within 'the in-the moment interpretations of how learners are engaging with classroom tasks and the actions that might assist that engagement' (Edwards 2010: 73). I have previously (Thompson 2013) defined categories that describe mediated activity within the classroom:

- direct instruction from a teacher or more capable peer. Whilst initially didactic the instructive voice can be internalised by the learner as part of their own inner speech
- modelling of a behaviour or task by an expert that the learner initially imitates and ultimately internalises
- feedback, either oral or written, that offers guidance on performance
- questioning to assess or assist performance
- reassurance and reinforcement of partially understood concepts
- joint exploration of meaning between teacher and learner or between students
- peer collaboration involving critical thinking, problem-solving or making decisions
- structuring of a task, or of part of a task, by the teacher in order to provide a constructive framework for the learner's developing mental processes

- redirection through the learning process
- conceptual restructuring whereby perception, memory, and action are re-evaluated and re-ordered. The internalisation of this structure becomes part of the learner's inner self-regulating voice.

*(Adapted from Thompson 2013: 272)*

These various forms of assisted performance are not mutually exclusive and successful mediation may include several of these elements. Some may appear to be more restrictive of students' creativity than others. The important point for considerations of task design for writing here is the relationship between these various forms of assisted performance and learners' mental development over time as their emerging psychological processes develop.

When working with my prospective teachers on task design for students' writing in their classrooms, we begin with a discussion of the function of the forms of writing that their students will write in the English classroom and the intended audience of that writing. In looking at the processes involved in writing, whether linguistic or psychological, Britton *et al.* (1975) reject the traditional rhetorical categories of writing: exposition, argument, description and narration. In reducing writing to these four levels of discourse, they argue, traditional theories of writing focus on the finished products of professional writers. The concern of traditional categorisation is the prescriptive tradition of considering what people should write rather than how they actually do write. In order then to counter the reductive impact of the traditional rhetorical categories Britton *et al.* attempt to devise a different system of categories in order to consider the processes and functions of pieces of writing. This categorisation takes the form of answers to the following questions considered critical to the process of writing: who is the writing for (audience) and why is it being written (function)? In the case of function, the broad categories identified are for mature writing: transactional (writing to get things done); expressive (revealing thought or feeling); and poetic (writing as an art form). Transactional writing is by far the dominant mode encountered by students in the secondary school curriculum. However, Britton *et al.* assert the primary importance of the expressive function in the development of a child's learning because it builds on 'linguistic resources – the knowledge of words and structures he has built up in speech' (1975: 82). The expressive mode, in terms of development, 'is a kind of matrix from which differentiated forms of mature writing are developed' (ibid: 83).

Much if not all writing is multi-dimensional and deploys various rhetorical and modal elements in composition. For example, a narrative may employ elements of exposition, argument and description to tell a story. Narrative lends itself to widely different forms of writing: a piece of fiction, a factual report, a scientific account, and so on. To illustrate this point the sequence for collaborative writing begins with a genre rewrite where, for example, a fairy story is retold as a hard boiled thriller or historical romance. The story is then retold in the form of a recipe and a newspaper report. These activities require an understanding of genre conventions of language use and narrative structures (Cope and Kalantzis 1993). The teacher begins by drawing on their students' current knowledge of the 'rules' of a genre type. In the writing task the students are encouraged to both use and break these rules as well as to draw on their individual and collective knowledge. In this way the students' everyday conceptual understandings of genre are challenged by scientific concepts of genre structures and functions.

The next part of the task design follows Britton *et al.*'s (1975) three elements or phases of the writing process: conception, incubation and production. The conception stage is the process that leads up to the act of writing. In school this is largely a request from a teacher, but the learner has to select from what they know and think: the ability to recall is critical at this stage. What previous knowledge or experience can students bring to the task? The learners' personal histories are integral to this process.

At the point that writers know what they are going to write, and for what purpose, they move into the incubation phase. In this phase the writers develop ideas and plan the outline of their writing through talk about their text. The structuring of this talk is crucial for this is the point of negotiation (Doyle and Carter 1984) where the teacher has to allow sufficient talk for the students to develop their ideas whilst maintaining their focus on the task demand. The pedagogical task design challenge for teachers here is when to structure talk as a significant other and when to allow the process of incubation to develop through peer group discussion as students' everyday concepts begin to converge with the higher order concept or scientific concepts required. Talk is the key to this process of incubation.

The final phase of production is the most crucial as far as the developing psychological processes are concerned. Britton *et al.* (1975) analyse Vygotsky's writing on the movement from inner speech (internalised thought) to outer speech (in spoken words or finally in writing) involving the deliberate control of semantics particular to the process of writing. Britton *et al.* describe this process as 'the dialectical interrelationship of thought and language' (1975: 39). For the individual writer an essential part of the writing process is explaining the matter to oneself. In this way the writer moves from the inner speech of incubation to the external form of written composition. However, talk in the form of the inner dialogue of inner speech remains central to this process. In collaborative writing students are required to verbalise thoughts as they negotiate the writing of text. The phases of conception, incubation and production are not linear stages in writing in that elements of redirection or redrafting can take place within talk about the content and composition of the text.

A sequence for collaborative writing might then be:

- an introduction to the task concepts
- examples of the conventions of the writing genre through work by an accomplished writer or modelling of the writing process by the teacher
- conception: introduction to the task, previous conceptual knowledge, personal history as writers
- incubation: ideas and plans, talk, inner speech

- production (paired or group writing): translation of inner speech to written text; negotiation of meaning; teacher feedback on the collaborative writing through whole class discussion of common problems or successes; written feedback for pairs/groups; revision of text.

### Task design for active reading: class readers, literature circles, and themed books

One of the most common targets set by English teachers for their students is a variant of the exhortation to read widely for pleasure. Of course the irony is that this target is often set for those pupils who most dislike picking up a book. For prospective secondary school English teachers it can be a shock to hear students say that they have never read a book in their life. Of course these students will have had books read to them: if not at home then certainly in their experience through the primary classroom and in secondary school English lessons. What they are telling us is that they have not actively engaged in the negotiation of meaning that is involved in the reading of a text.

The class reader provides English teachers with several interrelated problems. What whole class reader will appeal to the divergent interests of my class? How do students working at different stages of reading comprehension work on a shared text? What cultural and social factors from the students' backgrounds need to be considered? What cultural and social concepts are important to develop a critical reading of the text? Should the text be read aloud? How do I get through the book in the allotted time? How do I ensure that my students are active readers? How do I plan talk around the text? What are my students learning when they read the text?

The task design dimension for the teacher when planning a scheme of work for the class reader is related to the objective of helping students understand the social, cultural and historical aspects of the novel studied as well as aspects of the author's craft as a writer, authorial intentions and literary quality. But the design also has to attend to the students' conceptual understandings of the past, cultures, social class and so on. It would be impossible to fully comprehend a Dickens novel without an understanding of Victorian conceptions of morality or justice as well as the prevailing social realities of class. The scientific concept of a literary critique requires the acquisition of the tool of a meta-language for analysis. Yet everyday concepts such as love, power, loss, or separation can be powerfully understood by the adolescent whether they are a refugee from Afghanistan or the flood plains of southern England.

In the UK, probably the most common novel read at Key Stage 4 (ages 14–16) is John Steinbeck's *Of Mice and Men*. This popularity is based on years of collective teacher knowledge of the power of Steinbeck's story to affect young readers including boys who previously showed little appetite for literary texts. It is also a powerful tale of the Great Depression in the US that confronts mature themes of friendship, belonging, gender, race and social class. The novel is short and readily available in the store cupboards of cash strapped English departments. For many years I taught the novel as an exam text to groups of underachieving 16 year-olds. I discovered that each 'chapter' (not a word Steinbeck uses for each section) could be read aloud to the class in a single lesson. Year after year I experienced the pleasure of seeing my captivated audience enjoy hearing a great story; many told me it was the first the book they had read. In this sense, it was an important experience for the students. Yet their engagement was at a purely receptive level and their critical reaction to the book when asked to write about it remained at an emotive level rather than analytical.

Of course another danger in whole class teaching is the tendency for teachers to rely on oral forms of reading where students take turns to read aloud from the text. In practice, this often means confident readers are allowed to read extended passages with students who struggle reading for a few lines prompted by the teacher. In play readings, the Mercutios and Juliets tend to be the same students who read extended passages of prose. What do these practices teach the students about reading or the teacher about the pupils' reading development? Virtually nothing of course. For the reluctant or unconfident reader, or the reader for whom English is not their first language, reading aloud in front of your peers can be a terrifying experience. Even for confident readers, this is an essentially passive form of reading that involves nothing more than reciting words from a page. In fact, as O'Donnell-Allen (2006) points out, student engagement is often minimal in this reading exercise. Collaborative reading, on the other hand, involves both active engagement on the part of students and effective task design from the teacher.

Applebee (1996) argues that in literature discussions, teachers often close down real debate about texts through a belief that they have the 'correct' interpretation. Miller (2003) picks up on Applebee's argument for conversation about literature to argue that talk focused on multiple perspectives about literature can help shape students' critical thinking about texts. Harvey 'Smokey' Daniels (1994) coined the term 'literature circles' to describe a task-based structured approach to small group reading developed by many US English teachers in the early 1980s. In his initial version of the literature circle, the teacher assigns specific reading roles to each group member designed to mirror the analytical and cognitive decoding tools used by experienced and successful readers. For example, Daniels lists the following student roles: Questioner, Connector, Literary Luminary, Illustrator, and Word Wizard. Students read chapters from the point of view of their particular role using open-ended prompts on role sheets and then join a group discussion on the chapters in question. Roles are to be rotated as the literature circle has progressed. Talk is student-centred in that discussions are led by the students through their reading roles. These roles are designed to be temporary supports or scaffolds. In this way the task design aims to recreate the cognitive reading processes of mature readers.

However, Daniels (2007 came to realise that in many classroom scenarios the reading roles were often dominating the work of literature circles and often limiting the type of talk about text that the circles were designed to foster. Excessive concentration on roles leads to a series of reports rather than a genuine discussion. Daniels in his later work advocates a form of teacher continual assessment of small group, student-led discussions. This then becomes an important purpose for the teacher in setting the task of collaborative reading. From a Vygotskian perspective this involves direct mediation with students as they talk about reading with their peers. Prospective teachers that are introduced to literature circles in the English PGCE course at the University of Oxford are encouraged to adapt the reading roles to the contexts of their classrooms and the learners within them. They are also encouraged to sit with the groups and intervene as part of their assessment of both actual and potential levels of students' understanding. The ability to listen to students think aloud is a powerful diagnostic tool for assessment.

O'Donnell-Allen (2006) posits an alternative approach of book clubs that allow small groups to four to six students to choose their own shared text. The role of the English teacher within the talk in a reading group is more interventionist than the student-centred task design of the literature circle. The English teacher provides a variety of cultural tools to respond to the text including reading logs, illustrations and talk. Perhaps above all, the task design principle in the book club is to promote sustained talk about the levels of meanings embedded in texts. This type of talk about meaning mirrors Barnes' (2008) and Mercer's (2000) definition of exploratory talk where students explore potential meaning through a dialogic process. Book clubs of this type use several texts in the same classroom often grouped around thematic links and so the teacher is able to make choices about the ability mix involved in particular groupings. Following John-Steiner (2000), O'Donnell-Allen (2006) makes a crucial distinction between co-operation and collaboration within student reading groups. In co-operative activities such as Daniels' early version of a literature circle, each member fulfils a separate task which then all piece together to create the complete reading experience. In contrast, a collaborative learning activity requires collaborative whole task completion. O'Donnell-Allen cites the research of Alvermann and her colleagues (1996) who found that open-ended tasks that require group collaboration, as opposed to division of labour among individuals, are an essential component of effective discussion in small groups. Edwards' (this volume) third quadrant is once again paramount in this design.

I would argue that both forms of reading group follow a social-constructivist approach to designing a learning activity and the learning environment in which that activity takes place. The task design element of each form of collaborative reading attends to the concern with active reading for meaning and for students to both engage with the cultures embedded in that text and to act on this knowledge through their collective interpretation. Collaborative reading engages students with concepts of genre and theme as well as literary analysis and interpretation. The object of this activity is the collaborative act of meaning making through interpersonal discourse. John-Steiner (2000) explains that collaborative learning is characterised by 'fully realized equality in roles and responsibilities' because participants 'see themselves engaged in a joint task' (p.13). But the conducting role of the teacher, as assessor and as prompt, is equally important.

## Conclusion

I have argued in this chapter that one of the key goals of English teaching is the development of students' conceptual understanding through communicative tasks that actively engage students with the cultural and social tools required for meaning making and interpretation. Concept formation is central to literate practices. The Vygotskian stress on the dialectical interaction between students' developing scientific and spontaneous concepts means that the focus of assessment is on the process of learning that leads development rather than the final products of literary tasks. Through assessing both the incubation of thought in reading for meaning and the development of writing through interaction it may be possible to glimpse the development of higher psychological processes.

The implication for task design in the English classroom is that whilst English teachers need to promote opportunities within their classrooms for students to write expressively for a defined audience or to read actively for meaning, students also have to have time for incubation and opportunities for talk. The task design models that I have presented here represent communicative tasks that involve students' interaction with the social, cultural and historical shaping of language and literature. Writing in this model is the ability to make our own thinking visible and talk is central to the process of developing thought into written language. Reading is primarily a receptive rather than a productive process: but collaborative reading requires active engagement on the part of the readers. Through collaborative activities of reading and writing these literacy processes can be internalised and appropriated through interpersonal or interpsychological activity that in turn develops intramental processes of psychological tool use. It follows then that the process of task design for students' active engagement in the processes of reading and writing involves an engagement with the dialectical interaction between the development of thought through inner speech and the mediational properties of interaction through talk. The teaching of meaning making within the social environment of the English classroom may be subject to the pressures of teaching towards summative tests, yet it is in the very complexity of literacy processes that the heart of the learning lies.

## References

Alvermann, D. E., Young, J. P., Weaver, D., Hinchman, K. A., Moore, D. W., Phelps, S. F., Thrash, E. C. and Zalewski, P. (1996) Middle and high school students' perceptions of how they experience text-based discussions: a multicase study. *Reading Research Quarterly*, 31: 244–67.

Andrews, R., Torgerson, C., Beverton, S., Freeman, A., Locke, T., Low, G. and Zhu, D. (2006) The effect of grammar teaching on writing development. *British Educational Research Journal*, 32(1): 39–55.

Applebee, A. N. (1986). Problems in process approaches: toward a reconceptualization of process instruction. In A. R. Petrosky and D. Bartholomae (eds) *The Teaching Of Writing. 85th yearbook of the National Society for the Study of Education*, pp. 95–113. Chicago: University of Chicago Press.

Applebee, A. N. (1996) *Curriculum as Conversation: Transforming traditions of teaching and learning*. Chicago, IL: Chicago University Press.

Barnes, D. (1976) *From Communication to Curriculum*. Harmondsworth: Penguin.

Barnes, D. (2008) Exploratory talk for learning. In N. Mercer and S. Hodgkinson (eds) *Exploring Talk in School*. London: SAGE.

Bazerman, C. (1994) Systems of genres and the enactment of social intentions. In A. Freedman and P. Medway (eds), *Genre and the New Rhetoric*, pp. 79–101. London: Taylor and Francis.

Bazerman, C. (2012) Writing, cognition and affect from the perspectives of sociocultural and historical studies of writing. In V. W. Berninger (ed.) *Past, Present and Future Contributions of Cognitive Writing Research to Cognitive Psychology*. New York: Taylor and Francis.

Brice-Heath, S. (2007) Afterword. In V. Ellis, C. Fox and B. Street (eds) *Rethinking English in Schools: Towards a new and constructive stage*. London: Continuum.

Britton, J., Burgess, T., Martin, N., McLeod, A. and Rosen, H. (1975) *The Development of Writing Abilities (11–18)*. London: Macmillan.

Bruner, J. (1996) *Culture, Mind, and Education*. Cambridge, MA: Harvard University Press.

Burgess, T. (2007) The picture of development in Vygotskyan theory: renewing the intellectual project of English. In V. Ellis, C. Fox and B. Street (eds) *Rethinking English in Schools: Towards a new and constructive stage*. London: Continuum.

Chaiklin, S. (2003) The zone of proximal development in Vygotsky's analyses of learning and instruction. In A Kozulin, B. Gindis, V. Ageyev and S. M. Miller (eds) *Vygotsky's Educational Theory in a Cultural Context*. Cambridge: Cambridge University Press.

Cope B. and Kalantzis, M. (eds) (1993) *The Powers of Literacy: A genre approach to teaching writing*. Pittsburgh, PA: University of Pittsburgh Press.

Daniels, H. 'S'. (2006) What's the next big thing with literature circles? *Voices from the Middle*, 13 (4): 10–15.

Daniels, H. (2007) 'Pedagogy.' In H. Daniels, M. Cole and J. Wertsch (eds) *The Cambridge Companion to Vygotsky*, pp. 307–31. New York: Cambridge University Press.

Daniels, H. 'S'. (1994) *Literature Circles: Voice and choice in the student–centered classroom*. Portland, ME: Stenhouse.

Derry, J. (2008) Abstract rationality in education: from Vygotsky to Brandom. *Studies in the Philosophy of Education*, 27: 49–62.

DES (1975) *A Language for Life: Report for the Committee of Inquiry Appointed by the Secretary of State for Science and Education under the Chairmanship of Sir Alan Bullock* (The Bullock Report). London: HSMO.

DES (1989) *Report of the English Working Party 5–16*. Retrieved from www.educationengland.org.uk/documents/cox1989/

DES and WO (1988) *The Kingman Report*. Retrieved from www.educationengland.org.uk/documents/kingman/kingman1988.html

Dixon, J. (1967) *Growth Through English*. Oxford: Oxford University Press.

Doyle, W. and Carter, K. (1984) Academic tasks in classrooms. *Curriculum Inquiry*, 14: 129–49.

Eagleton, T. (1983) *Literary Theory: An introduction*. Oxford: Blackwell.

Edwards, A. (2010) 'How can Vygotsky and his legacy help us to understand develop and teacher education?' In V. Ellis, A. Edwards and P. Smagorinsky (eds) *Cultural-historical Perspectives on Teacher Education and Development*. London and New York: Routledge.

Ellis, V. (2007) More than soldiering on: realising the potential of teacher education to rethink English in schools. In V. Ellis, C. Fox, and B. Street (eds) *Rethinking English in Schools: Towards a new and constructive stage*. London: Continuum.

Ellis, V. (2009) *Subject Knowledge and Teacher Education*. London: Continuum.

Freedman, A. and Medway, P. (1994) *Learning and Teaching Genre*. Portsmouth, NH: Heinemann.

Gove, M. (2013) Michael Gove speaks about the importance of teaching. Retrieved from www.gov.uk/government/speeches/michael-gove-speaks-about-the-importance-of-teaching.

Graves, D. (1994) *A Fresh Look at Writing*. London: Heinemann.

Halliday, M. A. K. and Hasan, R. (1989) *Language, Context and Text: Aspects of language in a social-semiotic perspective*. Oxford: Oxford University Press.

Halliday, M. A. K. (1993) Towards a Language-based Theory of Learning. *Linguistics and Education*, 5: 93–116.

Hodge, R. and Kress, G. (1988) *Social Semiotics*. Cambridge: Polity.

John-Steiner, V. (2000) *Creative Collaboration*. Oxford: Oxford University Press.

Kress, G. (1988) *Communication and Culture: An introduction*. Kensington, NSW: New South Wales University Press.

Kress, G., Jewitt, C., Bourne, J., Franks, A., Hardcastle, J., Jones, K. and Reid, R. (2005) *English in Urban Classrooms: A multimodal perspective on teaching and learning*. London: RoutledgeFalmer.

Marshall, B. (2006) What do we know in English: facts and fiction in an arts based English curriculum. *English in Education*, 40(3): 7–20.

McCallum, A. (2012) *Creativity and Learning in Secondary English: Teaching for a creative classroom*. London and New York: Routledge.

Mercer, N. (1995) *The Guided Construction of Knowledge: Talk amongst teachers and learners*. Clevedon: Multilingual Matters.

Mercer, N. (2000) *Words and Minds: How we use language to think together*. London: Routledge.

Miller, S. M. (2003) How literature discussion shapes thinking: ZPDs for teaching/learning habits of heart and mind. In A. Kozulin, B. Gindis, V. S. Ageyev and S. M. Miller (eds) *Vygotsky's Educational Theories in Context*. Cambridge: Cambridge University Press.

Murray, D. (1972) Teach writing as a process not a product. *The Leaflet* (Nov. 1972): 11–14.

Myhill, D. (2001) *Better Writers*. Westley: Courseware Publications.

Myhill, D. A., Jones, S. M., Lines, H. and Watson, A. (2012) Re-thinking grammar: the impact of embedded grammar teaching on students' writing and students' metalinguistic understanding. *Research Papers in Education*, 27(2): 139–66.

Newman, D., Griffin, P. and Cole, M. (1989) *The Construction Zone*. Cambridge: Cambridge University Press.

O'Donnell-Allen, C. (2006) *The Bookclub Companion: Fostering strategic readers in the secondary classroom*. Portsmouth, NH: Heinemann.

Office for Standards in Education (Ofsted) (2012) *Moving English Forward: Action to Raise Standards in English*. Retrieved from www.ofsted.gov.uk/resources/moving-english-forward

Prior, P. (1998) *Writing/Disciplinarity: A sociohistoric account of literate activity in the academy*. Mahwah, NJ: Lawrence Erlbaum.

Russell, D. R. (2010) Writing in multiple contexts: Vygotskian CHAT meets the phenomenology of genre. In C. Bazerman (ed.) *Traditions of Writing Research*. New York: Routledge.

Schwab, J. J. (1978) *Science, Curriculum and Liberal Education: Selected essays*. Chicago, IL: University of Chicago Press.

Smagorinsky, P. (2002) *Teaching English by Principled Practice*. New Jersey: Merrill Prentice Hall.

Smagorinsky, P. (2008) *Teaching English by Design*. Portsmouth, NH: Heinemann.

Swales, J. (1990) *Genre Analysis*. Cambridge: Cambridge University Press.

Thompson, I. (2012a) Stimulating reluctant writers: a Vygotskian approach to teaching writing in secondary schools. *English in Education*, 46(1): 84–91.

Thompson, I. (2012b) Planes of communicative activity in collaborative writing. *Changing English*, 19(2): 209–20.

Thompson, I. (2013) The mediation of learning in the zone of proximal development. *Research in the Teaching of English,* 47(3): 247–76.
Vygotsky, L. S. (1978) *Mind in Society: The development of higher psychological processes.* Boston: Harvard University Press.
Vygotsky, L. S. (1987a) Thinking and speech. In *L.S. Vygotsky, Collected Works* (Vol. 1). New York: Plenum Press.
Vygotsky, L. S. (1987b) *Educational Psychology.* Boca Raton, FL: CRC Press.
Williams, R. (1977) *Marxism and Literature.* London: Oxford University Press.

# 7
# PRACTICAL THEORISING
## Designing tasks for science explanations

*Ann Childs and Jane McNicholl*

**Introduction**

> Nearly every science teacher would agree that explaining things is fundamental to a science teacher's job. It is not of course the whole job but it is a central and crucial part of it.
>
> *(Ogborn, Kress, Martins and McGillicuddy 1996: 2)*

This chapter focuses upon task design in relation to explaining concepts in science; the importance of which is highlighted in the quotation from Ogborn *et al.* above. The chapter begins by looking at an important body of literature in science education on pedagogical content knowledge (PCK) to look in detail at the knowledge teachers have to design appropriate tasks to facilitate pupil learning of important concepts in science. It then goes on to link this body of knowledge to science explanation and to key writers in science education who have looked at, described and analysed the processes involved in explaining science in the classroom and, in particular, the kinds of tasks which might be used in such science explanations. The chapter then looks in detail at one initial teacher education programme, the Oxford Internship scheme, and unpicks how the university and school context, through the process of practical theorising, is designed to help student teachers to develop their knowledge and understanding about how to explain science to learners, and to help them build a repertoire of tasks in order to do this. In the conclusion we look at what implications there are for future work and research in this area.

## Experienced teachers' knowledge

### Pedagogical content knowledge

Science teachers' subject matter knowledge has been identified to be a critical indicator of teacher quality (The Royal Society 2007), the implication being that teachers with poor subject matter knowledge teach dull and uninspiring lessons that do little to inspire future potential scientists and engineers (Institute of Physics 2002; DfES 2006). Grossman, Wilson and Shulman (1989) identified four components that they believed subject matter knowledge comprised: content knowledge (factual information); substantive knowledge (explanatory frameworks); syntactic knowledge (how knowledge develops); and beliefs about the subject matter. Alternatively Schwab's (1978) definition delineates subject matter knowledge into substantive knowledge (the facts, theories and disciplines of the sciences) and syntactic knowledge (the procedures of investigating and experimenting). In the case of science, there are arguments for scientific literacy and the nature of science to be also included in any definition of subject matter knowledge (Gess-Newsome 1999).

Clearly then, subject matter knowledge is important in ensuring teacher quality; however, in itself it is not sufficient. Subject matter knowledge has to be made accessible to learners and to do this requires teachers to have a special type of knowledge. To distinguish this special knowledge, Lee Shulman (1986; 1987) introduced the term pedagogical content knowledge (PCK) or 'the special amalgam of content knowledge and knowledge of general pedagogy that a teacher needs to be the best possible teacher' (Nilsson 2008: 1282). Shulman's original definition of PCK, the 'most useful forms of content representation, the most powerful analogies, illustrations, examples, and demonstrations' (1986: 9) has for many years been particularly powerful in the science education literature across the world (see Berry, Loughran and van Driel 2008). Indeed no other area seems to have devoted more effort investigating it. For example, in 2008 a special issue of the *International Journal of Science Education* was entirely devoted to PCK. Given that making scientific concepts and phenomena accessible to learners (or 'explaining') has been shown to lie at the heart of exemplary science teaching, this focus is hardly surprising (Gilbert, Boulter and Rutherford 1998; Glynn, Duit and Thiele 1995; Treagust 1992; Harrison and Treagust 1993).

In spite of the wealth of research into PCK, it is contested as 'an academic construct' (Nilsson 2008: 1282), not least in terms of how it has been defined and conceptualised (see Grossman 1990; van Driel, Verloop and De Vos 1998; Magnussen, Krajcik and Borko 1999; Barnett and Hodson 2001; Hashweh 2005; Loughran, Berry and Mulhall 2006; Loughran, Mulhall and Berry 2008; Lee and Luft 2008). Some of the models employed to conceptualise PCK see it as comprising four main areas: 'subject matter for instructional purposes; students' understanding of subject matter; media for instruction in the subject matter (the texts and materials); and instructional processes for the subject matter (Marks 1990 cited in Turner-Bisset 1999: 42) or pedagogy, subject matter, students and the environmental context. Alternatively the constructivist view emphasises student misconceptions as an important aspect. Experienced science teachers identified seven PCK components – knowledge of: subject matter, teaching strategies, resources, purpose, learners, curriculum organisation and assessment (Lee and Luft 2008). However, whatever model one adheres to, the consensus appears to be that the components are difficult to separate – its constitutive components are highly integrated and interrelated (for example Cochran, De Ruiter and King 1993; Lee and Luft 2008); in fact, the teachers in Lee and Luft's study would interweave the different components together when describing PCK.

While many agree that this amalgam of highly integrated components results in PCK being more than a sum of its parts, some scholars have gone further and argued that it is much more sophisticated and subtle. What they argue is that such knowledge possessed by expert teachers enables them to be sensitive to differences – differences that inevitably occur between individual teaching situations that teachers encounter. As Shulman argued in 1987, PCK encompasses knowledge about 'how particular topics, problems, or issues are organised, represented, and adapted to the diverse interests and abilities of learners and presented for instruction' (p. 8); it is 'highly topic, person, and situation specific' (van Driel and Berry 2012: 26; also see Abell 2007; Kind 2009). Because there is not only one way to teach certain subject matter, expert teachers with a repertoire of pedagogies are able to meet the needs of learners on a day-to-day basis (Hashweh 2005). For this reason, terms such as subject specific pedagogical knowledge (Burn, Childs and McNicholl 2007) or topic specific pedagogy (Lock, Soares and Foster 2009) have been used to define the knowledge that science teachers have.

Clearly PCK is a highly complex and contextualised (Barnett and Hodson, 2001) form of professional knowledge. While its exact nature remains contested, in our own research we have found Summers, Kruger and Mant's (1998) description particularly useful – it will become clear later in the chapter why this description, with its focus upon explanation, particularly resonates with our work:

- appropriate scientific terms and language to use with children
- what to emphasise (not just what is the case but what is not the case)
- how to simplify validly what are often complex ideas
- simple technical knowledge (e.g. why nominally identical bulbs do not glow equally and what to do about this).

*(Summers et al. 1998:171)*

It does have to be recognised, however, that despite all that is already known about it as the knowledge base of science teachers, PCK is still regarded as somewhat elusive knowledge, as Kind (2009) argues, 'finding out exactly what it comprises and using this knowledge to support good practice in teacher education is not easy' (p. 170). As is the case with other sorts of teachers' knowledge, it is often considered to be tacit and a rather obscure type of personal knowledge. Some recent work has taken a different view: for example, rather than seeing it as a personal possession, PCK might in fact also be held at the group level (Loughran, Mulhall and Berry 2008). Our own research into teacher learning within school departments has also shown that it can be the product of a social process and as such, shared, distributed and held across people, material artefacts and social settings (McNicholl, Childs and Burn 2013). Notwithstanding this, whether it is individualistic or shared, in being defined as the 'amalgam of content and pedagogy that is uniquely the providence of teachers' (Shulman 1987: 8), PCK remains a useful concept. As Abell (2008) argues, in moving away from vagueness or imprecision, re-defining it in more robust terms can only serve to help in researching the knowledge base of expert teachers, for example by shaping the 'questions researchers ask and the ways they design their studies' (p. 1407) and by informing the development of research instruments (Henze, van Driel and Verloop 2008; Lee and Luft 2008; Padilla 2008).

## Explanations in science

The section above has explored in detail PCK and the knowledge teachers need in order to teach science. But what is at the heart of a science teacher's job? The quotation from Ogborn *et al.* at the beginning of this chapter signals that a key part of a science teacher's job is to explain and it is this job and implications for task design that the remaining part of this chapter will focus on. Tobin and Garnett (1988) in their research on characterising exemplary practice in science link together the ability to explain with PCK when they say:

> These results highlight the importance of ensuring that high school science teachers have the knowledge needed to explain science phenomena, demonstrate science principles, probe student understandings, diagnose partial understandings and misunderstandings from student responses, and expand on student understandings of given science concepts. This type of content knowledge, which Shulman (1986) called pedagogical content knowledge, is the professional knowledge of the science teacher.
> 
> *(Tobin and Garnett 1988: 206)*

So too do Wellington and Osborne (2001) where they refer to it as the 'wisdom of practice':

> Being able to explain the ideas of science is one of the great arts of teaching i.e. putting difficult concepts in terms pupils can understand.... Through observation, practice and experience teachers develop a repertoire of ways of explaining things. If one doesn't work, then perhaps another will. This wisdom of practice (Shulman 1986: 9) develops over time – teachers acquire a whole armoury of examples, illustrations, explanations and analogies.
> 
> *(Wellington and Osborne 2001: 36)*

Why is a focus on explaining science important? Firstly, much of the work on exemplary science teachers has confirmed that along with all the other skills they bring to classroom, including being knowledgeable about student learning, employing a varied repertoire of teaching strategies, creating safe and structured learning environments, using assessment information effectively, exemplary teachers also explain science well (Garnett and Tobin 1988; Tobin and Fraser 1988; Fraser, Tobin and Lacy 1988; Tobin and Fraser 1990; Berliner 2004; Alsop, Bencze and Pedretti 2005; Bishop and Denley 2007; Waldrip, Fisher and Dorman 2009). This has been reinforced by more recent work by Wilson and Mant (2011) who discovered that one of the key skills that marked out exemplary science teachers was their ability to be 'explainers' of the subject. Secondly, other research has shown that students' attitudes/motivation improved when teachers are enthusiastic and explain well (Murphy and Beggs 2003; Osborne, Simon and Collins 2003).

What is an explanation in science? Mortimer and Scott (2003) define explanation in science as involving 'importing some form of theoretical model or mechanism to account for specific phenomenon' (p. 30). Horwood (1988) draws on Bateson's work when he says that 'to explain a thing is to map the thing onto a logical system of causality' (p. 41). Ogborn *et al.* (1996) highlight that in science 'there is a lot of explaining to do' and explaining involves answering questions like 'Why can metal ships float even though metals sink? How can we catch colds? What keeps the Moon going around the Earth?' (p. 2). Therefore, explanations in science could be seen as focusing on answering the what, how and why of the natural world using theoretical models or mechanisms.

How do teachers explain? Ogborn *et al.* argue that, in the science education of the time, 'the act and art of explaining to a class is much less discussed than the scientific ideas to be explained' and that 'there is no body of evidence on which to base arguments about how explaining can be done, and what different ways there are of doing it' (ibid: 2). Their research seeks to address this gap by providing 'a language to describe and compare different cases of explaining in the science classroom' (p. 3). Drawing on their empirical work with teachers in classrooms they offer a theoretical framework for describing explanations which has three components:

- scientific explanations as analogous to 'stories'
- an account of meaning-making in explanation, itself with four parts
  - creating differences
  - constructing entities
  - transforming knowledge
  - putting meaning into matter
- variation and styles of explanation.

*(Ogborn et al. 1996: 8–9)*

The full details of their model are explained in the book but we want here to pick up on a few key points we will pursue later in this chapter. Firstly, Ogborn *et al.* see explanations fundamentally as storytelling and this resonates with other writers such as Mortimer and Scott (2003) who draw on Ogborn *et al.*'s work when they say:

> As we see it, school science offers an account, a kind of story, of familiar natural phenomena expressed in terms of ideas and conventions of the school science social language.
> 
> *(Mortimer and Scott 2003: 18)*

Osborne and Millar (1998) also talk about the value in conceiving of 'explanation as story' for student learning:

> By using the word 'stories' we do not, of course, wish to suggest that the explanatory accounts provided by science are 'mere fictions'. Rather we want to emphasise the value of the narrative in communicating ideas and in making ideas coherent, memorable and meaningful.
> 
> *(Osborne and Millar 1998: 13).*

A second point to highlight at this stage is that Ogborn *et al.*'s framework focuses on the idea of 'creating differences':

> one essential difference is that between what the student knows and what they 'ought' to know. It is assumed that the teacher can bridge this difference. There is also a second difference: that between what the student ought to know and what the student wants to know.
> 
> *(Ogborn* et al. *1996: 12)*

Thus teachers are not only in the business of explaining what students 'ought' to know but they are also in the business of persuading the students away from previously held preconceptions, misconceptions or alternative frameworks towards the scientific understanding of ideas or concepts. Indeed Posner, Strike, Hewson and Gertzog (1982) distinguish between conceptual change as assimilation or accommodation. In assimilation, a 'student's current concepts are inadequate to allow him to grasp some new phenomenon successfully' (p. 212). Accommodation, however, requires that 'the student must replace or reorganise his central concepts' (p. 212). In order to achieve accommodation Posner *et al.* suggest that four important conditions that must be fulfilled. Firstly, the students must be dissatisfied with their 'existing conceptions' in that they 'are unlikely to make major changes until they believe that less radical changes will not work' (p. 214). Secondly, the new concept must be intelligible and Posner *et al.* stress the importance of analogies and metaphors, for example, in 'lending initial meaning and intelligibility to new concepts' (p. 214). Thirdly, the new concept must be 'initially plausible' and finally, it must be fruitful in that it may 'open up new areas of inquiry' (p. 214).

These notions about conceptual change along with the idea of 'creating a need to explain' and motivating students to want to learn we will return to later. As

Ogborn et al.'s work in particular shows, explaining science is a complex process and, as Wellington and Osborne (2001) indicate, teachers 'acquire a whole armoury of examples, illustrations, explanations and analogies' in order to explain (p. 36). Indeed other writers in science education also identify the use of metaphor, analogy, and modeling as important in giving science explanations and these have been shown both to aid the learning of scientific concepts and ideas, and also, as seen in Posner et al.'s work, as being important in making new concepts intelligible (see for example, Duit 1991; Harrison and Treagust 1993; Jarman 1996; Ogborn, Kress, Martins and McGillicuddy 1996; Tobin and Fraser 1990; Treagust, Harrison and Venville 1998). Again we will come back to teachers' use of examples, illustrations, explanations and analogies and so on later.

## Talk in the science classroom

In the discussion on PCK and the nature of explanations, we might have implied a focus on teacher-led approaches but that was not intended. Rather we view science teaching explanations as being often co-constructed by teachers and learners. To explore the ways in which teacher and students do this and so develop understandings or meanings of concepts in science we draw, in particular, on the work of Mortimer and Scott (2003). Their concerns in looking at meaning making in the science classroom arose out of their work with schemes of work and textbooks, where many tasks aimed at helping students learn science focused on the task or the activity. This focus drew attention away from what they perceived as 'the *key* feature of *any* science lesson' namely:

> The way in which the teacher orchestrates the talk of the lesson, in interacting with students, to develop the scientific story being taught.
> *(Mortimer and Scott 2003: 1)*

Although they perceive the choice of task as important, Mortimer and Scott argue that it is in the teachers' and students' talk around those activities where learning occurs. We would argue that this needs to be thought about as much as the actual task. In order to explore this talk, they adopted a Vygotskian perspective in their research into science classrooms and developed a new analytical framework based upon socio-cultural perspectives (from Bakhtin and Vygotsky) to analyse classroom talk in order to identify the ways in which teachers and students make meanings visible and hence co-construct explanations. By doing this the emphasis moved away from 'a time when the science teacher presented scientific facts to the class, and the students listened' (ibid: 1). The framework is elaborated in their book and we will be drawing on sections of this later in the chapter. Finally, as well as talk as a means of communication and sense making teachers also use other modes of communication to explain their subject; for example, diagrams, demonstrations, images from books, gestures, and so on (Kress, Jewitt, Ogborn and Tsatsarelis 2001) and we will touch on these too later.

In summary we have described a key framework, PCK, which describes the knowledge base that teachers need to transform their science subject knowledge to make it accessible to students in the process of explaining. One of the domains of this knowledge base is experienced teachers' knowledge of 'the most powerful analogies, illustrations, examples, and demonstrations' (Shulman 1986: 9) which we have shown has been added to from the work of Summers *et al.* (1988) to include tasks like practical work and demonstrations. These, for the purposes of this chapter, we argue are the tasks that teachers use in 'the art of explaining' (Ogborn *et al.* 1996: 2). But we have also drawn attention to the work of Mortimer and Scott (2003) who have emphasised that no matter how good the task(s) designed might be in explaining science, it is talk in the classroom between teacher and students, and how this is orchestrated, that is fundamental in achieving student progress and learning; we will come back to Mortimer and Scott's framework later as well.

## Differences between experienced teachers and beginning teachers

As we have seen above, exemplary teachers possess 'stores of powerful explanations, demonstrations, and examples for representing subject matter to students' (Borko and Livingston 1989: 491). But what about less than exemplary teachers – novices and teachers teaching outside of their subject specialism? Research (see for example, Hasweh 1987; Lee 1995; Sanders, Borko and Lockard 1993) has shown a number of issues and challenges faced by novice teachers and those teaching outside their specialism. Firstly there is a tendency for this group to teach lessons that are limited, unadventurous and lacking in sufficient cognitive challenge. For instance, Hashweh (1987) showed how when teaching outside of subject specialism, teachers' questioning practices were more closed and cognitively less demanding. Secondly, other studies have shown that within the classroom there was less dialogic teaching and safer, seat-based strategies were employed (Carlsen 1991; Lee 1995; Sanders *et al.* 1993). In our own research teachers would talk about this, for example:

> I try to keep it, I suppose, not consciously, but I keep it buttoned down more and I don't stray so much from subject.
> *(Experienced chemistry teacher, in Childs and McNicholl 2007: 11)*

> Outside of my specialism [the students] learn by rote... therefore you know you can't be inspiring and therefore [for the students] the subject is dull.
> *(Newly qualified physics teacher, in Childs and McNicholl 2007: 11)*

Because teachers felt unable to respond to students accurately and in sufficient depth they would 'close things down' and adopt rigid and safe teaching strategies. This point is obviously significant in relation to Mortimer and Scott's work which shows the importance of dialogue and talk in a science classroom. Thirdly, our research found that feeling like a novice was particularly intense when teachers had to deal with student misconceptions by providing explanations of the scientific ideas to remedy these misconceptions (Childs and McNicholl 2007; McNicholl, Childs and Burn 2013). In our early study, we found teachers talking about the importance of having two and three different ways of explaining – being able to explain in lots of different ways, or as Sanders, Borko and Lockard (1993) say, being able to use ideas, examples, analogies from off the top of one's head; this also resonates with Wellington and Osborne's 'wisdom of practice'. It was these powerful explanations – or effective *science teaching explanations* – that appeared to be lacking when teachers were teaching outside of subject specialism.

Fourthly, we identified another aspect of PCK that was under developed in this group and that was the ability to 'see the bigger picture'. What we mean by this is, having a level of knowledge and understanding that goes beyond the content of individual lessons or individual topics of work – seeing the 'bigger picture' refers to understanding the larger scientific story that spans the curriculum which means that a significant part of what Ogborn *et al.* and Mortimer and Scott see as crucial to explanation, the telling of stories, is problematic for this group. This challenge is nicely articulated by one of the teachers we worked with in our research:

> The first time you teach a particular module outside of your specialism… you don't have firm concepts of where it's all going and what seeds to sow early on because you know you are going to use them later.
> *(Experienced biology teacher, in Childs and McNicholl 2007: 9)*

Knowledge of curriculum organisation, that is knowledge of how ideas are developed through and across the curriculum, was also one of the seven components of PCK identified by the experienced teachers in Lee and Luft's study (2008). It would seem that multiple opportunities to plan, teach and review topics (Hashweh 2005; Park and Oliver 2008) combined with increasing familiarity with the curriculum are required for the development of 'expert' PCK and which is why some writers, for example Kind (2009) claim that 'several years must pass before PCK is fully developed' (p. 184).

## How to bridge the gap

### Internship

In common with many other Initial Teacher Education (ITE) programmes around the world, the one year Post Graduate Certificate of Education (PGCE) course, the major route into secondary school teaching in the UK, is provided by universities in partnership with schools. The intention is that over the year graduates bring their developing pedagogical knowledge and skills to bear on their subject matter knowledge obtained during their degree studies in order to transform it for students. In the case of novice science teachers this intention is complicated by the fact that many do not have graduate level knowledge of all the science subject matter taught in schools. Consequently many have to learn how to teach subject matter not studied since their own school days (Dennick and Joyes 1994) and this presents a major challenge for many novice teachers (Lock, Salt and Soares 2011). As we have already mentioned, such concerns are not confined to novices, there are times when even experienced teachers have limited subject matter knowledge, for example, when teaching outside their area of certification (or outside of their subject specialism). In the UK concerns have been raised about the extent to which non-specialists are teaching chemistry and physics lessons and the implications of this for the stream of future scientists and engineers (TES 2010; The Royal Society 2007). The Government's response has been to look to ITE as part of the solution; making ITE courses financially attractive to physical science graduates and encouraging providers to 'ensure that subject specific pedagogical training receives a high priority' (Department for Business Innovation and Skills 2010: 10).

For ITE partnership programmes, such as the PGCE course, this poses challenges for what each partner, school mentors and university tutors, can bring to student teachers' learning. The Oxford Internship Scheme addresses this issue by looking at what expertise each partner can contribute to the learning of student teachers. As Hayward (1997) says, prospective teachers work with both mentors (experienced school teachers) and university tutors and in this partnership 'the mentor is primarily required to discuss suggestions for practice in the context of their school' whilst the university tutor's role is 'to introduce them (the student teachers) in a systematic, rigorous and rational way to theoretical arguments about why certain practices, for example, mastery learning, are important and worthy of consideration' (p. 20). The student teachers take the more decontextualised and theoretical ideas from the university with the contextualised ideas from school and these are tested against each other in a dialectical approach called 'practical theorising'. As McIntyre (1993), writing about this process says:

> no knowledge, whatever the nature or source, should be assumed to be valid, but instead should be questioned in relation to a range of criteria.
> *(McIntyre 1993: 42)*

The role of the student teacher then is 'to understand, to theorise about, and most especially to evaluate the various suggestions for practice' (McIntyre 1993: 49) in the process of practical theorising. There is potential here for there to be contradictions or even disagreement between the different sources of knowledge, but, as Hayward argues, rather than problematic, differences need to be embraced since 'many of the problems associated with the lack of coherence in PGCE programmes stem from an unrealistic and unhelpful assumption that a straightforward continuity of perspective between schools and university is possible and desirable' (p. 19). We will look at how the potential of practical theorising works in developing student teachers' practice in explaining in science in the next section.

## Developing explanations in internship

We will now show how the process of practical theorising works in the case of helping beginning teachers 'develop a repertoire of ways of explaining things' (Shulman 1986).

## In the university context

We begin in the first weeks of the course by introducing the theoretical framework of PCK as a heuristic device to allow the beginning teachers to understand exactly what knowledge it is that they need to develop in their education as teachers. Early on in the course we also begin the work on explanation in science and we ask student teachers to work in small groups to complete the template which can be found in Appendix 1. This template has been designed to begin to get the student teachers to think about what an explanation might involve and makes key links to the literature and to key theoretical frameworks we have discussed above. Section 1 involves the student teachers identifying an area of the curriculum that they have found challenging to teach and asks them to write out what the explanation is in their own terms in order to begin to think themselves what might be difficult to explain to learners. In this section we also ask the student teachers to try and link this to a real life phenomena or a question to be answered. This is in part to create, as in Ogborn *et al.*'s framework, a difference or a need to explain in order to make students feel there is something worth learning. To support section 1, throughout the course our student teachers, in small groups, research and present what we call 'Amazing Science' where they are asked to find out an amazing science question/fact/news item and so on which could be used as a basis to begin a science explanation. At the end, all of the presentations are collated in a book for the student teachers to take away and use in their own teaching in school.

Section 2 of the template then introduces student teachers to a major distinction in science teaching between description and explanation. Description and explanation can cause problems for both teachers and students as Horwood reports:

> It is commonplace to see science teachers and pupils use the description of an event to process as equivalent to explaining it.
>
> *(Horwood 1988: 45)*

As indicated above, explanation has been defined as requiring the mapping of 'thing onto a logical system of causality' (Horwood, 1988: 41) or as involving some form of theoretical model or mechanism (Mortimer and Scott 2003). Description is different and Mortimer and Scott define description as involving:

> Statements that provide an account of a system, an object or a phenomena in terms of its constituents, or the spatiotemporal displacements of those constituents.
>
> *(Mortimer and Scott: 30)*

So a key purpose of section 2 is to get student teachers to begin to understand the issues and challenges that the difference between explanation and description poses for pupils' learning and for their own teaching. Therefore, in section 2 student teachers are asked to think about tasks that they can do with students which describe the phenomena to be explained. For example, they might choose a practical task using electric circuits to show that the current in a series circuit is the same in all parts of the circuit, or they might choose 'the ball in a ring' demonstrations which allow pupils to actually see that solids expand when heated. These are clearly not explanations but they are tasks which describe the phenomena and are, as Mortimer and Scott say, 'providing an account' of the system only. Similarly a demonstration which shows how diffusion, conduction or convection occur are all also descriptions – what they are not are explanations.

Section 3 of the template then requires the student teachers to use the extensive literature in science education on student preconceptions and/or misconceptions (see for example, Driver, Squires, Rushworth and Wood-Robinson 1994) to find out what specific issues, challenges, existing conceptions or alternative frameworks students will have in the area to be explained. This we hope enables our student teachers to begin to think about what kinds of tasks, activities and resources they will need to use to address these issues. In section 4, the student teachers are encouraged to get to the heart of the matter – to think about task/activities/ resources they will actually use to explain the phenomena. For example, they might choose to use a role play where students act as particles in solids to explain why a solid expands on heating or they might choose an analogy (and there are many) of how an electrical circuit works to explain why current is the same anywhere in a series circuit. Finally, section 5 uses the literature, such as Duit (1991), Posner *et al.* (1982), to ask student teachers to really critically evaluate the tasks they have chosen in section 4 in relation to their effectiveness in helping to explain the phenomena, for instance, in addressing the challenges for pupil learning highlighted in section 3 but also to identify potential limitations of the task in question. This template is also completed in a university session much later in the course, when student teachers are more aware of the challenges of explaining. On this occasion the templates are collected and produced as a booklet for the student teachers; this is designed to help to extend their repertoires in giving explanations in the classrooms in the future (Wellington and Osborne 2001).

This whole activity very much focuses on tasks that can be used for describing and explaining and, crucially, evaluating each task using a range of criteria drawn from the literature. At the heart of this activity are learners – student teachers have to continually consider how the needs of pupils are being addressed – as we have seen, a key element of co-constructing science explanations in the classroom. But, as we have seen, Mortimer and Scott also emphasise the importance of how these tasks can facilitate talk in the classroom and that this talk must also be planned into the shaping of the task. In order to address this issue we require our student teachers to do two things. Firstly, we ask them to present their explanation to other student teachers so that they can have some direct experience of what they will say, what questions they need to ask and what type of talk their explanation has the potential to stimulate. Second, during the course we ask our student teachers to tape or video themselves in the classroom while explaining and to analyse their talk using Mortimer and Scott's framework. In particular, we focus their analysis of their explanations in terms of how interactive the talk was and how questioning was used, both of which are also key aspects of Mortimer and Scott's own analytic framework.

However, the template we have used is limiting in one important aspect in that it does not really capture the notion of explanation as story. In order to inculcate in the student teachers the notion of explanation as story we have built into our lesson planning sessions both in school and in the university the idea of lessons being able to 'tell a story' not only within the lesson but between and across lessons. Mentors and tutors have also developed lesson planning templates which help to reinforce this focus on storylines too. In addition, for the presentations given at the university, student teachers are also encouraged to consider the need to present their explanation (both sections 2 and 4) as a story but further to think about how the different tasks for both description and explanation can be linked to create a narrative.

## *In the school context: science departments*

We have shown how the university input in the form of student teachers completing an explanation template draws on some key theoretical ideas and also the literature, for example, the work that looks at the distinction between explanation and description, pupils' preconceptions in science and the use of models, analogies and metaphors. The internship model described also demands that the student teachers use contextual knowledge from their mentors and experienced teachers in the process of practical theorising to develop their practice in giving explanations in science. But how might this happen? How do teachers learn PCK in the school context as they develop their own professional practice? In fact little research has been carried out into how science teachers learn PCK for explaining in their workplace and our research (see for example Burn, Childs and McNicholl 2007; Childs, Burn and McNicholl 2013; McNicholl, Childs and Burn 2013) has begun to unpick this important site for learning. In particular, this research has shown us that a key source for teachers to learn PCK was the interactions they routinely had with colleagues. Factors that facilitated this learning were, for example, the presence of a team room to bring teachers together to discuss PCK, a collaborative culture and leadership in the department which encouraged trust and openness amongst colleagues to share practice. Our research also showed that it was the knowledge domain of the 'most useful forms of content representation, the most powerful analogies, illustrations, examples, and demonstrations' (Shulman 1986: 9), including practicals and demonstrations (Summers *et al.* 1998) that teachers shared most often in the interactions with their colleagues. Our research also showed that these interactions were often very short, serendipitous and in the moment and usually occurred when a teacher realised they were teaching something fairly imminently; it would be at this point that they would then ask a subject specialist about suitable tasks.

However, the research also showed teachers meeting after school, for example for considerable lengths of time talking about how they would teach topics and sharing their PCK with others in the department. We also identified particular times of the day when teachers were likely to sit down and share practice and this was normally before or after school in the team rooms. These interactions around the learning of PCK in the school context are an important potential learning resource for our student teachers but this type of learning also presents, we would argue, two significant challenges. Firstly, the interactions were often short, serendipitous and focused on describing tasks and how to do them – teachers would not often explain why they chose these tasks – clearly also important for student teachers' learning. A possible reason why teachers did not articulate the 'why' part of their practice could because of time pressures but also because this wisdom or craft knowledge is often deeply buried, implicit and difficult to access, presenting significant problems for student teachers' learning (Brown and McIntyre 1993). Second, the interactions focused predominantly on only one aspect of PCK, the actual tasks, and important areas such as pupil learning/preconceptions, curriculum, purpose (and storyline) and so on were often absent from these interactions.

To respond to these challenges, we first of all, as said above, make the framework of PCK available to our student teachers as a heuristic device enabling them to understand what it is they need to learn and to help them to understand what questions they might need to ask while in their schools. Secondly, we direct our student teachers towards the potential of the informal interactions in the team room at break, lunchtime and after school as sources of learning PCK, particularly in relation to explaining science. We also try to get them to recognise the value in taking part in the day-to-day discussions within their departments and that frequenting the team room (if there is one, of course) will allow them access to these important professional discussions.

However, given that teachers' 'wisdom' or craft knowledge has been shown to be difficult to access and teachers' interactions tend to be fast and short-lived and hence unlikely to support deeper learning of PCK, we have decided to further develop the explanations activity described above. For instance, the next step is to get student teachers to take their template, completed during the university session, into school and to then further develop it alongside experienced teachers and/or their mentor. It is anticipated that in the process of working through each section, teachers will be required to explain their rationale and access and expose their craft knowledge more systematically to the student teachers than the more informal interactions described above. For example, the student teacher might ask their mentor about their views on the role play task commonly used when explaining the expansion of solids when heated. The mentor may see the advantages of this task but may also, using his/her contextual knowledge, consider that the activity is too difficult for the particular group of pupils involved or that the classroom

Designing tasks for science explanations **121**

laboratory might prove a difficult space to do a role play in or the group's dynamics might not be suitable to attempt such a lively activity. The teacher/mentor may also be able to talk much more specifically about what aspects of the scientific idea or concept the particular group of learners might find challenging and why, thus adding to the student teacher's understandings gleaned from the literature on pupil preconceptions when completing section 3. This is significant, we argue, because again this is another domain of experienced teachers' knowledge not observed in the many informal interactions in our research. More experienced teachers may also offer a range of other possible tasks that can be used for both describing and explaining the concept thus further building the student teachers 'repertoire of ways of explaining' (Wellington and Osborne 2001).

We hope these revisions to our original university-based activity will help our student teachers to develop their ideas of suitable tasks for explaining using theoretical ideas firstly in the university but to then test them in the realities of the context of their schools, where disagreements/different ideas have the potential to emerge leading to deeper and richer understandings about explaining science in the classroom. In using the template and, in particular the questions in section 5, the student teacher, as already mentioned, will also have better access to teachers' craft knowledge and 'wisdom', for example, their reasons for choosing particular tasks as well as their limitations. For example a student teacher might select a particular analogy to use to explain to pupils the difference between current and voltage. In taking this analogy to an expert physics teacher in school the teacher may, for example, have another analogy that has worked well for them which the student teacher can consider. The experienced teacher may also be able to spot particular issues and challenges that the pupils on which the analogy will be used may experience and work with the student teacher to adjust the analogy or even abandon it.

By using the template, the student teachers will explore how one particular explanation might be developed by drawing upon theoretical ideas in the university combined with professional contextualised ideas in practice. However, as we have previously pointed out, this so-called practical theorising can be fraught with problems, not least within the two different contexts there might be tensions and alternative view points to disentangle. For a student teacher, as indicated by Furlong and Maynard, this is very challenging:

> With a kind of postmodernist relativism, the Oxford scheme leaves it to the student to make up his or her own mind about what are appropriate forms of practice.
>
> *(Furlong and Maynard 1995: 50)*

It is therefore important that we address this point and to do this we will ask our student teachers in the future to bring their templates back to the university for final presentations where the aim is to discuss the issues and tensions that have emerged during the process of practical theorising in order to support them to 'understand, to theorise about, and most especially to evaluate the various suggestions for practice' (McIntyre 1993: 49) with their peers and university tutors.

Finally, the template could also provide a framework or a language that student teachers 'have in mind' when they are working with experienced teachers' on other occasions. In addition, it could also be 'borne in mind' and become a mental schema (in part or as a whole) for the more informal interactions we have described that frequently occur in science departments. While we have always been cautious about imposing more formality on these informal interactions in departments (Childs and McNicholl 2007), we believe that giving student teachers this framework and the language to ask questions of teachers, does not necessitate formality. Rather if used flexibly, the template can become a middle way – in providing a structure, it might give the interactions more formality while maintaining much of the informality, thereby making these interactions more useful for student teachers but also, we would argue, for experienced teachers as well.

## Conclusion and ways forward

The previous sections highlight the importance of ensuring that high school science teachers have the knowledge needed to explain scientific concepts and phenomena, demonstrate scientific principles, probe student understandings, diagnose partial understandings and misunderstandings from student responses, and expand on student understandings of given science concepts. This type of content knowledge, which Shulman (1986) called pedagogical content knowledge (PCK), is the professional knowledge of the science teacher and in this chapter we argue that secure PCK underpins effective classroom tasks – their design, selection and use. As Barnett and Hodson (2001) showed, science teachers' PCK is inextricably linked to context, such as the concepts to be taught, the learners teachers work with and the resources available and it was for this reason that they coined the term pedagogical context knowledge. Given the importance of context, it is surely the case that there is no one 'right task' to explain a scientific concept, idea or phenomenon, rather there might be a 'right' task for one group of learners and yet another equally effective task for a different group of learners. Also teachers might have to adapt the 'right' task if resources in their school are limited.

Moreover, designing tasks to explain is in actual fact a process and, in our research, we have shown how teachers learn from colleagues the tasks to explain science concepts as they work in their subject departments. This process of learning we have also seen has two principle challenges for student teachers which we have outlined above: the nature of the teacher–teacher interactions and the narrow focus on one aspect of PCK only. Therefore, we have argued that within the context of an initial teacher education programme there should be a more systematic, inquiry-led process, whereby tasks are taken to describe and explain a particular science concept and then subjected to rigorous critique based upon ideas from the literature (for example Duit, Posner *et al.* and so on) in a university session. In addition, such a critique must also be based on particular contextual issues found in school, for example, in relation to a particular group of students, or even individual learners and also to the resources available. The expertise drawn on to do this, we have argued, lies with the experienced school teachers and mentors that student teachers work with in science subject departments. It is important in the early days of their training that student teachers are led through this process, which we have called practical theorising, so that by the end of their course, this process has become almost second nature – it has become part of the mental schema of beginning science teachers which they can carry into and adapt in their careers.

A final implication is how we develop this more inquiry-led process to include all teachers to facilitate their continuing professional learning. In particular how can we, as university-based teacher educators, work with the informal learning we have seen in subject departments and embed a more inquiry-led process into teachers' day-to-day interactions? In other words, rather than formalising the learning, thereby risking constraining its usefulness for teachers, can we find a 'middle way' to support the informal learning we have seen? For example, this might include finding ways to encourage a richer discussion of PCK beyond the 'most useful forms of content representation, the most powerful analogies, illustrations, examples and demonstrations' (Shulman 1986: 9) which in our research dominated the teacher interactions. Furthermore, work by Hobson and McIntyre (2013) has shown that in some schools departmental cultures fail to encourage collegiality and the sharing of teacher knowledge; it seems that performativity-driven school cultures can lead to science teachers becoming fearful about seeking assistance from colleagues and in some cases, resulting in teacher fabrication. Clearly such departmental cultures will impede teacher learning since the kind of inquiry-led collegial approaches to learning we are advocating for both experienced and student teachers would be particularly challenging. How can we work with departments such as these and with the teachers there given the current climate as described by Hobson and McIntyre to facilitate the learning of PCK to benefit both the teachers and the student teachers in these contexts? The use of the template described above has the potential to facilitate focused communication between student teachers, their mentors and experienced teachers on an important aspect of science teaching. Therefore, for departments where collaboration is problematic, for whatever reason, this could be a useful device to open up the sharing of practice. However, it is only a first step and how we make fundamental and deep rooted inroads into the facilitation of purposeful sharing of practice as a regular and valued professional development for all science teachers is challenging and, as yet, a distant ambition.

# References

Abell, S. K. (2007) Research on science teacher knowledge. In S. K. Abell and N. G. Lederman (eds) *Research on Science Teacher Education*. New York: Routledge.

Abell, S. K. (2008) Twenty years later: does pedagogical content knowledge remain a useful idea? *International Journal of Science Education*, 3010, 1405 16.

Alsop, S., Bencze, L. and Pedretti, E. (2005) *Analysing Exemplary Science Teaching,* Maidenhead: Open University Press.

Barnett, J. and Hodson, D. (2001) Pedagogical context knowledge: towards a fuller understanding of what good science teachers know, *Science Teacher Education,* (85)4: 426–53.

Berliner, D. (2004) Describing the behaviour and documenting the accomplishments of expert teachers, *Bulletin of Science Technology Society,* (24)3: 200–12.

Berry, A., Loughran, J. and van Driel, J. H. (2008) Revisiting the roots of pedagogical content knowledge, *International Journal of Science Education,* (30)10: 1271–9.

Bishop, K. and Denley P. (2007) *Learning Science Teaching: Developing a professional knowledge base,* Maidenhead: Open University Press.

Borko, H. and Livingston, C. (1989) Cognition and improvisation: differences in mathematics instruction by expert and novice teachers, *American Educational Research Journal,* (26)4: 473–98.

Brown, S. and McIntyre, D. (1993) *Making Sense of Teaching,* Buckingham: Open University Press.

Burn, K., Childs, A. and McNicholl, J. (2007) The potential and challenges for student-teachers' learning of subject specific pedagogical knowledge within secondary school subject departments, *The Curriculum Journal,* (18)4: 429–45.

Carlsen, W. S. (1991) Effects of new biology teachers' subject-matter knowledge on curricular planning, *Science Education,* 75, 631–47.

Childs, A, Burn, K. and McNicholl, J. (2013) What influences the learning cultures of subject departments in secondary schools? A study of four subject departments in England. *Teacher Development,* (17)1: 35–54.

Childs, A. and McNicholl, J. (2007) Science teachers teaching outside their subject specialism: challenges, strategies adopted and implications for initial teacher education. *Teacher Development,* (11)1: 1–20.

Cochran, K. F., De Ruiter, J. A. and King, R. A. (1993) Pedagogical content knowing: an integrative model for teacher preparation, *Journal of Teacher Education,* 44, 263–72.

Dennick, R. and Joyes, G. (1994) New science teachers' subject knowledge, *School Science Review,* (76)275: 103–9.

Department for Business Innovation and Skills (2010) *Science and Mathematics Secondary Education for the 21st Century,* Report of the Science and Learning Expert Group, London: HMSO.

Department for Education and Skills, DfES, (2006) *The Science, Technology, Engineering and Mathematics (STEM) Programme Report,* London: HMSO.

Driver, R., Squires, A., Rushworth, P. and Wood-Robinson, V. (1994) *Making Sense Of Secondary Science: Research Into Children's Ideas,* London: Routledge.

Duit, R. (1991) On the role of analogies and metaphors in learning science, *Science Education,* (75)6: 649–672.

Fraser, B., Tobin, K. and Lacy, T. (1988) A study of exemplary primary science teachers, *Research in Science and Technological Education,* (6)1: 25–38.

Furlong, J. and Maynard, T. (1995) *Mentoring Student Teachers: The growth of professional knowledge,* London: Routledge.

Garnett, P. J. and Tobin, K. (1988) Teaching for understanding: exemplary practice in high school chemistry, *Journal of Research in Science Teaching,* (26)1: 1–14.

Gess-Newsome, J. (1999) Secondary teachers' knowledge and beliefs about subject matter and their impact on instruction, in J. Gess-Newsome, and N. G. Lederman (eds) *Explaining Pedagogical Content Knowledge,* Dordrecht, The Netherlands: Kluwer Academic.

Gilbert, J. K., Boulter, C. and Rutherford, M. (1998) Models in explanations, Part 2: whose voice? Whose ears? *International Journal of Science Education,* (20)2: 187–203.

Glynn, S. M., Duit, R. and Thiele, R. B. (1995) Teaching science with analogies: A strategy for constructing knowledge, in S. M. Glynn and R. Duit (eds), *Learning science in the schools: Research reforming practice*, Mahwah, NJ: Erlbaum.

Grossman, P. L. (1990) *The making of a teacher: teacher knowledge and teacher education*, New York: Teachers College Press.

Grossman, P. L., Wilson, S. M. and Shulman, L. E. (1989) Teachers of substance: subject matter knowledge for teaching, in M. C. Reynolds, (ed.) *Knowledge Base for the Beginning Teacher*, New York: Pergamon.

Harrison, A. G. and Treagust, D.F. (1993) Teaching with analogies: a case study in grade-10 optics, *Journal of Research in Science Teaching*, (30)10: 1291–1307.

Hashweh, M. Z. (1987) Effects of subject-matter knowledge in the teaching of biology and physics, *Teaching and Teacher Education*, (3)2: 109–20.

Hashweh, M.Z. (2005) Teacher pedagogical constructions: a reconfiguration of pedagogical content knowledge, *Teachers and Teaching: Theory and practice*, (11)3: 273–92.

Hayward, G. (1997) Principles for school focused initial teacher education: some lessons from the Oxford Internship Scheme, in T. Allsop and A. Benson (eds) *Mentoring for Science Teachers*. Buckingham: Oxford University Press.

Henze, I., van Driel, J. H. and Verloop, N. (2008) Development of experienced science teachers' pedagogical content knowledge of models of the solar system and the universe, *International Journal of Science Education*, (30)10: 1321–42.

Hobson, A. J. and McIntyre J. (2013) Teacher fabrication as an impediment to professional learning and development, *Oxford Review of Education*, (39)3: 345–65.

Horwood, R.H. (1988) Explanation and description in science teaching, *Science Education*, (72)1: 41–9.

Institute of Physics (2002) *Physics Teacher Supply*, A report of the Institute of Physics.

Jarman, R. (1996) Student teachers' use of analogies in science instruction, *International Journal of Science Education*, (18)7: 869–80.

Kind, V. (2009) Pedagogical content knowledge in science education: perspectives and potential for progress, *Studies in Science Education*, (45)2: 169–204.

Kress, G., Jewitt, C., Ogborn, J. and Tsatsarelis, C. (2001) *Multimodal Teaching And Learning. The rhetorics of the science classroom*, London: Continuum.

Lee, O. (1995) Subject matter knowledge, classroom management, and instructional practices in middle school science classrooms, *Journal of Research in Science Teaching*, (32)4: 423–40.

Lee, E. and Luft, J. A. (2008) Experienced secondary science teachers' representation of pedagogical content knowledge, *International Journal of Science Education*, (30)10: 1343–63.

Lock, R. Salt, D. and Soares, A. (2011) *Acquisition of Science Subject Knowledge and Pedagogy in Initial Teacher Training*, Report to the Wellcome Trust, University of Birmingham.

Lock, R., Soares, A. and Foster, J. (2009) Mentors' written lesson appraisals: the impact of different mentoring regimes on the content of written lesson appraisals and the match with pre-service teachers' perceptions of content, *Journal of Education for Teaching: International Research and Pedagogy*, (35)2: 133–43.

Loughran, J., Berry, A. and Mulhall, P. (2006) *Understanding and Developing Science Teachers' Pedagogical Content Knowledge*, Rotterdam: Sense Publishers.

Loughran, J., Mulhall, P. and Berry, A. (2008) Exploring pedagogical content knowledge in science teacher education, *International Journal of Science Education*, (30)10: 1301–20.

Magnusson, S., Krajcik, J. and Borko, H. (1999) Nature, sources, and development of pedagogical content knowledge for science teaching, *Examining Pedagogical Content Knowledge: The construct and its implications for science education*, 6, 95–132.

McIntyre, D. (1993) Theory, theorizing and reflection in initial teacher education, in J. Calderhead and P. Gates (eds) *Conceptualizing Refection in Teacher Development*, London: Falmer Press.

McNicholl, J., Childs, A. and Burn, K. (2013) School subject departments as sites for science teachers learning pedagogical content knowledge, *Teacher Development*, (17)2: 155–75.

Mortimer, E.F. and Scott, P. (2003) *Meaning Making in Secondary Science Classrooms*, Maidenhead: Open University Press.

Murphy, C., and Beggs, J. (2003) Children's perceptions of school science, *School science Review*, (84)308: 109–16.

Nilsson, P. (2008) Teaching for understanding: the complex nature of pedagogical content knowledge in pre-service education, *International Journal of Science Education*, (30)10: 1281–99.

Ogborn, J., Kress, G., Martins, I. and McGillicuddy, K. (1996) *Explaining Science in the Classroom*, Buckingham: Open University Press.

Osborne, J. and Millar, R. (1988) *Beyond 2000*, London: Kings College. Available online at: www.nuffieldfoundation.org/sites/default/files/Beyond%202000.pdf

Osborne, J., Simons S. and Collins S. (2003) Attitudes towards science: a review of the literature and its implications, *International Journal of Science Education*, (25)9: 1049–79.

Padilla, K. (2008) Undergraduate professors' pedagogical content knowledge: the case of 'amount of substance', *International Journal of Science Education*, (30)10: 1389–1404.

Park, S. and Oliver, J. S. (2008) Revisiting the conceptualisation of pedagogical content knowledge (PCK): PCK as a conceptual tool to understand teachers as professionals, *Research in Science Education*, 38, 261–84.

Posner, G. J., Strike, K. A., Hewson, P. W. and Gertzog, W. A. (1982) Accommodation of a scientific conception: towards a theory of conceptual change, *Science Education*, (66)2: 211–27.

Royal Society, The (2007) *A 'State Of The Nation' Report: The UK's Science and Mathematics Teaching Workforce*, London: The Royal Society.

Sanders, L.R., Borko, H. and Lockard, J. D. (1993) Secondary science teachers' knowledge base when teaching science courses in and out of their area of certification, *Journal of Research in Science Teaching*, (30)7: 723–36.

Schwab, J. J. (1978) *Science, Curriculum And Liberal Education*, Chicago: Chicago University Press.

Shulman, L. S. (1986) Those who understand: knowledge growth in teaching, *Educational Researcher*, (15)2: 4–14.

Shulman, L. (1987) Knowledge and teaching: foundations of the new reforms, *Harvard Educational Review*, 57, 1–22.

Summers, M., Kruger, C. and Mant, J. (1998) Teaching electricity effectively in the primary school: a case study, *International Journal of Science Education*, (20)2: 153–72.

Times Educational Supplement (2010) *Maths and Science Often 'Uninspiring', Says Ofsted*, published on 26 November. Available online at: www.tes.co.uk/article.aspx?storycode=6064259 (accessed 20 January 2012).

Tobin, K. and Fraser, B.J. (1988) Investigation of exemplary practice in science and mathematics teaching in Western Australia, *Journal of Curriculum Studies*, (20)4: 369–71

Tobin, K. and Fraser, B. (1990) What does it mean to be an exemplary science teacher? *Journal of Research in Science Teaching*, (27)1: 3–25.

Tobin, K. and Garnett, K. (1988) Exemplary practice in science classroom, *Science Education*, (72)2: 197–208.

Treagust, D. F. (1992) Science teachers' use of analogies: observations from classroom practice, *International Journal of Science Education*, (14)4: 413–22.

Treagust, D. F., Harrison, A. G. and Venville, G. J. (1998) Teaching science effectively with analogies: an approach for preservice and inservice teacher education, *Journal of Science Teacher Education*, (9)2: 85–101.

Turner-Bisset, R. (1999) The knowledge bases of the expert teacher, *British Educational Research Journal*, (25)1: 2, 39–55.

Van Driel, J. H. and Berry, A. (2012) Teacher professional development focusing on pedagogical content knowledge. *Educational Researcher*, (41)26: 26–8.

Van Driel, J. H., Verloop, N. and De Vos, W. (1998) Developing science teachers' pedagogical content knowledge, *Journal of Research in Science Teaching*, (35)6: 673–95.

Waldrip, B., Fisher, D. and Dorman J. (2009) Identifying exemplary science teachers through their students' perceptions of the assessment process, *Research in Science and Technological Education*, (27)1: 117–29.

Wellington J. and Osborne, J. (2001) *Language and Literacy in Science Education*, Buckingham: Open University Press.

Wilson, H. and Mant, J. (2011) What makes an exemplary teacher of science? The pupils' perspective, *School Science Review*, (93)342: 121–5.

# APPENDIX 1

### Explanations activity

**Section 1:** What are you explaining? What key stage? Clear statement of the science at the 'correct level'. What's your key question? Where's the real life context?

**Section 2:** Description of the phenomenon (what activity or activities? Why?)

**Section 3:** Student preconceptions/misconceptions/why is this hard? (with references)

**Section 4:** Explanation

**Section 5:** What does the task (e.g. metaphor, analogy, role play, practical, simulation etc,) explain? What does it not explain? How does it address the challenges for student learning identified in section 3? What misconceptions does it have the potential to cause?

# 8
# DESIGNING TASKS TO PROMOTE LEARNING IN THE FOREIGN LANGUAGE CLASSROOM

*Trevor Mutton and Robert Woore*

**Introduction**

What are the principles underpinning effective task design in second language (L2) classrooms in the secondary school? How can beginning teachers learn to design effective tasks for L2 learning in this context? These are the key questions addressed by this chapter.

Our central arguments are that designing language learning tasks is a thoughtful process which must draw on knowledge from a wide range of sources; that language learning differs from the learning which takes place in some other subjects in important respects; and that the knowledge sources that inform task design should therefore include an understanding of how languages are learnt, taking account of research findings in second language acquisition (SLA). It follows that learning to design effective tasks for the languages classroom has to be thought of as an intellectual exercise; it is not something which will occur simply by beginning teachers observing and imitating more experienced practitioners.

It is important to note at the outset that the contexts of instructed L2 learning vary widely. For example, on the one hand there are classes of adult students with different first languages and strong, instrumental reasons for learning an L2 (often English); and on the other hand, there are classes of younger learners with a shared first language (L1) and little interest in L2 learning. Many modern foreign language (MFL) students in UK secondary schools fit the latter description. Further, they often perceive language learning to be a 'difficult' and essentially frustrating experience (Graham 2004) which gives little enjoyment (Williams, Burden and Lanvers 2002). As a consequence, the take-up of languages in the UK beyond compulsory age has fallen steadily over a number of years (Tinsley and Han 2012; Tinsley 2013). There is some evidence that the recent introduction (in January 2011) of the 'English Baccalaureate' – a performance measure for schools – may be reversing this trend (Tinsley and Han 2012; Clemens, 2011); however, this does not necessarily indicate a greater eagerness of students' part to learn languages. Ideally, we would like students to opt to learn a language because they enjoy it and feel they are making good progress, not simply because they or their school feels they ought to.

What explains the apparent reticence of UK students to learn languages? Whilst some have argued that they do not recognize the value of learning a foreign language, given the global dominance of English (e.g. Stables and Wikeley, 1999), others have suggested that part of the problem may lie in the nature of language learning in MFL classrooms. Curriculum aims are often translated into schemes of work that reflect a narrow, topic-based approach to language learning. Such an approach is heavily dependent on published course books and affords insufficient opportunity for learners to use new language with any degree of spontaneity (Ofsted 2011b). Our own experience, as teachers and teacher educators, is primarily rooted in this UK context. Nonetheless, we would argue that the principles of task design outlined in this chapter apply to instructed language learning contexts more widely.

The chapter itself is divided into three sections. The first explores a number of issues which we believe to be central to an understanding of effective task design, including a focus on the nature and purposes of a 'task' (section 1.1); the distinctive nature of language learning and why task design in the MFL classroom might be different to task design in many other subject areas (1.2); the ways in which SLA research evidence might be used to inform task design (1.3); and the range of other factors that may be taken into account in designing L2 learning tasks, including a 'visualisation' of how the task might work in practice with a particular group of learners (1.4). The second section presents and critically analyses two concrete examples of language learning tasks. These are used to illustrate some of the complexities involved in designing tasks for L2 classrooms and some of the pitfalls that may arise. Finally, section 3 offers some concluding reflections and implications for both beginning teachers and Initial Teacher Educators.

# 1 The factors underpinning effective task design

## 1.1 Defining 'language learning tasks'

The term 'task' has particular resonances in the field of L2 learning. In recent years, there has been considerable interest in 'task-based' approaches to language teaching (see, for example, Skehan 1998; Ellis 2003; Nunan 2004; Samuda and Bygate 2008). Various researchers within this tradition have offered a definition of what task-based language teaching (TBLT) entails, or have outlined the key characteristics or underpinning principles of such an approach. While demonstrating some differences in the degree of specificity as to what a task is, most highlight the following aspects of TBLT: the predominance of meaning; the achievement of a task outcome; and the use of the learner's own linguistic capabilities and resources in order to achieve such an outcome. For example, learners working in a small group might be asked to discuss and agree on an itinerary for a day out in Paris, drawing on tourist websites and maps of the city.

Ellis (2009) discusses the way in which tasks can be either 'focused' (tasks which allow for the use of a particular linguistic feature) or 'unfocused' (that is to say, provide the opportunity for more general language use in a communicative way). He also distinguishes between 'input-providing' and 'output-prompting' tasks, thus addressing a commonly-held perception that tasks need to be predominantly speaking activities:

> Input-providing tasks engage learners in listening or reading, while output-prompting tasks engage them in speaking or writing. Thus, a task can provide opportunities for communicating in any of the four language skills. Many tasks are integrative; they involve two or more skills.
>
> *(Ellis 2009: 224)*

Finally, Nunan (2004) adds another distinction, between 'real world' tasks taking place in the world beyond the classroom and 'pedagogical' tasks, the latter occurring within the classroom and designed to provide opportunities to understand or use the L2. These pedagogical tasks can, in turn, be either 'rehearsal tasks' – in which learners in the classroom rehearse for a real-world communicative task – or 'activation tasks', in which learners take part in genuine communicative interaction in the classroom for its own sake. Nunan also suggests that teachers should help learners develop the knowledge and skills that will ultimately support their performance as they engage in communicative tasks. He calls these 'enabling skills', which may be developed through 'language exercises' and 'communicative activities'. For Nunan, such exercises and activities are both types of 'form-focussed work' rather than tasks in themselves: that is, they are focussed on the development of particular linguistic forms or structures.

In this chapter, we adopt a broad conception of language learning tasks, which includes all of the different types outlined above. Further, it encompasses not only 'tasks' as conceptualized within the TBLT approach, but also Nunan's 'exercises' and 'activities'. Thus – notwithstanding Nunan's criticism that Breen's (1987) similar definition of a pedagogical task is too broad, since it covers almost anything that the learner might do in an L2 classroom – we define a language learning task as *any activity that is intended to promote language learning*. We do so because we believe that all kinds of classroom tasks may, in the right circumstances, be valuable for language learning and that all require careful thought in their design. Defined in this way, tasks become the central pedagogical units in all L2 teaching. Nonetheless, as will be made clear later, we agree with Nunan's underlying argument (though not his terminology) that there are different orders of tasks, with some 'enabling' tasks preparing the way for later, 'higher order' ones. Therefore, it is important to think in terms of designing not only effective tasks, but also effective sequences of tasks.

## 1.2 The distinctiveness of L2 learning in the MFL classroom

Before proceeding, let us pause to consider the justification for this particular chapter within the book as a whole. In other words, what makes designing tasks for languages classrooms different from designing tasks in other subject areas? We would argue that language learning is distinctive in at least four interrelated respects.

First, socio-cultural theory sees language as the quintessential tool through which learning is mediated (Lantolf 2000). In languages classrooms, therefore, the L2 may be both the object of learning itself and the medium of communication through which the teacher mediates this learning. Indeed, as will be explored in section 1.3 below, a widely-held view is that it is precisely through understanding and producing the L2 (whilst also paying attention to linguistic forms) that language learning happens. This has an important implication for task design: comprehending a teacher's procedural instructions in the L2 (and perhaps negotiating this understanding by asking for clarification or repetition, etc.) can itself be considered a valuable language learning task. However, this conception of a task does not readily fit within the quadrant model of task design proposed by Edwards (this volume: 21).

Second, there is an intimate connection between the language(s) we speak and our social and cultural identity. Learning a new language is, therefore, potentially disruptive to that identity. As Norton and McKinney (2011: 73) argue, 'every time learners speak, they are negotiating and renegotiating a sense of self in relation to the larger social world'. Of course, other subject areas (such as history) may cover controversial material which challenges students' cultural assumptions and sense of identity; but (at least when operating in a 'traditional' L1-based classroom) language is the tool which mediates the students' relationship to this material, and which allows them to adopt a critical stance towards it. By contrast, to speak (or even to comprehend) a 'foreign' language is publicly to take on 'the behavioural characteristics of another cultural group of people' (Gardner 2001: 6). Thus, motivation – which is of course a prerequisite for successful learning in any subject area – may be a particularly complex issue for language learners. Ways of motivating learners must therefore be a key consideration when designing language learning tasks (Dörnyei 2003).

Third, the knowledge that learners are aiming to 'acquire' in languages lessons has a different status compared to that in some other subject areas; it is not contested or open to debate in the same way as, say, one's understanding of a historical event or one's interpretation of a piece of literature. Having identified a particular variety of a language as the object of learning, there is no argument over the target forms that the learner should acquire (such as the morphology of a particular past tense verb form or the realization of a particular phoneme). It follows that the nature of learning associated with this knowledge is also different. Pring (2013) argues that one goal of education is to initiate learners into the distinctive 'disciplines of inquiry' associated with individual subject areas; '[b]iologists, for example, see the field system differently from the medieval historian and will pursue different kinds of investigation' (p. 105). However, languages do not straightforwardly fit this view of education. Language can of course be an object of inquiry and investigation in itself, as in the various branches of linguistics; but the aim of language teaching is to produce linguists, not 'linguisticians'. The explicit 'knowledge about language' resulting from linguistic inquiry (in both L1 and L2) is arguably distinct from the implicit knowledge which drives one's communicative use of those languages; and the nature of the interface between these two types of knowledge remains a contested area of SLA research. Therefore, there is reason to be wary of designing tasks (or too many tasks) which are framed primarily in terms of the development of explicit knowledge about language.

Fourth, related to the previous point, the ability to use an L2 communicatively requires the automatisation of various processing operations. Automatic (as opposed to 'controlled') processing is rapid, effortless and subconscious (Schneider and Shiffrin 1977). It places low demands on attention and working memory, thus freeing up more of these limited resources for other, potentially more valuable processing operations. Thus, a beginner learner who uses up all their attention trying to articulate a sequence of L2 sounds or to form the future tense (because these processes are not yet automatic) has no mental resources left for conceptualising the content of their next utterance. By contrast, the development of automaticity is less important in many other subject areas, for example in those which see learning as the initiation of the learner into a particular 'discipline of inquiry'. As in other instances of skill development (such as learning to play a musical instrument or to swim front crawl), automaticity in L2 processing results from repeated practice. A language learner might therefore benefit from tasks which provide repeated 'controlled practice' in forming, say, past tense sentences or in reading aloud words containing particular symbol-sound correspondences (Dörnyei 2013), much as a beginner guitarist might repeatedly practise playing the F major chord. However, this is not to imply that the automatisation of skills is *all* that is involved in becoming a proficient linguist or musician. Therefore, such tasks should form only part of a wider repertoire of tasks, which, we would argue, must also include opportunities for genuine communicative use of the L2.

## *1.3 Second language acquisition research and language learning task design*

When designing classroom tasks, teachers in all subject areas draw upon a complex web of knowledge derived from multiple sources. We would argue that these sources should include knowledge of theory and research concerning the nature of learning: that is, an understanding of *how learners learn*. In relation to language teaching in particular, we argue in this section that task design should take into account the large body of SLA research conducted over the past 50 years or so: that is, research addressing the specific question of *how learners learn second languages*.

In making this case, we certainly do not wish to suggest that SLA research can tell teachers what to do when designing specific tasks for specific classrooms on specific occasions. Too many contextual factors must be taken into account for this to be possible (see next section); and in any case, all learners are different in various respects. Rather, we follow VanPatten's (2010: 36) belief that, 'with an understanding of the linguistics and psycholinguistics of [L2] acquisition, teachers can have a more informed reason underlying their instructional efforts and decisions'. Further, we would argue that such an approach might help guard against a number of specific dangers, as outlined in the following paragraphs.

First, knowledge of SLA theory and research may allow teachers to maintain a critical perspective on official policy and guidance, especially where these shift over time (as in the case of the varying prescriptions regarding teachers' use of the L1 and L2 in UK MFL classrooms: see Macaro 2001). Further, where detailed official guidance is followed by teachers without any deeper vision of learning on their part (see Chater, this volume), a 'checklist' approach to teaching and an incoherent model of the learners' progression may result.

Third, sound theoretical underpinnings may help teachers avoid the tendency to replicate uncritically the kinds of tasks which they themselves experienced as learners (as observed by Long 2009). For example, we often find that our student teachers are drawn towards the kind of explicit grammar teaching syllabus under which they feel they prospered as learners. However, student teachers of languages are likely to be a rather unusual, self-selecting group within the wider population of L2 learners; it is therefore important to explore what research has to say about the effectiveness of explicit grammar instruction for L2 learners more generally.

Finally, keeping SLA research in mind helps guard against the over-dominance of other, more practical concerns when designing classroom tasks. For example, there may be a strong attraction towards tasks which seem to keep learners quiet or happy. We consider this to be a perfectly valid concern (indeed, we have already mentioned the central importance of motivation in L2 learning); however, teachers must also consider the extent to which the tasks they set are effective in promoting L2 learning in the longer term.

## *Insights from SLA research*

What insights, then, does SLA research provide that may be of use when designing language learning tasks? Unfortunately, there is no simple answer to this question. As Ellis (2005: 210) says, 'research and theory do not afford a uniform account of how instruction can best facilitate language learning'. Indeed, there are many areas of controversy, even in respect of fundamental issues such as the benefits of developing learners' explicit (conscious) knowledge of grammatical rules or the role of the L1 in supporting L2 learning. Various explanations may be sought for these disagreements, such as the relative infancy of SLA research (compare, for example, the evidence base available to support medical decision-making); the diverse contexts in which SLA studies have been conducted; and the competing theoretical frameworks adopted by different researchers (see Atkinson 2011).

Whatever the reasons, it would be easy to conclude that the available evidence is so fragmented and contradictory as to be of little practical use for teachers, and that the safest option (insofar as research is consulted at all) is to adopt a 'pick-and-mix' approach, whereby lessons include a range of tasks consistent with various different research findings. Such an approach, however, is likely to suffer from a lack of overall coherence. Further, we would suggest that, notwithstanding the various controversies and disagreements, a certain degree of consensus can be identified in the SLA literature. This is reflected in several recent attempts to formulate an overall set of research-informed principles to guide L2 instruction (for example, Ellis 2005; Long 2009; Dörnyei 2009, 2013). Some might contest these research syntheses on the basis that they reflect the particular, cognitivist approach that has historically tended to dominate 'mainstream' SLA research: that is, an approach focussing on what happens in the mind of the individual learner and neglecting the socio-cultural dimensions of language learning (see, for example, Lantolf 2011; Larsen-Freeman 2011). Nonetheless, we would argue that these attempts to identify overarching principles for L2 teaching represent a reasonable starting-point when seeking evidence to inform classroom task design – whilst acknowledging that they cannot be seen as definitive or complete. Further, though they do not speak in perfect unison, considerable common ground may be discerned between them. For example, they broadly concur in areas such as the following[i]:

- Learners need plentiful opportunities for high-quality oral interaction in the L2, comprising extensive, rich input and spontaneous, meaningful output.
- Learners should be encouraged – whether orally or in writing – to produce language freely to communicate their own meanings, not just to produce language in the context of controlled exercises.
- Learners should be given opportunities to 'focus on form' (that is, attend to linguistic forms) in the context of meaningful, communicative language use, for example through effective error correction.
- By contrast, teachers should not assume that explicitly teaching linguistic forms according to a pre-ordained structural syllabus will necessarily enable students to use those same forms communicatively.
- Learners need instruction which responds to their individual needs.

We consider this last point to be of pivotal importance. Many SLA studies within the cognitivist paradigm are based on mean effects, in which learning outcomes are aggregated across a group. The details of individual learners are thus lost, just as a beach made up of myriad different-coloured pebbles may look a uniform brownish-grey when viewed from a distance. As a result, such studies cannot tell us which teaching approach will be most effective for a specific learner in a specific context. All classrooms contain individuals with different levels of L2 proficiency, different motivational profiles and different learning preferences (to name just a few such variables).

In practical terms, we would suggest that one way of responding to the needs of individual learners is to analyse their L2 output resulting from free (rather than controlled) language production. The errors they make will provide the teacher with valuable insight into their 'interlanguage' (Selinker 1972) – that is, the current state of their L2 linguistic system. Such errors are also valuable to the learners, because they provide the opportunity for corrective feedback from the teacher; this in turn provides them with an opportunity to modify their interlanguage and to make it more target-like. In this central role of the teacher as a mediator of L2 learning, we see a point of intersection between the cognitivist and socio-cultural perspectives on SLA.

We would also argue that, where research appears to offer contradictory implications for designing specific classroom tasks, these may often be resolved through a finer-grained conceptualisation of the task's objectives. These objectives will, in turn, depend on the particular context of the task. We illustrate this point with an example drawn from the field of L2 reading (discussed at greater length in Woore 2014). Three distinct implications for task design have been derived from research in this area.

First, various studies of reading comprehension in both L1 and L2 have highlighted the central importance of vocabulary knowledge (for example Schmitt, Jiang and Grabe 2011). According to this view, L2 readers automatically 'access' reading skills and strategies which they have already developed in their L1, provided that they know enough of the words in an L2 text (Walter 2007). The priority for teachers is therefore to develop students' vocabulary knowledge; instructing them in reading skills and strategies is 'more or less a waste of time' (Swan 2008: 267).

Second, reading research strongly indicates that automatic word recognition is essential for fluent reading (see Grabe 2010), because it frees up more of the brain's limited attentional resources for higher-level comprehension processes (for example inferencing; relating text content to existing knowledge). Since automatic word recognition develops through extensive practice, it has been argued that L2 learners need to read very large amounts of simple texts composed of mainly familiar language (Grabe and Stoller 2011).

Third, in contrast to both these views, recent studies such as Macaro and Erler (2008) have found that systematic instruction in comprehension strategies can help learners become more confident when approaching the kinds of texts they might encounter in 'real life' settings – texts in which the language used is likely to be considerably above their current productive level. In order for this to be achieved, learners need both (a) plenty of exposure to challenging L2 texts, containing considerable proportions of unfamiliar words and structures; and (b) systematic support in developing their use of a range of comprehension strategies (in effective combination) to help them tackle such texts.

At face value, then, these strands of SLA research suggest diametrically opposed implications for L2 reading instruction; they cannot possibly all be right. It is important, however, to consider the context in which the reading instruction is taking place. Many studies of L2 reading have investigated advanced learners with high levels of instrumental motivation for learning to read the L2 (usually English). In such contexts, the development of vocabulary knowledge and automatic word recognition may well be appropriate instructional priorities. By contrast, Macaro and Erler's (2008) study into strategy instruction was conducted with young, near-beginner learners in UK MFL classrooms – a setting which is characterised by extremely limited curriculum time and (as noted above) generally low levels of learner motivation, attainment and progress. It could take a very long time for students in this context to acquire sufficient vocabulary knowledge to read anything but the most basic texts fluently; in the meantime, restricting their reading diet to texts composed mainly of familiar language may take a further toll on their motivation: why bother learning to read in another language, if the texts are always so trivial? Yet texts which are more engaging in terms of content are also likely to be more challenging linguistically; and without explicit instruction in this area, learners may not learn to deploy effective strategies to help them approach such texts with confidence.

Taken together, the bodies of research described above also remind us that the broad aim of 'developing L2 reading proficiency' encompasses a number of sub-goals, including (amongst other things) building wide vocabulary knowledge, developing automatic word recognition and ensuring that learners are able to engage in effective strategic behaviour for dealing with unfamiliar language. The decision facing teachers is then which particular sub-goal(s) to focus on in a given context at a given time; this will depend in turn on an analysis of the learners' needs, resulting from the assessment of their previous work. Indeed, we would argue that a clear identification of the desired learning outcome(s) lies at the heart of effective task design. A task (and associated text) for developing fluent word recognition in the L2 will look different from one designed to develop the 'strategic L2 reader'. In other words, it is not enough simply to 'do a reading activity', though there may sometimes be a strong temptation to conceive of task design in this way.

## 1.4 Other factors to be taken into account when designing language learning tasks

Research into task-based language teaching has highlighted the need to take into account a number of factors when designing tasks. As the previous section began to explore, this decision-making must be informed by a clear understanding of what the task itself is aiming to achieve. Some researchers have identified various features of tasks and task variables that are seen to be effective in determining particular aspects of language acquisition, such as the fluency, accuracy or complexity of the learners' output (Skehan 2003). For example, Skehan identifies that tasks which are structured effectively (for example with a clear time-line) may be used to promote accuracy while those which include familiar information can lead to increased fluency. However, research has not yet been able to identify whether specific aspects of task design can be linked to more effective overall L2 learning; indeed, this is unsurprising given the wide range of contextual and learner-related variables that may intervene.

Others, adopting a more socio-cultural approach to language acquisition, have argued that it is precisely the *interaction* between learners and task that is important (rather than individual elements of a task being seen to determine particular outputs); and that it is the way in which the process of learning is mediated that determines the nature of the learning that arises through completing a task (Lantolf 2000). While it could be argued that there is 'the *propensity* of certain tasks to lead to particular types of language behaviour' (Ellis 2000: 214), there are clearly many potential factors which might influence the way in which learners engage with tasks, making it difficult to attribute particular outcomes to specific task variables.

Our approach in this chapter is to suggest a model of task design that enables teachers to plan for their students' learning by taking critical account not only of SLA research evidence, but also of those contextual factors that may have a significant influence on the desired learning outcomes. In so doing, we favour a 'dialogical model' of planning (John 2006). This envisages the process of planning as one of 'a thought-experiment tied to the specifics of the discourse-community in which it is embedded' (John 2006: 494). In practice, we see task design within such a model as beginning with a series of questions that the teacher will need to address, based on complex professional knowledge. For example:

- Based on recent lessons with the class, what in particular do you want to achieve in this lesson?
- What relevant previous knowledge should the students be able to draw on in terms of:
  - vocabulary
  - structure(s)?
- What do the students need to learn in terms of:
  - vocabulary
  - structure(s)
  - being able to communicate effectively in the target language (i.e. specific communicative skills)
  - aspects of the target culture?
- What, specifically, should all students be able to do by the end of the lesson?
- What might some students be able to do in addition to the above?
- Are there any specific contextual factors that need to be taken into account?
- What knowledge and understanding of the learners (as a group and as individuals), including their approach to learning, need to be taken into account in order to support their L2 learning effectively?

This 'dialogic' approach will enable the teacher to identify two key things: first, the nature of the task itself and its specific demands (including the nature of the intended outcomes; the way in which the task might develop what has gone before;

how it might lead to further learning; etc.); second, what the learners might bring to the task (by way of their existing knowledge and understanding; their previous achievements; the nature of the errors they make; their learning dispositions; their anticipated level of engagement with the task; and so forth).

Further, the complexity of thinking required during the planning of a lesson (Clark and Yinger 1979) requires a focus not only on the design of the task itself but also on what might actually occur within the classroom in terms of the way in which the students interact with the task. In this respect, 'planning as visualization' (Mutton *et al.* 2011: 408) enables the teacher to anticipate what *might* happen (rather than to determine what *will* happen), with this anticipation being rooted in strong pedagogical understandings which draw on knowledge from a range of sources, including the experience of having used similar tasks in the past. In addition the teacher will, whilst actually teaching any lesson, draw on further knowledge (such as that derived from the effective use of assessment strategies) in order to modify as necessary the conditions of the task. For example, she or he may provide extra support or scaffolding if any learner appears to be experiencing difficulty. Figure 8.1 represents this whole process in diagrammatic form.

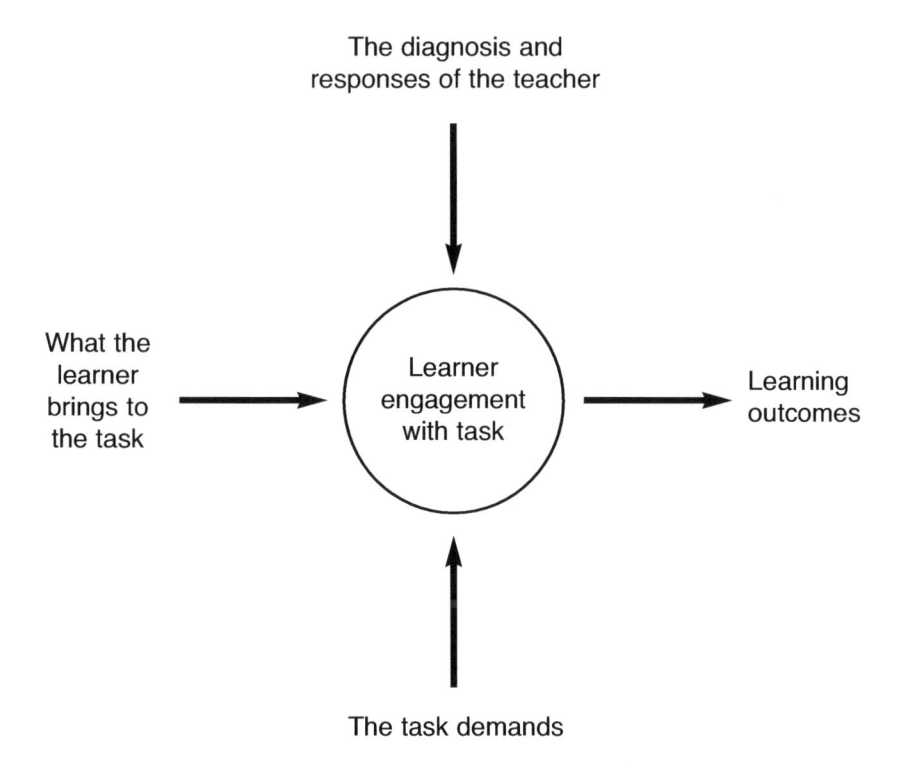

**Figure 8.1** A dialogical approach to foreign language task design

One consequence of this dialogical approach to task design is that it is difficult to take any task 'off the shelf' and expect to be able to use it effectively to develop students' learning: teachers themselves have to be closely involved in the design of tasks and of any accompanying materials (Ellis 2009).

Finally, given the limited time available for L2 teaching in many instructed contexts, we believe that it is also important to consider how to use this time most effectively and efficiently. Thus, when in the classroom, students will benefit most from those tasks that can *only* be carried out in this context (for example, tasks involving oral interaction with the teacher or other learners; tasks requiring high levels of mediation by the teacher). Tasks which learners can complete relatively independently may as well be completed outside the classroom (for example as homework) – provided, of course, that the learners are adequately motivated to do so. To give an example, in the classrooms we visit, we often find that a lot of time is spent practising the spoken forms of new vocabulary through a sequence of listening, repetition and questioning activities. It could be argued, however, that the time spent on these activities could be reduced if students themselves were better able to generate accurate pronunciations for the new language by decoding the written forms (Woore 2013). The scarce lesson time might therefore be better spent on helping learners develop their L2 decoding proficiency, thus equipping them to learn new vocabulary more independently.

## 2 Task design in action: a critical evaluation of two language learning tasks

In this section, we present two examples of languages tasks, both of which were designed (and tried out) as part of a collaborative project between teachers and university researchers (PDC in MFL 2013). The aim of the project was to explore ways in which L2 teaching might be made more consistent with research-based principles, specifically in the context of MFL classrooms in UK secondary comprehensive schools. In each case, we provide a brief description of the task, its aims and its context, followed by a critical discussion of the ways in which it responds both to SLA research findings and to particular contextual factors. There is no attempt to suggest that these are 'perfect' tasks or that they are the only ways of achieving their respective aims; rather, our purpose in this section is to explore, through concrete examples, some of the issues that we have raised in previous sections.

### 2.1 A French decoding task

This task was designed for a class of thirty beginner learners of French (age 14). Though in their third year at secondary school, they had only been learning French for two-and-a-half trimesters (approximately 27 weeks), with about two hours' lesson time per week. At the start of a new topic – 'food and drink' – the teacher wanted learners to become familiar with the spoken and written forms of some key vocabulary items which they would use later in paired role play dialogues, where they would order items from a printed café menu. By practising these forms in this preparatory task, the teacher was thus pre-empting pronunciation problems which might arise in the subsequent communicative task. An additional, on-going aim to which this preparatory task responded was to develop the accuracy and fluency of learners' print-to-sound decoding in the L2.

Learners were presented with a worksheet containing fifteen vocabulary items such as *café* (/kafe/, 'coffee' 4), *bouteille* (/butɛj/, 'bottle'), *champignon* (/ʃɒ̃piɲɔ̃/, 'mushroom') and *prendrai* (/pʁɒ̃dʁe/, '[I] will take'). Their task, to be completed collaboratively with the person sitting next to them, was to try to pronounce the words accurately and to sort them into four categories according to the sounds they contained, these being represented by anglicised spellings on the same worksheet: 'ay', 'uh', 'oo' and 'sh', representing the French phonemes /e/, /ø/, /u/ and /ʃ/ respectively. The task was stopped after six minutes and feedback was provided in a whole class setting. Here, the teacher projected a digital version of the worksheet on an interactive whiteboard. Learners were invited to come up to the board and 'drag' the vocabulary items into the relevant sound categories, eliciting further suggestions from the class if they got the answer wrong. The teacher also provided correct pronunciations of all fifteen words as part of the feedback process.

As a means of introducing new vocabulary, the task addressed the teacher's concerns that more 'traditional' forms of vocabulary presentation for beginners (such as choral repetition) were unpopular with this class of adolescent learners, and were in any case not the most efficient use of class time: asking them to work out the pronunciations for themselves was intended to develop their autonomy as learners, rather than relying upon the teacher to provide a spoken model. This follows the principle that learners should gradually be empowered to decode the pronunciations of unfamiliar words for themselves, since this can be argued to be an important facilitator of both intentional and incidental vocabulary acquisition (Woore 2013).

The rationale for doing the task in pairs was twofold. First, it was hoped that learners would support each other when thinking about the sounds of the French words and that they would peer-correct at least some mispronunciations. However, this relies on high levels of task engagement; it may be that, with certain classes or in certain circumstances, an alternative, more controlled, teacher-fronted task would be more appropriate. (We would, however, note that sitting quietly and facing the front do not necessarily indicate high levels of task engagement). Second, learners could attempt to pronounce the French words in a 'safe' environment, rather than in front of the whole class: attempting to 'sound French' when saying words aloud may feel more threatening when done in public, especially given the implications for learners' sense of identity (see The distinctiveness of L2 learning in the MFL classroom, page 132). In order to assess the learners' progress in decoding, however, the teacher must circulate and listen to the pairs' discussions. The insights thus gained into the learners' errors will in turn inform the design of subsequent decoding tasks.

The task's focus on print-to-sound decoding responds to several recent studies which have found that, in the absence of systematic decoding instruction, beginner learners of French in English MFL classrooms have low L2 decoding proficiency and make little progress in this area, relying instead on English decoding conventions to (mis)pronounce French words (Erler 2003; Woore 2009, 2011). In turn, this has been found to have a negative impact on various other aspects of L2 learning, including overall motivation (Erler and Macaro 2011). Specifically, the task aimed to help learners overcome the automatic activation of English symbol-sound correspondences, targeting specific graphemes which had been identified as posing particular problems for the class: for example, they needed to learn that the French realization of <ch> is not /tʃ/, as in English, but /ʃ/. Of course, this task would not be suitable for complete beginners; these learners had previously worked on the symbol-sound correspondences in question and already knew various other words containing the same graphemes, which they could draw on as a source of analogy for working out the pronunciations of the new words.

We would, however, argue that the decoding task described here may not be without its problems. First, it seems possible that the use of English spelling conventions to represent French phonemes on the worksheet ('ay' for /e/, etc.) might be counter-productive, actually encouraging learners to produce (and entrench) anglicized realizations of those phonemes. Alternative ways of representing French sounds might therefore merit consideration, such as the mnemonic pictures and physical actions developed for primary school learners by Cave and Haig (2012). At the very least, we would encourage the teacher to make clear that the anglicized representations are only approximations of the correct sounds. These sounds should therefore be clearly modelled for the learner.

Second, tasks such as this one – which aim to develop learners' knowledge of L2 symbol–sound correspondences – must be followed up by opportunities for them to apply this knowledge in practice and to do so with increasing automaticity. This will in turn free up attentional resources for other processing operations, such as integrating textual information with existing world knowledge when reading (see The distinctiveness of L2 learning in the MFL classroom, page 133 ). Therefore, this decoding task might be followed up with a reading comprehension task based on a text containing the fifteen target words, together with other words exemplifying the same symbol–sound correspondences. In our experience, L2 reading tasks often focus on the comprehension of meaning and neglect the development of learners' phonological representations of the written words, which have in fact been argued to play an important role in supporting the comprehension of difficult written material (Baddeley and Logie 1999).

Third, the use of isolated words rather than words-in-context as the basis for this task may be questioned. For example, the words *café* and *prendrai* might have been integrated into a simple meaningful clause, which learners could use communicatively in the subsequent role play task (for example *Je prendrai un café*, 'I'll have a coffee'). Learners could then be encouraged to progress (at their own pace) from the initial sound categorisation task to reading the phrases aloud (in pairs or to themselves), thus helping them to develop their knowledge of relevant pre-formulated 'chunks' of language. These are believed to play an important role in fluent language production (for example Dörnyei 2009). To accommodate the use of phrases rather than individual words, however, the task might require some modification, for example by asking learners to use different-coloured highlighter pens to identify particular sounds within the phrases.

Finally, the learners in this class performed the task in their L1. Since the main aim of the task was to develop their knowledge of four French grapheme–phoneme correspondences, it seems reasonable to allow them to use their L1 as a mediating tool. However, by repeating similar tasks over time, it might be possible for learners to start to conduct their discussions in the L2. The teacher might introduce some set phrases to scaffold this process, such as *Je pense que … se prononce … comme dans le mot…* (I think that … is pronounced … as in the word …) and Tu es d'accord? (Do you agree?). This would in turn open up new possibilities for implicit learning through the communicative use of the L2.

## 2.2 A French 'classroom language' task

The second task was again designed for a large class of beginner learners of French (28 in number), aged 11. The students had all arrived at secondary school a few months earlier and the majority of the class had had limited previous experience of learning the language. The task took place at the beginning of the second trimester (after about 12 weeks' learning). At this stage, the teacher wanted to develop the students' capacity to use the target language as the predominant means of communication within the classroom, particularly in relation to 'authentic' classroom interactions (for example asking permission to do things in the classroom, apologising for being late or having forgotten a book, seeking clarification of the teacher's instructions, etc.). In previous years, the teacher had introduced similar students to this classroom language through lists of phrases which they had copied down and which had been displayed prominently in the classroom. However, the teacher had been frustrated to find that, despite these efforts, little spontaneous use of the L2 had ensued. For the current cohort, the teacher therefore decided to try an alternative approach and planned a series of tasks that, it was hoped, might lead to more effective acquisition and use of the classroom language phrases.

For the task presented here, the teacher had already presented the new classroom language on the interactive whiteboard, using a combination of their written forms and visual representation of their meanings; this was followed by oral repetition practice. The task itself then involved learners playing a board game to strengthen their mental representations of the target phrases and to develop their fluency in producing them. Students played the game in groups of four, throwing the die to determine how many squares they could advance around the board. Many of the squares had written on them an example of classroom language, which students had to read out if they landed on them; they then had to follow the accompanying instructions, as in the following examples:

*Jai oublié mon cahier'* – *reculez de deux cases*
(I've forgotten my book – go back two squares)

*J'ai fini l'exercice* – *avancez de trois cases*
( I've finished the exercise – move forwards three squares)

A further element of the task involved the students having to use appropriate language as required to play the game itself: for example, saying whose turn it was; expressing pleasure or regret at what each respective square instructed them to do, and so forth. They were asked to use the L2 where they could, using language which they already knew as individuals (for example *très bien*: 'very good'; *quel dommage*: 'what a shame') or by drawing on the knowledge of others in the group by way of mediation (Lantolf 2000). Where this did not lead to the speaker being able to express a response in the L2 because the language was unknown (for example, to say 'You have to miss a turn'), learners were asked to make a note (in L1) of what it was that they wanted, but were unable, to say. Following the first run-through of the task, the teacher went through the unknown words or phrases that learners had noted down and taught these as necessary. The task was then repeated and the students were encouraged to use the newly-taught language wherever possible.

In devising the task (and the wider task sequence) in this way, the teacher was hoping to address a number of aims at different levels. First, as noted above, the longer-term aim was to establish the L2 as the predominant means of classroom communication with this class, in order to demonstrate to the learners that the language was not simply an object of study, but could be a genuine means of communication. In turn, it was hoped that using the language to communicate spontaneously in the classroom would provide additional opportunities for language learning, associated for example with Long's (1996) interaction hypothesis. Further, the teacher was keen to address the 'insufficient use of the target language in secondary schools' highlighted in recent national inspection findings (Ofsted 2011: 1). Second, a more immediate aim was to provide an opportunity for learners to practise the classroom language phrases they had just been taught, contributing to the wider aim described above. Third, the task aimed to help students learn the procedural language required to play the board game itself. The idea of allowing the learners first to identify the language needed to play the game, before being taught it for use in the second iteration, draws on Swain's (2000) 'output hypothesis', whereby learners 'notice, so to speak, a "hole" in their interlanguage' (p. 100) and so have a specific purpose for learning the language that will fill this hole. Of course, playing the game through the medium of the L2 (particularly when playing for the second time) also involves using the L2 for genuine communication.

The game format was designed to allow language to be used and practised in a 'low stakes', small group context which would be as unthreatening to them as possible. It could also be repeated in future to practise other language forms besides the classroom language phrases, with the learners' ability to use the L2 as the medium of communication for game playing increasing each time; through task repetition, it is argued that more complex language may be produced (Ellis 2000). Further, repetition of a game such as this would be unlikely to result in the students feeling that they were merely repeating something they had done previously: in the world outside the classroom, a board-game can be played over and over again with the element of chance adding the novel aspect to any re-run of the same activity.

As in the previous example (see A French decoding task, page 140), however, there are a number of issues to consider before using this task in the classroom. First, careful thought would need to be given to the way in which the procedural instructions for the task were delivered. While the teacher might consider it important to maximise L2 use as a means of exposing the students to more target language input (Ellis 2005), the complexity of the instructions for a class such as this, which has limited experience of the language to date, might present some problems. Indeed, research has found that teachers often revert to L1 in order to provide procedural instructions for classroom tasks (Macaro 1997). However, this does not necessarily have to be the case with this particular example: the teacher has the advantage of explaining a board game, a concept that should be familiar to many in the class; where this is not the case, other learners may be able to mediate the understanding of what a board game entails. Modelling the game with appropriate use of mime and gesture should also facilitate comprehension of the procedural instructions. It may be, however, that some use of L1 is required to explain the aspect of the task that relates to the noting down of the unknown words and phrases needed to play the game itself; here the teacher's judgement will be required to decide to what extent the understanding of the task will be facilitated by L1 use (Cook 2001). Of course, many UK classrooms now include considerable (and increasing) numbers of students with English as an additional language (NALDIC 2013), in which case it cannot be simply assumed that a shared L1 can be used to deliver procedural instructions to all students quickly and efficiently. This may provide additional incentives for using the L2 in the classroom, since it levels the playing field for learners who may struggle to understand English.

Second, the nature of the task means that the students are likely to be highly motivated to play the game irrespective of its linguistic purposes (as a vehicle for acquiring specific pieces of classroom language), which may result in them interpreting the task in their own way (Brooks and Donato 1994) and focussing only on the goal of winning the game. In turn, this may tend to sideline the opportunities to practise the L2. Careful explanation as to the language learning potential of the task might help, but it will also be important to consider the ways in which the activity is monitored to ensure that the students are using the target language appropriately when playing the game. The teacher might also need to consider some mechanism for each of the groups to self-monitor and/or reward the L2 contributions of individual students.

Finally, consideration will need to be given to the ways in which both of the task's linguistic foci (the classroom language that forms the basis of the board game; the language needed to play the game itself) are followed up. In the case of the former, learners need to be encouraged to use the L2 wherever appropriate and the teacher needs to insist on this during normal classroom interactions. In the case of the second, students will need to be given further opportunities to play similar board games, in order to develop their capacity to use the language with increasing levels of spontaneity, complexity and automaticity.

## 3 Reflections on designing tasks for language learning

In this section, we draw together the ideas discussed in this chapter and offer some reflections on designing – and learning to design – effective tasks for instructed L2 learners.

### 3.1 The nature of tasks in the L2 classroom

We have adopted a broad definition of a 'language learning task' and the examples in Task design in action, page 140, are deliberately different from those which may be familiar from the field of task-based language teaching. In doing so, we hope to have highlighted the wide range of learning experiences that a teacher must provide in order to promote language learning, as well as the depth of thinking that lies behind the design of such experiences.

Not all tasks, so defined, are of the same order; they must be seen in terms of a wider learning sequence. For example, some may be 'enabling' tasks which prepare the ground for subsequent communicative tasks; they may focus on the development of specific aspects of linguistic knowledge; or they may provide opportunities for controlled practice in a particular skill. (The decoding task presented in A French decoding task, page 140 exemplifies all three of these categories). By contrast, we would classify as 'higher order' tasks those which involve the use of the L2 for genuine (or simulated genuine) communication: for example, telling someone about your holiday, booking a hotel room over the telephone or reading a text to find out about its content. The spontaneous classroom communication which is the ultimate goal of the classroom language sequence presented above (see A French 'classroom language' task, page 143) is an example of such a higher-order task.

In our view, teachers must ensure that learners have frequent opportunities to engage with such higher order, communicative tasks. This follows from our view that the primary purpose of language teaching is to develop learners' ability to use the L2 for genuine communication. Thus, in the words of the final, overarching principle formulated by PDC in MFL (2013), 'the teaching of linguistic knowledge (knowledge of grammar and vocabulary) should act in the service of skill development, not as an end in itself'. To adopt a culinary analogy, in the 'higher order' task of cooking a lasagne, the lower order tasks of making white sauce and grating cheese reveal their full value only through the tasting of the finished product.

## 3.2 Factors influencing task design

We hope to have shown that – potentially at least – designing both lower- and higher-order tasks for language learning is an intricate and thoughtful process which draws on a wide range of knowledge sources. These include, for example: knowledge of the students' learning dispositions, motivational profiles and previous attainment; knowledge of the affordances and constraints of the particular learning context; and knowledge of how languages are learnt. We have argued that knowledge in this last category should be informed by the (constantly developing) insights from SLA research. Of course, a task might also be designed as a result of less thorough and less detailed thinking. However, we would suggest that such tasks are less likely to be successful in terms of L2 learning. Rather, it is likely that, as the range and depth of the knowledge on which the teacher draws increase, so too will the quality or extent of learning arising from the task. It follows that the most effective tasks will always be 'bespoke' creations, tailored to the needs of individual classes or learners; 'off-the-peg' tasks, such as those provided in textbooks, cannot be responsive in this way, at least if they are used unthinkingly.

We have also argued that, in relation to some other subject areas, L2 learning is distinctive in some important respects. Consequently, some of the principles of effective task design which apply to other subjects may not always apply so readily to languages. For example, in our work with schools, we have often observed a general expectation that effective lessons will engage students' 'higher order thinking skills', as advocated in official guidance (for example Ofsted 2011a). Yet, as we have argued, some valuable language learning tasks do not require such conceptual thinking: for example, those that involve controlled practise to develop automaticity; or the use of language to communicate simple information. This highlights the danger of language teaching being evaluated against generic, rather than languages-specific criteria. Indeed, it could be argued that those who make judgments on language teachers' practice – with increasingly high stakes in a context where inspection outcomes may determine not only a teacher's career progression but also the success of the school as a whole – should themselves have a detailed, research-informed understanding of the processes involved in L2 learning.

## 3.3 Implications for initial teacher education

The ideas discussed above have a number of implications for beginning teachers and teacher educators. First, beginning teachers need opportunities to design tasks. A context in which they are simply asked to implement pre-existing tasks – such as those included in a textbook or scheme of work – will not afford opportunities to engage with the complexities of task design; and grappling with these complexities, we would argue, lies at the heart of learning to be an effective teacher. There are grounds for ensuring that beginning teachers' initial steps in task design are manageable in scale (for example planning a single task forming a short teaching 'segment' rather than being 'thrown in at the deep end' with whole lessons); nonetheless, since tasks can only be understood in terms of the wider sequence of learning of which they form part, they must be given an understanding of the learners' longer-term goals (for example. a communicative task through which they will put into practice the language they have learnt in a particular segment).

Second, helping beginning teachers to design tasks effectively must mean acknowledging the wide range of knowledge sources involved and must involve providing them with opportunities to develop their knowledge in all these areas. This implies a model of ITE which encourages beginning teachers to access various kinds of evidence – for example, by observing experienced teachers, talking to learners, analysing learners' linguistic errors and finding out about SLA research – and to critically analyse and synthesize this information. This of course raises important questions about how such learning might be instantiated – an issue which is, however, beyond the scope of this chapter.

Third, tasks can be seen as a workspace for the kind of 'deliberate practice' (Dunn and Shriner 1999) which 'both leads to and maintains teaching expertise' (p. 647). Both the process of designing a task and the subsequent evaluation of the task provide opportunities for teachers to broaden and deepen the range of knowledge on which they draw when designing future tasks; thus, there can be a progressive enriching and refining of the teacher's pre-active visualisation of task outcomes. There is not space here to explore further the process of evaluating tasks; however, we would suggest that this should take into account both the specific aims of the task and its contribution to wider language learning – understood, as argued above, as the progressive development of learners' ability to use the L2 for genuine communication.

Finally, we repeat the point made earlier that instructed language learners may have very limited contact with the L2, both inside and outside the classroom. They lack the opportunities for intensive linguistic input and output which allow some (especially young) learners to acquire an L2 naturalistically in immersion contexts. By contrast, recent evidence suggests that older learners have certain cognitive advantages which facilitate language learning in instructed settings (for example Muñoz 2006; Muñoz and Singleton 2011). However, it is the quality of the tasks in which these learners engage in the classroom which will determine whether (and to what extent) language learning actually occurs. Task design therefore lies at the very heart of language teaching.

## References

Atkinson, D. (2011) Introduction: cognitivism and second language acquisition, in D. Atkinson (ed.), *Alternative Approaches to Second language Acquisition*. Abingdon: Routledge.

Baddeley, A. D. and Logie, R. H. (1999) 'Working memory: the multiple component model', in A. Miyake and P. Shah (eds), *Models of Working Memory: Mechanisms of active maintenance and executive control*, pp. 28–61. Cambridge: Cambridge University Press.

Breen, M. (1987) Learner contributions to task design, in C. Brumfit (ed.) *General English Syllabus Design*. Oxford: Pergamon Press.
Brooks, F. B. and Donato, R. (1994) Vygotskyan approaches to understanding foreign language learner discourse during communication tasks, *Hispania,* 77, 262–74.
Cave, S. and Haig, J. (2012) *Physical French Phonics*. Dunstable: Brilliant Publications.
Chater, M.(2014) Curriculum crisis? Yes please: policy perspectives on task design, this volume.
Clark, C. M., and Yinger, R. J. (1979) *Three Studies of Teaching Planning*. East Lansing, MI: Institute for Research on Teaching, Michigan State University.
Clemens, S. (2011) *The English Baccalaureate and GCSE Choices*. DfE Research Brief.
Cook, V. J. (2001) Using the first language in the classroom, *Canadian Modern Language Review,* (57)3: 402–23.
Dörnyei, Z. (2003) Attitudes, orientations, and motivations in language learning: advances in theory, research, and applications, *Language Learning,* (53)1: 3–32.
Dörnyei, Z. (2009) *The Psychology of Second Language Acquisition*. Oxford: Oxford University Press.
Dörnyei, Z. (2013) Communicative language teaching in the twenty-first century: the 'principled communicative approach', in J. Arnold and T. Murphey (eds) *Meaningful Action: Earl Stevick's influence on language teaching,* pp. 161–71. Cambridge: Cambridge University Press.
Dunn, T. G. and Shriner, C. (1999) Deliberate practice in teaching: what teachers do for self-improvement, *Teaching and Teacher Education,* (15)6: 631–51.
Ellis, R. (2000) Task-based research and language pedagogy, *Language Teaching Research,* (4)3: 199–220.
Ellis, R. (2003) *Task-based Language Learning And Teaching*. Oxford: Oxford University Press.
Ellis, R. (2005) Principles of instructed language learning, *System,* (33)2: 209–24.
Ellis, R. (2009) Task-based language teaching: sorting out the misunderstandings. *International Journal of Applied Linguistics,* (19)3: 221–46.
Erler, L. (2003) *Reading in a Foreign Language – Near-Beginner Adolescents' Experiences of French in English Secondary Schools*. Unpublished doctoral thesis, University of Oxford, Oxford.
Erler, L. and Macaro, E. (2011) Decoding ability in French as a foreign language and language learning motivation. *Modern Language Journal,* (95)4: 496–518.
Gardner, R. (2001) *Language Learning Motivation: The student, the teacher and the researcher*. Keynote address to the Texas Foreign Language Education Conference, University of Texas, Austin.
Grabe, W. (2010) Fluency in reading – thirty-five years later. *Reading in a Foreign Language,* (22)1: 71–83.
Grabe, W. and Stoller, F. L. (2011) *Teaching and Researching Reading*. Second Edition. Longman: Harlow.
Graham, S. J. (2004) Giving up on modern foreign languages? Students' perceptions of learning French, *Modern Language Journal,* (88)2: 171–91.
International Phonetic Association (2005). *Handbook of the International Phonetic Association: A guide to the use of the International Phonetic Alphabet*. Cambridge: Cambridge University Press.
John, P. (2006) Lesson planning and the student teacher: re-thinking the dominant model, *Journal of Curriculum Studies,* (38)4: 483–98.
Lantolf, J. P. (2000) Second language learning as a mediated process, *Language Teaching,* (33)2: 79–96.
Lantolf, J. P. (2011) The sociocultural approach to second language acquisition: sociocultural

theory, second language acquisition and artificial L2 development, in D. Atkinson (ed.) *Alternative Approaches to Second language Acquisition*. Abingdon: Routledge.

Larsen-Freeman, D. (2011) A complexity theory approach to second language acquisition/development, in D. Atkinson (ed.) *Alternative Approaches to Second language Acquisition*. Abingdon: Routledge.

Long, M. H. (1996) The role of the linguistic environment in second language acquisition, in W. C. Ritchie and T. K. Bhatia (eds) *Handbook of Second Language Acquisition*, pp. 413–68. New York: Academic Press.

Long, M. (2009) Methodological principles for language teaching, in M. H. Long and J. Doughty (eds) *The Handbook of Language Teaching*, pp. 373–94. Oxford: Blackwell.

Macaro, E. (1997) *Target Language, Collaborative Learning and Autonomy*. Clevedon: Multilingual Matters.

Macaro, E. (2001) Analysing student teachers' codeswitching in foreign language classrooms: theories and decision making, *Modern Language Journal*, (85)4: 531–48.

Macaro, E. and Erler, L. (2008) Raising the achievement of young-beginner readers of french through strategy instruction, *Applied Linguistics*, (29)1: 90–119.

Muñoz, C. (2006) The effects of age on foreign language learning: the BAF project, in C. Muñoz (ed.) *Age and the Rate of Foreign Language Learning*, pp. 1–40. Clevedon: Multilingual Matters.

Muñoz, C. and Singleton, D. (2011) A critical review of age-related research on L2 ultimate attainment, *Language Teaching*, (44)1: 1–35.

Mutton, T., Burn, K. and Hagger, H. (2011) Learning to plan, planning to learn; the developing expertise of beginning teachers, *Teachers and Teaching: Theory and Practice*, (17)4: 399–416.

NALDIC (2013) Retrieved from www.naldic.org.uk/research-and-information/eal-statistics/eal-pupils

Norton B. and McKinney, C. (2011) An identity approach to second language acquisition, in D. Atkinson (ed.) *Alternative Approaches to Second language Acquisition*. Abingdon: Routledge.

Nunan, D. (2004) *Task-based Language Teaching*. Cambridge: Cambridge University Press.

Office for Standards in Education (Ofsted) (2011a) *Learning: Creative approaches that raise standards*. Available online at: www.ofsted.gov.uk/resources/learning-creative-approaches-raise-standards

Office for Standards in Education (Ofsted) (2011b) *Modern languages: achievement and challenge 2007–2010*. Available online at: www.ofsted.gov.uk/Ofsted-home/Publications-and-research

Pring, R. (2013) *The Life and Death of Secondary Education for All*. Abingdon: Routledge.

Professional Development Consortium in Modern Foreign Languages (PDC in MFL) (2013) *PDC in MFL: Research for language teaching*. Available online at: http://pdcinmfl.com/

Samuda, V. and Bygate, M. (2008) *Tasks in Second Language Learning*. New York: Palgrave Macmillan.

YSchmitt, N., Jiang, X. and Grabe, W. (2011) The percentage of words known in a text and reading comprehension, *Modern Language Journal*, (95)1: 26–43.

YSchneider, W. and Shiffrin, R. M. (1977) Controlled and automatic human information processing: I. detection, search, and attention, *Psychological Review*, (84)1: 1–66.

Selinker, L. (1972) Interlanguage, *International Review of Applied Linguistics*, (10)3: 209–31.

Skehan, P. (1998) *A Cognitive Approach To Language Learning*, Oxford: Oxford University Press.

Skehan, P. (2003) Task based instruction, *Language Teaching*, (36)1: 1–14.

Stables, A. and Wikeley, F. (1999) From bad to worse? Pupils' attitudes to modern foreign languages at ages 14 and 15, *Language Learning Journal*, (20)1: 27–31.
Swain, M. (2000) The output hypothesis and beyond: mediating acquisition through collaborative dialogue, in J. Lantolf (ed.) *Sociocultural Approaches To Second Language Research*, pp. 97–115. Oxford: Oxford University Press.
Swan, M. (2008) Talking sense about learning strategies, *RELC Journal*, (39)2: 262–73.
Tinsley, T. (2013) *Languages: The State of the Nation*, London: British Academy.
Tinsley, T. and Han, Y. (2012) *Language Learning in Secondary Schools in England. Findings from the 2011 Language Trends Survey*. Available online at: www.cfbt.com/evidenceforeducation/our_research/evidence_for_government/national_policy_reforms/language_trends_survey.aspx.
VanPatten, B. (2010) Some verbs are more perfect than others: why learners have difficulty with ser and estar and what it means for instruction, *Hispania*, (93)1: 29–38.
Walter, C. (2007) First- to second-language reading comprehension: not transfer, but access, in *International Journal of Applied Linguistics*, (17)1: 14–37.
Williams, M., Burden, R. and Lanvers, U. (2002) 'French is the language of love and stuff': student perceptions of issues related to motivation in learning a foreign language, *British Educational Research Journal*, (28)4: 503–28.
Woore, R. (2009) Beginners' progress in decoding L2 French: some longitudinal evidence from English Modern Foreign Languages classrooms, *Language Learning Journal*, (37)1: 3–18.
Woore, R. (2011) *Investigating And Developing Beginner Learners' Decoding Proficiency in Second Language French: An evaluation of two programmes of instruction*. Unpublished DPhil Thesis, University of Oxford, Oxford.
Woore, R. (2013) *Decoding, Vocabulary Learning And Vocabulary Learning Strategies in Beginners' L2 French*. Paper presented at EUROSLA 23, University of Amsterdam, 28–31 August 2013.
Woore, R. (2014) Developing reading and decoding in the MFL classroom, in P. Driscoll, E. Macaro and A. Swarbrick (eds) *Debates in Modern Languages Education*. London: Routledge.

# Notes

1 This choice – usually of a 'prestige' or 'standard' variety – is of course socially and politically charged; however, this is not usually part of the L2 teacher's day-to-day decision-making.
2 Readers interested in the full sets of principles are referred to the publications cited above.
3 These are state-funded secondary schools with non-selective intake.
4 French words are given in italics and are followed, in parenthesis, by (a) a representation of their pronunciation, where relevant, using the phonetic alphabet of the IPA (2005); and (b) an English translation.

# 9
# NEGOTIATING KNOWLEDGE
## Task design in the history classroom

*Jason Todd*

Locating this inquiry into task design for history students in epistemological concerns serves two purposes. On a practical level it informs the development of teacher education programmes, continuing professional development and pedagogical development. On a more political level it engages with debates about the nature of history and how these inform curriculum change contestations and the broader nature of teachers' work. I will seek to broaden the idea of task design to encompass the notion of 'historical enquiry'.

### Historical disciplinary knowledge and task design

Underpinning any thinking about task design is a discussion about the nature of knowledge in general terms and specifically in relation to the study of history. In one model of teaching it is assumed that teachers are the guardians of a body of knowledge and their role is to help the pupil access that body of knowledge – a simple form of transmission to Cartesian empty vessels waiting to be filled. Yet it is evident that learning, teaching and the knowledge associated with both, exists in a much messier, nuanced and situated set of circumstances. Work by Durkheim, Vygotsky and Bernstein directs us to the elusive and diffuse nature of knowledge in school settings. In developing specific pedagogies for the history classroom it is important for teachers to interpret debates about history as a discipline alongside ideas about how school students learn history. Prospective teachers will need to make sense of theory and research in these areas alongside practice and observed experiences. Reconciling theoretical knowledge with practical knowledge can be problematic especially where they appear to contradict eachother. This is further complicated by the way in which wider discourses serve to shape and constrain; firstly through institutional processes that serve to emphasise particular narrowly prescriptive outcomes. A second complication is in the ways in which debates are framed in the form of simple binaries with no sense of the complications of contexts or settings.

Oancea and Furlong's (2007) work in trying to understand the diversity in the field of educational research and the different ideas of quality in this area returned to the ideas of Aristotle. The synergies they describe between different domains of knowledge are useful in helping teachers thinking about task design and discussing the multiple tensions involved. They highlight that alongside *episteme theoretike* (knowledge that is demonstrable through valid reasoning) and *techne* (technical skill, or a trained ability for rational production) consideration should also be given to *phronesis* (practical wisdom, or the capacity or predisposition to act truthfully). Phronesis also suggests strong ethical dimensions to teacher thinking. Moreover, a consideration of phronesis might also offer a space in which we help teachers negotiate the complex processes involved in task design in the history classroom.

What is emerging is a contestation about knowledge, about knowing. History as a discipline is contested and diverse; while knowledge of the learners and how they learn is complex and needs to take account of the range of contexts in which learning and knowledge are constructed. In reflecting this epistemological ambivalence, task design in history means eschewing a didactic approach; 'this is how it's done', models of 'best practice'. Rather we need to cultivate teachers who are capable of asking questions of themselves, their contexts, their own learning, and their school students' learning as well as the nature of their subject.

An increasing interest in teachers' prior knowledge has shown how powerfully teachers' own perceptions of the nature and purpose of history impact on their approaches to the teaching of history (Evans 1994). While individual case studies of teachers (Gudmundsdottir and Shulman 1989; Wilson 1990) explore the complex ways in which individual teachers made sense of their own knowledge in their classrooms. Wineburg and Wilson's work (1991), as part of series of wisdom in practice studies, gives an indication of the multifaceted nature of history teaching and the possibilities, rather than constraints that this offers. It illustrates two contrasting teachers, invisible and visible, making sense of both epistemological representations and contextual representations, the subject and the learner. While the lessons are very different in nature, both teachers share an understanding of history as a human construction that involves an act of judgement related to questions of historical significance. Both also share a common process, an act of pedagogical reasoning, of turning inwards towards an examination of the nature of the subject, but to fashion this into a pedagogical form they also need to turn outwards into the minds and settings of the learners in their classrooms. While other factors are relevant (Shulman 1986) within the scope of this chapter I shall look at this turning in towards the subject and turning outwards towards the learner.

In the process of turning out one quickly realises that history, perhaps more than any other subject on the curriculum attracts a great deal of heated debate. The title of Taylor and Guyver's (2012) book, *History Wars and the Classroom*, indicates the international and political nature of the debates.

Disciplinary history seeks to focus on the processes and conceptual underpinnings of history; it allows school students to think about how knowledge is constructed not simply handed down. It can offer school students powerful levers to understand the world they inhabit but also to better it '...history holds the potential, only partly realised, of humanising us in ways offered by few other areas in the school curriculum'. (Wineburg 2001: 5) Sometimes set against this is the idea of history as a body of knowledge that students need to acquire to orientate themselves in the culture (Hirsch 1987).

The need to be aware of the tensions and questions at play is critical to the development of history tasks in the classroom. Prospective teachers need to take account of the societal and school contexts in which these debates take place. They must reflect on their biographies and how these shape their own dispositions to these questions. Smagorinsky (2010) highlights the importance of both teacher biographies and the ways in which they may internalise the values of goal-orientated colleagues. Pendry, Kitson and Husbands' work on prospective history teachers (1998, 2003) echoes the importance of teacher biographies and the ways in which they bring prior values and aspirations into their training. Evans' (1994) work, in the US, examines the important ways in which history teachers' understanding and beliefs about the nature of the subject play out in the classroom.

If teachers are unaware of the basis of their beliefs they can often remain unexamined and given. The importance of getting prospective teachers to examine their own preconceptions can support their development in two important ways. The first is by helping them to examine the teaching and teachers they are working with; to understand what more experienced teachers' craft or classroom practice is based on. Guy Claxton's (1990, 1993) work highlights the place of 'mini-theories', ideas that school students and teachers hold that help explain the world. To evaluate these mini-theories it is important to access what they are based on, to situate this knowledge. For Claxton this process 'involves a gradual process of editing these minitheories so that they come to (i) contain better-quality knowledge and skill, and (ii) to be better "located" with respect to the area of experience for which they are suitable' (1990: 66).

Editing can also be useful as a tool to examine what might be seen as the tacit knowledge that an experienced teacher holds, giving prospective teachers an insight into the expectations of that teacher and the source of those expectations. Secondly it can heighten awareness for the prospective teacher of the ways that possible defaults and habituated practice can evolve, and encourage them to adopt a critical aproach to the development of their own 'mini-theories'.

In order to raise the question of historical knowledge and examine their own biographies prospective history teachers, as part of the Oxford University Department of Education (OUDE) History programme begin the programme with the theme of preconceptions. The handbook states:

The purpose of our work on preconceptions is to help you:

- to become aware of your own preconceptions

- to recognise that the preconceptions of your peers may well be different to yours
- to examine the sorts of assumptions about, for example, the nature of teaching and learning that are implicit within them
- to think about their appropriateness and usefulness to you as a teacher and
- to begin to think critically about these ideas in the light of your developing knowledge about education and your expertise as a teacher.

The structure of the programme is designed to prompt prospective teachers to draw from different sites of learning – from their reading; from the school-based mentors and their own classroom experiences; and from their university-based tutors. The week is structured around an introductory session, school-based tasks following the theme during the course of the week and a follow-up session at the end of the week. This follow-up is critical to giving space for prospective teachers to explore the different contexts of their placement schools, the comparative element guarding against normalising individual experience.

Course evaluations comments on the preconceptions course are typically favourable: 'My understanding of the richness and diversity of History has been rejuvenated and extended this year. Very grateful for this' (Prospective teacher 2013). Some comment on how valuable it has been to alert them to their own preconceptions: 'Very useful as it's not really something I'd spent much time thinking about before', while others have gone further to place this work in its wider context: 'Essential, given the current raging debates and DfE (government) output'.

The structure also provides a space in which to make sense of the different forms of Aristotelian knowledge that the prospective teachers are encountering in the course of their training, their reading of theoretical and research-based literature, the lessons they have observed and the technical skills they have witnessed or deployed. The space at the end of the week could be seen as a phronetic space in which to reconcile and explore the relationship between the different forms of knowledge and relate it to the particularities of the range of school experiences. John Hattie (2012) makes the case that teachers talking to each other about teaching can have an impact on student achievement suggesting that it should be developed in schools. The openness of dialogue is important and can be inhibited by associated notions of 'good' or 'bad' practice. It can be enhanced when teachers are prepared to be open about problems and difficulties they are experiencing. Extending this dialogue into schools can be a major challenge for both finding spaces and guarding against performative and normative criteria that close down discussion.

Michael Young (2008) has usefully contributed to epistemic debates with the 'powerful knowledge', 'knowledge of the powerful', dyad. Knowledge of the powerful is canonical in its nature. Establishing the content of which is regarded, by some, to be of critical importance. Powerful knowledge, as described by Young, has emancipatory potential and is linked to ideas of social justice. In a history context, powerful knowledge might be characterised as a content-rich curriculum that emphasises the procedural and conceptual processes at the heart of history, that allows school students not just to see what we know, but how knowledge is created and how further knowledge might be developed. Its emancipatory potential comes with the ability to generalise.

> As with other disciplines, only when young people can generalise appropriately (Shemilt 2009), find explanatory power and challenge the grounds of other's generalisations can they hope to engage with serious political discourse.
>
> *(Counsell 2011: 202)*

Disciplinary history is under threat from both wider public discourses and a range of internal pressures, for example in debates about greater access and engagement with the curriculum (Counsell 2011). Teachers need to be able to think things through to resolve possible tensions.

The internal pressures indicate the need for teachers' intellectual work on task design to operate on a range of levels. Counsell highlights the pressure in UK schools to reduce history to generic skill sets, sometimes in the interests of providing engagement. A disciplinary approach is further curtailed by over-simplifying in the name of access, the unintended consequences of assessment, the persistence of a distracting dichotomy between historical skills and historical content and the problem of teachers acting on 'third hand' ideas. These problems are not unique to the UK; in Australia attempts to implement a broader integrated social education echoed what Counsell describes as 'genericism'. Teachers need to work at the intersection, implied here, between knowledge of the subject and knowledge of the school students in terms of how they access the curriculum.

Taylor and Guyver's book (2012) outlines the polarisations that surround the teaching of history in ten different countries and serves as a reminder of the contested nature of historical knowledge and the international scope of these debates. However a range of contributors to the book reminds us that the public debates themselves can serve to obscure more nuanced positions. The polarity and tension of the debates in public suggest a schism in history education and it is possible to overstate this and obscure a great deal of consensus. For prospective teachers the public debates about what should be taught can distract from thinking about why we should study history at all (Wineburg 2001) and how to make history relevant to young learners.

Both Barton and Sandwell in their chapters on American and Canadian history teaching respectively (Taylor and Guyver 2012) point out that many of the wider debates have relatively little impact in the classroom. What might be of more significance are the internal threats, some relating to the teachers' own biographies, others relating to the institutional context of schooling. Any approach to task design and preparing teachers for the classroom needs to be attentive to these tensions without overplaying some and overlooking others. Developing an approach that encourages thought about how macro debates are played out at a micro classroom-based level. As part of the OUDE History programme prospective teachers' first assignment requires them to examine ways in which public debates about history manifest themselves in their school contexts.

The potential of powerful knowledge, as presented in the guise of disciplinary history, needs careful consideration. Prospective teachers need clarity in their own thinking about what it might involve, while also being attentive to the needs of the learner. Young's own work has received criticism from both White (2012) and Beck (2013). Beck highlights three tensions at the heart of Young's approach. The intrinsically esoteric nature of disciplinary knowledge that makes it challenging for school students to access; secondly, the danger of over-simplification which is exacerbated by a culture of performativity and thirdly, the potentially regressive role of esoteric knowledge of maintaining social hierarchies, even while its proponents allude to its socially emancipatory possibilities.

These are useful to bear in mind; Young's response in the same journal offers some ways forward. He suggests that the idea of powerful knowledge invites the curriculum designer to 'take account of both social relation and the epistemic relation of knowledge thus allowing for the emergent properties of knowledge' (Young 2013: 196). Simply conveying how history works is not enough. Any attempt at emancipatory task design must also involve learners in the construction of knowledge. In addition he warns that 'any attempt to develop a pedagogy that imagines it can avoid, rather than work with, the 'epistemic constraints' of a subject will be doomed to fail.' (Young 2013: 197). Exploring the relationship between powerful knowledge and knowledge of the powerful is the critical judgement; we should not simply a focus on one or the other.

## Epistemological problems in task design

The first epistemological problem the history teacher has to tackle in task design is reconciling Young's knowledge dyad, crudely put, between content and concept. In wanting the work to be socially informed, the teacher also needs to think about issues of power and its exercise through forms of representations. The debates in England over the inclusion of Clive of India as part of the compulsory curriculum may serve to illustrate this point. Speaking at the Hay Literature Festival the historian Simon Schama, initially drafted to advise on the new UK history curriculum, describes Clive of India as 'a sociopathic corrupt thug and of dubious inclusion for study in the curriculum' (Schama 2013–transcript available from HistoryWorks). He goes on to make the case that Clive's inclusion might serve to obscure more pertinent questions about how the British came to be in India in the first place.

History task design involves designing enquiries where the concepts and processes are embedded in meaningful historical contexts, while recognising that what gives these contexts their meaning is an exercise of power. This does not mean, however, that the investigation into Clive of India cannot be framed in such a way as to reveal these power relations. This is where wrestling with the history education device of the enquiry question forms a first step of task design (Byrom and Riley 2003).

An example of taking a socially informed approach to a study of a topic riddled with tradition is Catherine Hall's (epistemic) study of the Macaulays (Hall 2012). Hall's own formation as a historian was in the radical and feminist politics of the 1960s. Her commitment remains to reveal the 'grammars of difference organised by class, gender, racial and ethnic identities', giving voice to those absent from the traditional narratives. Yet in turning her gaze to someone like Thomas Babington Macaulay, whose narrative history of Britain speaks so eloquently to Michael Gove the recent British education secretary, she acknowledges how 'the theoretical shots of the late twentieth century had not sufficiently disrupted established orthodoxies' (Hall 2012: xv) and that the centre needed to be addressed more directly if history was to be critically de-centred.

It reminds us that while the inclusion and particularly the exclusions of history are important, work should still be done on the most traditional of topics. It is the form the treatment and analysis takes that is important. Arguing about whether Clive of India should or should not be in the curriculum is less important than exploring the form an enquiry may take. Schama himself arrives at a possible enquiry question regarding the process by which the British government succeeded the East India Company. 'How was it that the business of government came to supplant the business of business?'; including a study of Robert Clive. But another approach, melding the ideas of historical significance and historical interpretation might be to ask 'Is Clive of India as significant as the Education Secretary thinks he is?' This allows an exploration of the nature of colonial rule but also invites students into a debate into the nature of history and its living vibrant legacy.

'Wrestling' with the enquiry question involves reconciling the different epistemic elements of history: the content and the discipline. For the prospective teacher it also includes what has been learnt about the technical aspects of the classroom that are context dependant. Underpinning both of these must be an exploration of the mini-theories and preconceptions that influence the development of practice (techne) and an awareness of context. Reconciling these elements, sometimes conflicting, and having a concern with the common good, requires space in which to reveal these different elements, to think and act phronetically.

A second epistemological problem regarding the idea of powerful knowledge, in the context of teaching history which includes a disciplinary focus, is the way in which the discipline of history is conceptualised. Levisohn (2010) in his study of historical narratives indicates that narrative presents an epistemological and pedagogical problem. The pedagogical problem relates to helping school students make a judgment about competing narratives. Wineburg and Wilson's (1991) approach is to return to the discipline to allow school students to be part of a broader cultural enterprise that enables participation on a range of levels. This acknowledges that school students are participants in a wider cultural enterprise. An introduction into the 'discipline' of history could therefore aspire to broader educational aspirations, enabling students to access important cultural tools. The process of internalisation as described by Edwards (2010) involves school students' taking on what is culturally valued, prior to acting on that knowledge.

The epistemological problem is how to define the discipline of history? Responding phronetically to these epistemological challenges, in the context of task design, involves an exploration of questions generated by the challenge. Or Wineburg's reflexive turn inwards to examine our own understandings of our subject.

Consideration should be given, in designing tasks that reflect the disciplinary nature of history, to a range of epistemological questions. Where do the boundaries of the subject lie? What consensus exists over how the discipline of history might be conceptualised? Is it possible to include methodologies drawn from other disciplines such as anthropology or sociology? If its boundaries are drawn too broadly history might lose it coherence as a discipline. Drawn too narrowly it becomes an inaccessible esoteric discipline as described by Beck (2013). How far should the history community engage with postmodernist critiques of its subjective nature but also the linguistic turn? Is historical knowledge only constructed in the academy? What then are the cultural tools? The range of questions here indicates how history exists as an 'abstract idea with many meanings' (Jordanova 2006: 58). Asking how and where disciplinary boundaries are drawn can reveal powerful investments and ideologies with new fields of investigation, like gender history, allowing for new forms of legitimation; these are also relevant in the classroom in the choices that teachers make regarding content. The diagram below suggests an approach that allows school students to study a common topic, the First World War, with an enquiry built around the question: How many different ways can the First World War be studied? This can be developed further in getting school students to think about why so many ways exist. It might serve to resolve the pedagogical problem of making superficial judgements about the relative merits of one account over another by instead judging the value of different approaches. While the enquiry opens up the diverse nature of the discipline it allows students to gain a shared sense of how sources are critical to the study of history and how questions can guide different approaches to the writing of history.

It might help, to enhance the process of internalisation described by Edwards (2010), to develop the enquiry by relating to popular manifestations of history. Educators like Counsell have a degree of ambivalence to more popular forms of historical knowledge seeing the place of disciplinary knowledge as a corrective to 'rawer forms of collective memory'. This contrasts with historians like Raphael Samuel (1994, 1998) who advocated a community approach to history making, an approach popularised by the British TV historian Michael Wood. In Wineburg's work the second reflexive turn, outwards towards the learner, might invite us to take a more catholic view of the possibilities offered by these more democratic forms of knowledge; to fashion tasks that resonate with the wide range of ways that history manifests itself.

Counsell indicates that the clearest place that the intersection of disciplinary and more colloquial/vernacular history can be found is in the 'Interpretations' strand of

**160** Jason Todd

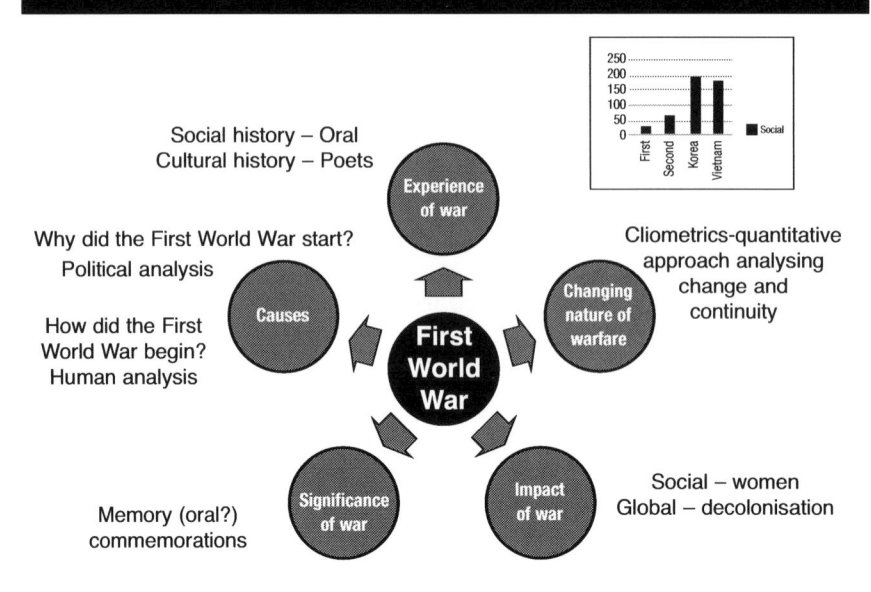

**Figure 9.1** Examining the First World War on different levels

the English national curriculum, first defined in the 1991 incarnation. In Ofsted's (the official body charged with inspecting schools in England) reporting on the state of history teaching in English schools 'Interpretations' was highlighted as causing most difficulty or variation in terms of quality (Ofsted 2007 and 2011). Counsell makes the point that exploration at this intersection was not in a bid for equivalence between vernacular forms of history and disciplinary informed history, which once again suggest an unspoken status afforded to one over the other. This is further complicated if we consider that perhaps not all forms of collective memory have equal value (Wertsch 1994). Just as not all accounts constructed within the discipline of history have equal value. Exploiting this intersection may serve to help school students and give value in their eyes to the study of history; by engaging with its popular manifestations and asking not only in what ways can disciplinary history contribute to reading collective memory but also in what ways can collective memory contribute to a more embedded critical reading of disciplinary history?

Samuel would certainly advocate an embrace of more popular forms of history for the potential they have not only to engage young people but to give them access to meaningful and powerful cultural tools. 'A history that was alert to its constituency would need to address not only the record of the past but also the hidden forces shaping contemporary understandings of it, the imaginative complexes in and through which it is perceived" (Samuel 1998: 222).

We have already talked about the place of the enquiry question in history task design when reconciling the knowledge dyad in socially informed ways. It can also be useful in reconciling the content issues inherent in history and especially the relationship between vernacular and official forms of knowing. Byrom and Riley (2003) highlight, in talking about professional intellectual wrestling, a range of questions that teachers need to ask in choosing content. They should develop a set of criteria to think about in terms of content selection. This includes thinking about pupil motivation: does the content make the students want to learn? Creating parallels to contemporary debates aids motivation in the way it signals that history is alive and kicking rather than inert and dead. Thinking is also required about pupil progression; what will the study of this content enable the school students to get better at? For diversity; does the content reflect the lives of the rulers and the ruled, men, women and children? Riley and Byrom (2003) also put forward 'Icons' – does our selected content help them to know about commonly accepted landmarks in history? This may aid the process of internalisation described by Edwards and act as a form of cultural tool. Riley and Byrom's second criterion 'Interpretations' involves a consideration of how the selected content or 'Icons' are interpreted differently, and therefore an engagement with how knowledge is constructed. The Icons and Interpretations criteria bring us back to the need to explore the relationship between knowledge of the powerful and powerful knowledge, rather than eschewing one in favour of another.

In the example above of the First World War, the second, more challenging question, is to ask Why? Why are there so many different ways of studying the First World War? Given the challenge, this question might be better focussed on contemporary vernacular manifestations of the First World War. This would allow school students greater access by enabling them to act in a space where formal and informal forms of knowledge are in play. And also, to allow them to go beyond simply taking on what is culturally valued and instead asking questions and acting on these. This year sees commemorations marking the beginning of the First World War with national and international events being organised. Asking the question 'How is the war commemorated and why?', having already considered the question 'How many different ways can the First World War be studied?', might enable students to take part in a broader discourse about history, commemoration and the First World War and to orientate themselves in these contemporary debates. School students would thus be able to acquire relevant cultural tools and use them to construct knowledge as part of a broader cultural enterprise.

## Learning the past

The second substantive area of knowledge is knowledge of how school students learn history. This knowledge is needed to develop a subject pedagogy that attends to the dynamic but contested nature of historical knowledge outlined above. Carter and Doyle's original work (1984) placed an emphasis on the social dimensions of the classroom structures; in particular pupil perceptions and attitudes towards subject matter. Work by British researchers as part of the evaluation of the Schools History Project (Shemilt 1980) or Project CHATA (Concepts of History and Teaching Approaches) has contributed greatly to our understanding of how school students learn history.

Within the scope of this chapter I want to examine the influence that socio-cultural factors have on how school students learn history and what impact this might have on task design. Following the socio-cultural perspective is a useful reminder of the importance of the teacher's own learning: of the way in which teachers use cultural tools inscribed with meaning and how these tools are acquired in 'settings of distributed expertise' that include other colleagues but also the young learners themselves (Ellis 2010). In terms of knowledge and phronesis it invites prospective teachers to explore the relationship between theory and method in collaboration with others but remains mindful of the need to be inclusive if pursuing the 'humanly good' (Gadamer, 1982: 278).

Prospective teachers need spaces in which to explore theory in light of experiences, and such spaces should be offered as part of the school-based mentor meeting. But they also need spaces where the particularities of the situation can be explored. The university-based session allows a sharing of context that hints at the complexities. This is further reinforced by an assignment that looks at a common issue in two different school settings.

In terms of pupil learning and socio-cultural perspectives, a body of research is emerging that alerts teachers to the social and interactive factors that exert a powerful influence on and mould young people's historical thinking. Such factors include the diversity of children's backgrounds especially with regard to racial and ethnic difference (Epstein 1997, Traille 2007) ; and how these intersect with debates about 'vernacular' or community history versus official versions of the past as a primary source of beliefs and thinking (Levstik 1999).

Given the increasingly diverse nature of classrooms, pupil perceptions and the different ways in which diverse communities relate to the subject, pupil perceptions are an important area. Grever, Haydn and Ribbens (2008) highlight a range of differences between young people's ideas about history and those advanced by policy makers. They also suggest that while most young people felt that history was meaningful and relevant to their lives, some discrepancies occurred when comparing school students from indigenous and ethnic minority backgrounds. In a DfES research paper 'Ethnicity and education' (2006) looking at evidence on minority ethnic school students, history was cited as the least favourite subject, behind mathematics, by students from Indian, Pakistani and Black African backgrounds.

Harris and Clarke's (2011) research into prospective teachers' stance towards diversity again highlights teacher biographies and suggests a 'self-perpetuating cycle' where prospective teachers' own commitment to a more diverse and inclusive curriculum is curtailed by their own biographies and school experiences. This might encourage the development of an approach that tended to identify 'traditional' landmark events and topics in English history. Epstein (1997, 2008) has shown how in the United States African-American school students either switch off or construct their own narratives when confronted with a dominant discourse that does little to include them.

The solution is not simply to alight on content that seems to give a better balance and representation. History is more than the study of our projected ideal selves. Samuel (1998: 222) highlights that 'it can also be a means of undoing and questioning, offering more disturbing accounts of who we are and where we come from than simple identification would suggest'. Real learning might also involve transformation. Kay Traille's (2007) work looking at African Caribbean students' experience of the topic of slavery being taught in school is cautionary. She highlights how in some cases the teaching of slavery could lead to imposed identities that often reflect negative value judgments; a degree of stereotyping and insensitivity with teachers' own attitudes or ignorance leading to carelessness and significant silences partly where the teacher wanted to avoid potential conflict.

What Traille's work also highlights is the need for teachers to be alert to the preconceptions that school students bring into the classroom. She reminds us that school students' own emotional and affective maturation can have an impact on the nature of their engagement with the topic.

> First and foremost, evidence from this study indicates that educators may need greater awareness of the ideas and prior conceptions that students of African-Caribbean descent bring to the history classroom. These include cognitive and emotional conceptions about what these students think history is for. A better understanding of the informal versions of history that students may bring to the classroom will enable us to improve the tailoring of the formal curriculum that we have to offer. Second, there is the need to put more effort into getting children of African-Caribbean descent to see the importance of the discipline in answering their questions. We need to work towards improving the ability of students of African-Caribbean descent to engage in analytical thought processes about formal and informal history learning, to evaluate all versions of the past critically and comfortably.
>
> (Traille 2007: 33–34)

Traille calls for an embrace of disciplinary history with recognition of history's emotional and affective power: a need for sensitivity but also cognitive engagement. The design of the task needs to take account of these dual elements, to help school students to acquire tools that enable them to challenge their own preconceptions, a form of mediated action (Wertsch 1994). As Carter and Doyle (1984) suggest, teachers need to relay the meaning and purpose of the work and in emphasising the social dimension of the task the teacher needs to show an awareness of the social competences needed. Direction can come from how the teacher conveys their own understanding of the nature of history. And a carefully worded and planted enquiry question can capture the interest of the learner whilst highlighting a particular aspect of historical thinking (Riley 2008).

Beyond that, particularly in relation to a sensitive topic like slavery, it helps if the question enables the students to see the relational aspects. Sometimes referred to as the 'big picture'(Corfield 2009); school students are encouraged to see that slavery has a longer history then simply the transatlantic slave trade, from Romans to the present day, highlighting the shifting nature of slavery; which might also allow pupil thinking about multiple and shifting selves. It should give some background context to societies, such as those in West Africa, prior to the advent of the transatlantic slave trade. Just as when teaching the Holocaust, some idea of pre-1930s Jewish life and a longer history of anti-Semitism, will enable school students to see the complexity of the issue deterring thinking that simplifies the issue into binaries of good and evil. The enquiry also needs to be attentive to the particularities of the topic, in the case of the transatlantic slave trade its scale, how it helps in understanding modern industrial Britain and the way in which it resonates in the students' contemporary lives from the fabric of the towns they live in to the ways in which race is conceptualised. This kind of connection is enabling, it encourages school students into mediated action, to act on the topic and construct their own understandings. Edwards (2010) describes this process of encoding, following Vygotsky, as involving connecting the everyday understanding of the learner to the established understanding of the experts.

The problem is the sheer enormity of the task, the associated levels of risk, ambiguity and the relationship between the major and minor tasks; in the case of history the relationship between the overarching enquiry question and the learning activities. Andrew Wrenn (2001) explores this in the context of planning teaching on the transatlantic slave trade. His approach is to embed the enquiry around a key individual, Olaudah Equiano. This approach can serve to concretise some of the more abstract ideas. Wrenn's overarching question is provocative 'Olaudah Equiano – African hero?' but allows a range of outcomes to be constructed. Using Equiano's own writing, he gives the slave agency but in getting school students to reflect on the status of Equiano's account he invites school students to think about the nature of historical evidence and interpretations while the question allows a discussion of historical significance and identity.

The concept of historical significance is useful in getting students to work at the intersection of the work of professional historians and manifestations of collective memory. It can enable school students to engage with history, by seeing the resonance of the debate in their contemporary world. With Equiano, Wrenn considered asking, during preparations for the Millennium celebrations and opening of the Millennium Dome[1], Why was Equiano (originally) chosen as a statue for the faith zone in the Millennium Dome? One could play, or wrestle with similar questions related to public debates. Why did the newspaper, the *Daily Telegraph* see the inclusion of Equiano in the national curriculum as 'a betrayal'?[2] More recently with regard to the commemorations of the abolition of the slave trade in March 2007 we could ask: 'Who is more significant, Equiano or Wilberforce?'

Students' historical knowledge is derived from contexts outside of classrooms (Epstein 1997, 2008; Levstik 2008; Barton, McCully and Conway 2003) from their homes, communities and the mass media. Students bring these narratives into the classroom and as such their understandings about topics like slavery are drawn from a range of circumstances including wider public discourses. In designing tasks for the classroom we should seek to tackle these preconceptions head on, both for the possibilities they offer in terms of engagement but also because of the opportunities they present to transform school students' learning. Situating the learning in a meaningful enquiry embedded in the nature of history as a discipline allows school students to examine their own narratives. Morgan's (2010) research into Holocaust education highlights the possibilities of this approach.

> By encouraging the students to behave more like real historians, engaging with the enormous diversity and complexity of this subject and the very difficult questions it raises, I have enabled them to participate in the continued challenge of shaping and testing new narratives...students are likely to have deeper and more valuable understandings about the human condition, about society and about the world around them if their reflections take account of the complexity of the past. Indeed, if students are able to properly contextualise a study of the Holocaust within secure knowledge and understanding of the events of that time they are likely to be better able to relate the Holocaust in meaningful ways to discussions about other genocides and on-going crimes against humanity.
>
> *(Morgan 2010: 30)*

Sensitive topics, such as the Holocaust and slavery, demand a consideration of the affective needs of school students. We have to move beyond technical or rational knowledge to open up a reflective conversation with the situation. The teacher needs an ability to be empathetic, to imagine how the learner might engage with and interpret the task is to think phronetically. This applies not only in the setting up of the task with an enquiry question. It is true also when the learning commences. The task needs to be structured to take account of the changing needs of the learners. Edwards (2010) highlights how the learning process is one of internalisation and externalisation. If school students are to acquire cultural tools and act upon them, in the case of history the tools of historical analysis, they need tasks that invite them to apply those tools to real historical problems.

It is a negotiation that the teacher needs to make. They can draw on technical and epistemological knowledge but they need to reconcile this to the particulars of the situation: their own biographies and preconceptions and to those of their school students.

## Conclusion: phronesis and the hermeneutic turn

I am advocating an approach that stresses the importance of the context of children's learning, both within and outside school, and of the disciplinary tradition with history. This approach requires a degree of circularity in teacher thinking, as the contexts shift both in terms of different school settings but also in terms of shifting public debates. This hermeneutic turn places an importance on an understanding of context, of situatedness that emerges through dialogue with school students and other professionals, across settings but also with literature. Space for dialogue is critical to the development of teachers and task design when teachers have to negotiate between epistemic knowledge about the subject and the more protean knowledge about school students to fashion this into classroom practice.

The analogy of the cabinet maker (Gadamer 1982, Heidegger 1992) alerts us to the risk of an overdependence on the techne or craft. The 'habituated familiarity' of the maker's craft, their decision determined by their techne with no allowance for context or circumstances. For the history teacher, at any stage of their career, habits might inhibit development so that they are not able to attend to exigent circumstances while routines support their actions.

The place for phronesis in the development of history teachers' task design begins with Byrom and Riley's idea of wrestling with the enquiry question. But it also follows Schön's ideas of the 'reflective practitioner' (1983) to explore its deeper meanings particularly when thinking about reflection both in action and on action. A hermeneutic conceptualisation of task design in history stresses the role of interpretation. It emphasises the place of context but also of openness. The task should allow for some elements of co-construction or Dewey's notion of operating as co-inquirers, thus allowing potential for students and teachers to be surprised. It suggests a teacher who is alert and attuned to the learner but also open to difference and change. Higgins (2010) combines Dewey's theory of vocation, which involves learning through one's work, with Gadamer's philosophy of the question to highlight a key dimension of phronesis, being receptive to the newness in new situations. Dewey's emphasis on vocation draws on techne but also returns task design to questions of what is right or good. Gadamer's focus on the open question has a direct application to the enquiry approach that I have been advocating. The question must therefore be open and retain an element of uncertainty. In addition it should have an object of enquiry, a real purpose, as well as content. A question like 'What are the causes of the First World War?' loses its power if it cannot be given a questioner, a person behind it who has a genuine desire to understand.

In introducing the enquiry question the teacher needs to highlight the provisionality of possible answers and their own interest in exploring the question. This might be done by situating the question and school students' responses to it within a wider public discourse. School students thereby also get a sense of what is at stake, the different debates (the provisionality) and their place within those debates, enabling encoding by connecting different forms of knowledge.

Teachers need to reflect on the social contexts in which knowledge is embedded, having some sense of the relationship between education, schools and social inequality. Reflection means having spaces and groups within which appropriate kinds of dialogue can happen. Reflection can be so much more if it attends to the enactive and felt experience of teaching, attending to theory through a connection to our feelings. Phronetic knowledge emerges out of the particulars of a situation, while episteme is concerned with eternal principles and techne with the application of these principles. Phronesis offers a situated way of thinking, an embedded engagement, about action that may attend to a wider set of concerns. It encourages the teacher to turn both inwards to explore the universal and the abstract and outwards to consider the particular and the concrete. It offers a negotiation between these two sites of knowing, avoiding reductive binaries. The highlighting of the 'common good' is both ethical and practical as a way of informing decisions about tasks and reconciling some of the inherent tensions thrown up by simple binaries.

## References

Arthur, J., Davies, I., Kerr, D. and Wrenn, A. (2001) *Citizenship Through Secondary History*. London and New York: Routledge.

Barton, K. C., McCully, A. W., and Conway, M. (2003) History education and national identity in Northern Ireland. *International Journal of Historical Learning, Teaching and Research*, 3.

Byrom, J. and Riley, M. (2003) Professional wrestling in the history department: a case study in planning the teaching of the British Empire at Key Stage 3. *Teaching History* 112: 6–19.

Beck, J. (2013). Powerful knowledge, esoteric knowledge, curriculum knowledge. *Cambridge Journal of Education*, (43)2: 177–93.

Carter, K. and Doyle, W. (1984). Academic tasks in classrooms. *Curriculum Inquiry*, 14: 129–49.

Claxton, G. (1990). *Teaching to Learn a Direction for Education*. London: Cassell.

Claxton, G. (1993) Minitheories: a preliminary model for learning science, in P. J. Black and A. M. Lucas (eds) *Children's Informal Ideas in Science*. London: Routledge.

Corfield, P. (2009) 'Teaching history's big pictures: including continuity as well as change.' *Teaching History*, 136: 53–9.

Counsell, C. (2011) Disciplinary knowledge for all, the secondary history curriculum and history teachers' achievement. *The Curriculum Journal*, (22)2: 201–25.

DfES (2006) Ethnicity and education: the evidence on minority ethnic pupils aged 5–16. Retrieved from http://dera.ioe.ac.uk/6306/1/0208-2006dom-en.pdf

Edwards, A. (2010) How can Vygotsky and his legacy help us to understand develop and teacher education? In V. Ellis, A. Edwards and P. Smagorinsky (eds) *Cultural-historical Perspectives on Teacher Education and Development*. London and New York: Routledge.

Ellis, V. (2010) Studying the process of change: the double stimulation strategy in teacher education research. In V. Ellis, A. Edwards and P. Smagorinsky (eds) *Cultural-historical Perspectives on Teacher Education and Development*. London and New York: Routledge.

Epstein, T. (1997) Sociocultural approaches to young people's historical understanding. *Social Education*, (61)1: 28–31.

Epstein, T. (2008) *Interpreting National History: Race, identity, and pedagogy in classrooms and communities*. London and New York: Routledge.

Evans, R. (1994) Educational ideologies and the teaching of history, in G. Leinhardt, I. L. Beck and C. Stainton (eds) *Teaching and Learning in History*. New Jersey: Lawrence Erlbaum Associates.

Gadamer, H, G. (1982) *Truth and Method*. Trans. G. Barden and J. Cumming. New York: Crossroad.

Grever, M., Haydn, T. and Ribbens, K. (2008) Identity and school history: the perspective of young people from the Netherlands and England. *British Journal of Education Studies*, (56)1: 76–94.

Gudmundsdottir, S. and Shulman, L. (1987) Pedagogical content knowledge in social studies. *Scandinavian Journal of Educational Research*, 31: 59–70.

Hall, C. (2012) *MaCauley and Son: Architects of imperial Britain*. New Haven: Yale University Press.

Harris, R. and Clarke, G. (2011) Embracing diversity in the history curriculum: a study of the challenges facing trainee teachers, *Cambridge Journal of Education*, (41)2: 159–75.

Hattie, J. (2012) *Visible Learning for Teachers: Maximising impact on learning*. London and New York: Routledge.

Heidegger, M. (1992) What calls for thinking? In *Basic Writings*. New York: Harper.

Higgins, C. (2010) The good life of teaching: an ethics of professional practice. *Journal of Philosophy of Education*, (44)2–3: 189–478.

Hirsch, E. D. (1987) *Cultural Literacy: What every American needs to know*. Boston: Houghton Mifflin.

Jordanova, L. (2006) *History in Practice*. London: Hodder.

Levisohn, J. A. (2010) Negotiating historical narratives: an epistemology of history for history education. *Journal of Philosophy of Education*, (44)1: 1–21.

Levstik, L. (1999) 'The well at the bottom of the world: Positionality and New Zealand (Aotearoa) adolescents' conception of historical significance.' Paper presented at the annual meeting of the American Research Association, Montreal, Canada

Levstik, L. (2008) Articulating the silences: teachers' and adolescents' conception of historical significance, in L. Levstik and K. Barton (eds) *Researching History Education Theory, Method and Context*. London and New York: Routledge.

Morgan, P. (2010) How can we deepen and broaden post-16 students' historical engagement with the Holocaust? *Teaching History* 141: 27–33.

Oancea, A. and Furlong, J. (2007) Expressions of excellence and the assessment of applied and practice-based research. *Research Papers in Education*, (22)2: 119–37.

Ofsted (2007) History in the balance: history in English schools 2003–7. London: Ofsted.

Ofsted (2011) *History for All*. Retrieved from www.ofsted.gov.uk/resources/history-for-all

Pendry, A. Husbands, C. Arthur, J. and Davison, J. (1998) *History Teachers in the Making, Professional Learning*. Buckingham: Open University Press.

Pendry, A. Kitson, A. and Husbands, C. (2003) *Understanding History Teaching*. Maidenhead: Open University Press.

Samuel, R. (1994) *Theatres of Memory*, Vol I. Verso.

Samuel, R. (1998) *Islands Stories*, Vol II. Verso.

Schama, S. (2013) Transcript of Hay Festival speech. Retrieved August 24 2013 http://historyworks.tv/news/2013/05/31/history_curriculum_debate_updates_new_bbc_r3_night/

Schön, D. A. (1983) *The Reflective Practitioner: How professionals think in action*. London: Maurice Temple Smith.

Shemilt, D. (1980) *History 13–16 Evaluation Study*. Edinburgh: Holmes McDougall.

Shulman, L. S. (1986) Those who understand: knowledge growth in teaching. *Educational Researcher*, (15)2: 4–14.

Smagorinsky, P. (2010). A Vygotskian analysis of the construction of setting in learning to teach, in V. Ellis, A. Edwards, and P. Smagorinsky (eds) *Cultural-historical Perspectives on Teacher Education and Development*. London and New York: Routledge.

Taylor, T. and Guyver, R. (2012) *History Wars and the Classroom: Global perspectives*. Charlotte, NC: Information Age Publishing.

Traille, E. K. A. (2007) 'You should be proud about your history. they made me feel ashamed': teaching history hurts. *Teaching History* 127, 31–7.

Wertsch, J. (1994) Struggling with the past: some dynamics of historical representation, in M. Carretero and J. F. Voss (eds) *Cognitive and Instructional Processes in History and the Social Sciences*. Marwah, NJ: Lawrence Erlbaum Associates.

White, J. (2012). An unstable framework: critical perspectives on the framework for the National Curriculum. Retrieved July 7 2012. Available online at: www.newvisionsforeducation. org.uk/2012/04/05/an-unstable-framework

Wilson, S. M. (1990) A conflict of interests: The case of Mark Black. *Educational Evaluation and Policy Analysis,* (12)3: 293–310.

Wineburg, S. (2001) *Historical Thinking and Other Unatural Acts: Charting the future of teaching the past.* Philadelphia: Temple University Press.

Wineburg, S. and Wilson, S (1991) Models of wisdom in the teaching of history. *The History Teacher,* (24)4: 395–412.

Wrenn, A. (2001) Slave, subject and citizen, in J. Arthur *et al.* (eds) *Citizenship through Secondary History.* London: Routledge.

Young, M. F. D. (2008). *Bringing Knowledge Back In: From social constructivism to social realism in the sociology of education.* London: Routledge.

Young, M. (2013) Powerful knowledge: an analytically useful concept or just a 'sexy sounding term'? A response to John Beck's 'Powerful knowledge, esoteric knowledge, curriculum knowledge. *Cambridge Journal of Education*, (43)2: 195–8.

## Notes

1 The Millennium Dome, in London, was originally built to house the 'Millennium Experience', a major exhibition celebrating the beginning of the third millennium that included an area called the Faith Zone.
2 See 'The "Betrayal" of Britain's History', *Daily Telegraph*, September 19, 1995; 'Heroic Virtues' and 'History Fit for (Politically Correct) Heroes', *Sunday Telegraph*, September 24, 1995.

# 10
# INSIDERS AND OUTSIDERS

Task design in learning about religions

*Nigel Fancourt*

### Learning about different religions

Over recent decades, many countries have come to recognise that pupils should have an impartial understanding of different religions and world views. This includes countries that have traditionally had close relationships between the state and religious organisations, such as England or Germany (Jackson *et al.* 2007), as well as those which have traditionally separated religion and the state, such as France (Willaime 2007) or America (Moore 2007). International organisations have also recognised the importance of such study, often in order to encourage increasingly diverse groups within society to live together harmoniously (Keast 2007; OSCE 2007). Supra-national human rights frameworks, through international courts, have also had a major impact. States are expected to juggle the pupils' right to freedom of and from religion with their parents' rights to these freedoms, and the pupils' right to an education (Hunter-Henin 2011; Jawoniyi 2012).

The wider political, cultural and historical relations between governments, religious organisations and educational systems mean that the study of religions is located within and across different subjects in the curriculum (Davis and Miroshnikova 2012; Fancourt 2013). In countries with a strong tradition of collaboration in education between religious organisations and the state, it most naturally falls within 'religious education', as in England, Germany or Holland; nevertheless, in these countries, its introduction is not straightforward or uncontested, as it may replace or merge with existing forms of religious nurture (Riegel and Ziebertz 2009). Sometimes a new name is used to denote this change, for instance the term 'Religion Education' in post-apartheid South Africa (Chidester 2003). It may only include religions, or also extend to secular world views, as in England (Watson, J. 2010). In countries with strong lines of demarcation between religious organisations and the state, and no recognised place for religious education, it falls in other subject areas. It may lie within citizenship, cultural or social studies, as in Singapore (Sim 2008) and the USA (Moore 2007; American Academy of Religion 2010). In France, which institutionalised the separation of church and state in the principle of *laïcité*, it has been particularly developed within history, as 'the teaching of facts about religion' (Debray 2002). In China, it falls within geography (Nanbu 2008). It inevitably pervades some cross-curricular issues, notably multicultural, human rights and intercultural education (Banks 2009), for instance in Norway (Leganger-Krogstad 2011) and Australia (Australian Curriculum and Assessment Reporting Authority 2013).

This chapter is not directly concerned with justifying the study of religions, whether as religious education or elsewhere. Instead, it starts from a practical classroom problem: how do pupils grasp beliefs that are not their own? This is applicable wherever it is located in the curriculum. Nevertheless this chapter assumes that it is important that pupils comprehend discrete religious beliefs or world views, and do not mix or confuse them. This is both because the accurate representation of an individual religion's framework of beliefs is of value *per se*, and also because, more instrumentally, harmonious living together will not be achieved if pupils merely gain a stereotypical, idealistic or erroneous image of religions, which does not match the realities of religious difference (Jackson *et al.* 2010). Genuine inter-religious understanding is neither served by eliding differences between religions nor by air-brushing out difficult issues in any of them. Accordingly, in this chapter, the term 'religion' is generally used to refer to particular religions, and not to a wider all-encompassing notion of all religions together (see Jackson 1997), though others may disagree with this approach. Further, non-religious world views are not excluded; it is simply less clumsy than constantly using a phrase such as 'religions and world views education'.

## Insiders and outsiders

The contemporary need to study a variety of religions has epistemological implications about the nature and status of knowledge for states both with and without a tradition of confessional religious education (Gearon 2013). Previously, in many countries, pupils were assumed to be of one religion and the purpose of religious education was familiarisation with its beliefs and practices, which were broadly considered to be true. Clearly, study within one religion could involve consideration of possible different internal perspectives, but nevertheless the broad conceptual, ethical and devotional framework was considered part of a shared tradition. By contrast, teaching about a range of religions must recognise that most of these beliefs and values are not those of the pupils themselves; thus, agnostic or Muslim pupils could be asked to understand the Hindu concept of *dharma*.

There is therefore an important distinction between insiders and outsiders, which Jackson (1997; 2004) developed explicitly. He argued that it is analogous to an ethnographer who as an outsider lives with and comes to understand the lives of the insiders, and then extends this to set out an 'interpretive' approach to religious education, modelled on social sciences. He particularly draws on Geertz's (1983) distinction between 'experience-near' concepts, meaning within the tradition, and 'experience-distant' concepts, those of people outside it, particularly 'concepts fashioned to capture the general features of social life' (Jackson 1997: 35). It is also important to distinguish between the three levels of the religion rather than assume that all think the same way or value the same aspects of their religious identity. These are: the religious tradition overall; the particular branch or movement; individual. Jackson's approach has been recognised widely as significant, underpinning much research and pedagogy (Weisse 2007; Miller, O'Grady and McKenna 2013), though he has also been criticised for relying on a secular, therefore potentially biased, social scientific model (see Wright 2004; Gearon 2013). This process can be shown diagrammatically (Figure 10.1).

This pedagogical distinction is paralleled in religious thought. The separation of insiders and outsiders is important within many religions, which demarcate the boundary between those who have accepted its claims and those who have not, particularly in terms of judgement and the afterlife. The uniqueness of any particular religion's claims is important for insiders, but the extent to which outsiders are excluded may vary both between and within religions. An exclusivist position often considers that particular beliefs have a soteriological dynamic: these beliefs are not simply true but their acceptance, and/or an individual's actions on the basis of them, affects what happens to that individual after death. This however is arguably a stronger feature of some religions. Hinduism is often seen as more inclusivist in recognising other beliefs (Sharma 2010), though most religions contain elements of both exclusivism and inclusivism (Gorsky 2004; Moser 2010; Kiblinger 2003). Further, the boundaries between particular denominations or branches within religions can be solid too; indeed intra-religious divisions can often be more conflicted than inter-religious ones. A further complication is that the separation between religions is not always clear-cut, particularly given the fluidity of membership of an established religion, what Davie (1994) termed 'believing without belonging', or the blurred boundaries between some Asian religions, such as Hinduism and Sikhism (Geaves 2005). Overall however, the truth of the particular claims often matters to those who hold them, and thus the pedagogical distinction takes seriously the self-understanding of many religious adherents.

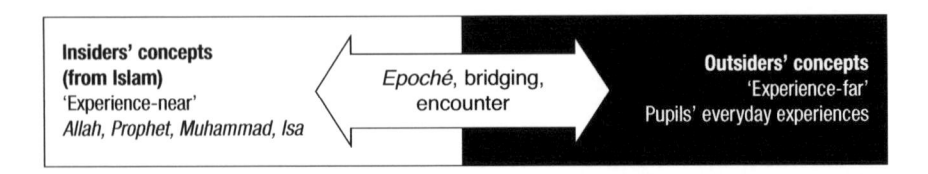

**Insiders' concepts (from Islam)** 'Experience-near' Allah, Prophet, Muhammad, Isa ⟵ *Epoché*, bridging, encounter ⟶ **Outsiders' concepts** 'Experience-far' Pupils' everyday experiences

**Figure 10.1** Insiders and outsiders in religious education

Clearly, pupils are not asked to accept these concepts as true, but instead they are asked to consider how these concepts allow others to make sense of their experiences and lives: pupils do not have to accept that Jesus died for humanity's sins, but that Christians believe that Jesus died for humanity's sins. Religious education researchers tried to develop pedagogical strategies for enabling pupils to grasp these other frameworks. The phenomenological notion of empathy has been significant here; for instance one English pedagogical model claimed that religious education 'uses the tools of scholarship in order to enter into an empathetic experience of the faith of individuals and groups' (Schools Council 1971: 21; see recently Lovat 2012). This approach suggested that pupils should suspend their own views in order to enter into the thoughts of others: 'it provides a more formal framework for what is put more concretely in a native American proverb: 'Never judge a man until you have walked a mile in his moccasins' (Smart 1986: 258), so pupils had to 'set [their own view] as it were "out of action" [to] "disconnect it", "bracket it"' in the process of *epoché*' (Husserl 1931: 108).

However, this approach has been critiqued. One criticism is that it merely gave pupils an imaginary insight into different religions, but did not enable them to tackle underlying epistemological or existential issues, notably the truth claims, precisely because it suspended the pupils' ability to make judgements on what they studied (for example Wright 2004). A related issue was that the phenomenological approach, particularly as developed in English religious education, placed too much emphasis on the experiential aspects of religions as opposed to 'doctrinal/confessional schemes' (Barnes 2001: 455; see also the debate between Barnes (2006, 2007, 2009), and O'Grady (2005, 2009). A third issue was the extent to which one could genuinely enter into another person's perspective: could agnostic pupils really put themselves into the position of a Vaishnite *dalit*? This epistemological issue of how pupils understand religions fully, such as whether a specific type of knowledge is required, is discussed by Walshe and Teece (2013).

Further the issue was blurred by the fact that empathy has two slightly different senses, one cognitive, a form of perspective-taking, and the second emotional, akin to concern or sympathy. For instance, one English policy document defined it as including:

- the ability to consider the thoughts, feelings, experiences, attitudes, beliefs and values of others
- developing the power of imagination to identify feelings such as love, wonder, forgiveness and sorrow
- the ability to see the world through the eyes of others, and to see issues from their point of view.

*(School Curriculum and Assessment Authority 1994: 5)*

The first is cognitive, the second is emotional, and the last combines them. This has meant that some critics assume that empathy always combines these elements (see Erricker 2010), rather than separating them out. Overall, while the term is not unproblematic, the focus here is on the pupils' development of an accurate understanding of the conceptual framework of any religion, and the most appropriate intellectual processes to achieve this. The terms bridging or encounter have also been used.

The value is in recognising both the significant differences between different positions, especially how pupils from one religious perspective may struggle when asked to understand another, and the need to enter into this different perspective in a reasonably unbiased way. Indeed, other subjects also require pupils to apprehend alternative conceptual frameworks. In history, pupils may be asked to understand the perspectives of people in the past – historical empathy (Barton and Levstik 2004; Endacott 2010). A difference however is that the synchronic nature of contemporary religions means that these 'others' are not separated off, closed in a distant time, but can speak and respond for themselves. This makes historical empathy less troubling, as there is clearly no intention to convert pupils to *being* Victorian or medieval. Pupils can engage with these perspectives, but this does not alter their identity. Further, no pupils will actually be Victorians, so there is no risk of causing anxiety by misrepresenting their own perspectives to them; thus it does not matter in quite the same way if pupils have a false understanding of a historical world view. There are also similarities with modern languages where pupils must grasp a different vocabulary and grammar (for example Ellis 2005; Lantolf and Thorne 2006). Pupils have to understand this other structure, appropriating for themselves, yet they do not thereby 'become' French or Spanish. Here the foreign words often apply to familiar concepts, and the nuances of translation only arise at a more sophisticated level, whereas in religious education the concepts themselves may be alien. There is neither space to develop these similarities further nor to consider the debates within each subject, but evidently there are wider curriculum parallels to be made.

Having undertaken the process of apprehending insiders' concepts, pupils may be asked to develop their conceptual understanding in four different ways. First, they would be asked to connect new concepts with other concepts within the same conceptual framework, for instance *dharma* with *bhakti* and *moksha,* or Allah with the Qur'an or Muhammad, what Smart (1986) called the 'web of ideas' (p. 258). It is vital to understand how the different concepts inter-relate for insiders, within that tradition. Jackson (1997) describes this as 'coming to an understanding of this pattern of conceptual inter-relationship or cultural "grammar"' (p. 35) echoing a linguistic analogy (see also Barnes 2001). Second, pupils may also be asked to relate concepts across different religions, between different groups of insiders: Hindu *dharma* and Buddhist *dhamma,* or Muhammad and Christ. This might be in order to make comparisons between these different conceptual systems: different concepts of God, for instance. Third, they may be asked to link insiders' claims to outsiders' concepts for the study of religion, for instance, *amrit sanskar* to the concept of 'rite of passage'. Jackson draws on Geertz to suggest that pupils would have to 'grasp concepts that are for another people "experience-near" well enough to place them "…in illuminating connection with experience-distance concepts"'

(Jackson 1997: 35, citing Geertz 1983: 58). Lastly, pupils may be asked to evaluate and reflect on the insiders' concepts, including considering how this affects their own views, in a broadly hermeneutical approach, termed 'reflexivity' and 'edification' by Jackson (1997: 133–4) but often labelled 'learning from religion' (Grimmitt 1987; QCA 2004): what do pupils think of the beliefs studied? How do they compare with their own beliefs? Such a process is neither a form of socialisation into nor transmission of shared religious beliefs and values. Pupils are to develop an understanding of concepts which do not necessarily match with their own and reflect on this process. The focus here is not on this secondary process, but on its value in achieving the former.

## Conceptual development and learning about religions

How can this process of empathy or bridging between insiders and outsiders be understood as a process of conceptual development? While there has been some careful attention to learning about religious concepts in religious education, in Cooling's (1994) 'concept-cracking' approach (focused on Christianity) and more recently in Erricker's (2010) 'conceptual and inter-disciplinary approach', very little attention has been paid to general pedagogical theories when considering pupils' learning about different religions. A systematic search revealed only a handful of references to the sustained use of theories of *conceptual* development. By contrast, there is much research since the 1960s using Piagetian models of intellectual development to analyse pupils' attitudes and religiosity, notably Goldman's work on 'readiness for religion' (1966), and Fowler's (1981) model of faith development. Such studies generally focus on whether and how pupils' broad cognitive development occurs (for example Van der Zee *et al.* 2008; Robbins and Francis 2010), rather than on classroom pedagogy. Put more provocatively, few 'pedagogies' of religion education (see Grimmitt 2000) pay much attention to wider pedagogical thought.

One of the most significant theories of pupils' conceptual development stems from the Russian psychologist, Lev Vygotsky and his work underpins much research on pedagogy across the curriculum, for instance, English (Thompson 2012), or mathematics (A. Watson 2010). He said nothing about religious education, which is unsurprising given the context of militant atheism in early Soviet Russia. Vygotsky himself had a Marxian perspective, though was not a doctrinaire Marxist (Blanck 1990; Kozulin 1997). He grew up as a Hebrew and Yiddish speaking, non-observant Jew in Imperial Russia, in an age of pogroms and Slavophilia, and in his early years was interested in issues of Jewish culture and history, contributing to Jewish journals (Blank 1990; Van de Veer 2007). Some argue that aspects of his psychology, notably the interplay between self and society, have religious roots, in the Russian Orthodox notion of 'conciliarity' (Lynch 2001) and the Rabbinic tradition of the dialogical self (Sampson 2000); he was indebted to the radical Jewish philosopher, Spinoza (Derry 2004). He often worked within ethnically diverse classrooms – a multiculturalist before his time (Kozulin 2003); his research with Luria on ethnic minorities within Soviet Central Asia was pivotal to later cultural-historical theory (Luria 1976). This focus on ethnic minorities has continued, for instance, Kozulin's (1997) work with immigrant Ethiopian Jews in Israel, and Hedegaard's (1999) study of Turkish immigrants in Denmark. Unfortunately, religion is often submerged within culture; thus Hedegaard simply identifies pupils as Turkish, though the examples she gives are impliedly Sunni Muslim. Overall, despite its roots in Soviet Russia, cultural-historical theory is potentially sympathetic rather than hostile towards religiosity issues.

Vygotsky's work and legacy has already been used by some writers on religious education, in three ways. In confessional religious education, Court (2009) has considered how a Vygotskian approach to conceptual development could sit alongside moral and spiritual development, and Rymarz (2013) uses it to justify 'direct instruction' of theological issues. More generally, Afdal (2010) has analysed the interrelationship between research and practice in religious education as two inter-acting activity systems, though he does not focus on classroom pedagogy. Various researchers use cultural-historical perspectives to analyse classroom data, for example Eke *et al.* (2005), Stern (2010) and Haakedal (2012). The learning of different religions' concepts can be more explicitly developed through a Vygotskian lens, drawing on some of these existing socio-cultural insights.

A basic question is how students acquire new concepts at all. Vygotsky's seminal work, *Thought and Language* (1986), was based on the distinction between spontaneous or everyday concepts and scientific concepts. The first were acquired and developed through the ordinary processes of socialisation, and are 'strongly based in the individual experiential history of the learner' (Moll and Greenberg 1990: 253). By contrast, 'scientific', also translated as 'generic', concepts were learnt in formal educational settings because pupils had to learn to grasp their 'generalizational structure' (p. 200). Vygotsky's point is not epistemological, as if only science were knowledge; these concepts 'do not necessarily relate to scientific issues – they may represent historical, linguistic or practical knowledge – but their organisation is "scientific"' (Kozulin 1990: 168). Significantly, the development of 'scientific' concepts is more mature than that of spontaneous ones because 'they benefit from the systematicity of instruction and cooperation' (Vygostsky 1986: 148). However, fully mature thinking only emerged when the two types of concepts flowed together: the everyday concepts work their 'slow way upward' toward scientific concepts, and the scientific concepts 'grow downward' (p. 194). Vygotsky emphasises that pupils have to learn the conceptual system of generic, non-everyday concepts formally, but full intellectual development is only complete when they appropriate them for themselves, as shown in Figure 10.2. His central point was that pupils did not move sequentially from one intellectual stage to the next; instead, they were able to grasp these generic systems through educational settings, and it was the teacher's role to support their learning, within the 'zone of proximal development' (Vygotsky 1986; Bozhovitch 2009).

From this one can suppose that pupils could also formally learn different systems of religious concepts. On one level, learning a different religion's concepts is the same as learning any new set of generic concepts. Nevertheless, this is likely to be

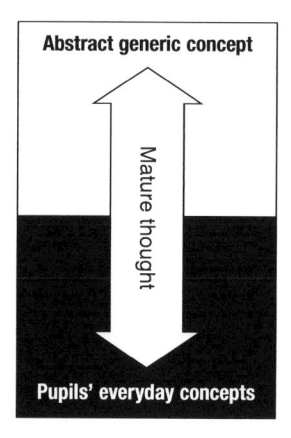

**Figure 10.2** Vygotskian model of concept formation

more challenging as there may be less overlap between pupils' everyday concepts and the conceptual system of any particular religion. Vygotsky's example is of everyday terms such as 'table' and 'chair', contrasted with the generic term 'furniture' (Vygotsky 1986: 198), but the generic concept here is still rooted in the pupils' everyday experiences. Clearly, the development of religious concepts *within* a particular tradition may also be culturally situated. For instance in Álvarez and del Río's (1999) analysis of Castilian cultural identity, they include various religious examples in their 'planes of activity', from the situated, marked by 'religious imagery in everyday contexts', to the symbolic, 'Christian and historical narratives', to the instrumentally mediated, including 'oral traditions such as praying in church' (p. 317). There is a strong contextual link between the different concepts and planes of activity. Nevertheless, the distinction between everyday concepts and a particular religious conceptual framework also helps explain why pupils who belong to a particular religion may not necessarily find the study of their own beliefs straightforward, since the conceptual framework may not be a significant part of their own everyday language (Court 2010; Rymarz 2013), or they may be familiar with a different denominational emphasis within it.

Pupils not brought up in a particular religious tradition will not be so intuitively familiar with the beliefs, dispositions and values that underpin its formal expressions, and their everyday language will not be infused with the same conceptual system. For instance, a Hindu pupil might be familiar with devotion to images of Rama, Shiva or Swaminarayan, and thus grasp the devotional importance of a Christian Orthodox icon more quickly than a Jewish child who was not used to seeing, and might have theological objections to, religious images. Thus it would be harder to find a meeting point between everyday concepts and insiders' generic concepts. The usual processes for the development of more abstract thought such as forming 'chain complexes' of related everyday concepts (Vygotsky 1986: 115) and 'pseudoconcepts' (p. 119), which children develop for themselves out of these complexes, would also not be possible.

Further, this kind of learning about different religions reverses the usual relationship between majority and minority conceptual frameworks. The challenge is not that disadvantaged or minority pupils have to access culturally mainstream generic concepts, but rather that all pupils have to access the generic concepts of a specific religious conceptual structure. It is not that the minority must access the majority's generic concepts, but that the majority have to access the minority's generic concepts: for example, all pupils have to learn about Muslim or Hindu perspectives. This lack of overlap between pupils' everyday concepts and generic concepts is reflected in a concern about the issues facing pupils from disadvantaged or minority backgrounds in education, because their classroom experiences do not help them to connect their own understandings with the ideas being presented to them. Hedegaard's work on Turkish immigrants in Denmark considers their dislocation (1999), and Moll and Greenberg's (1990) study of Hispanic pupils in America argues that their own 'funds of knowledge' are ignored by schools in formal learning. The challenge for such students may be that they have to learn another 'minority' framework – though of course they may not find this a challenge.

What does this Vygotskian perspective contribute to the insider/outsider distinction? These issues are shown diagrammatically (Figure 10.3).

This combines the Vygotskian generic or everyday distinction (Figure 10.2) with the insider/outsider distinction (Figure 10.1), and by way of example is applied to learning about Sikhism. The purpose of the diagram is to conceptualise and explore these positions, though inevitably they are somewhat over-dichotomised. What is classed as pupils' everyday language may actually be a reasonably sophisticated level of generalisation and prior learning. Nevertheless, the image is helpful in drawing out some potential patterns. This juxtaposition creates four quadrants. The bottom right corner represents the outsiders' everyday concepts, the 'non-Sikh' in this case, who has to be brought into contact with the top right quadrant, which is a Sikh conceptual framework. The term 'concept' is intended to cover a range of terms for beliefs, values, doctrines and practices, and is not limited to beliefs in a narrow sense. The significant process of conceptual development is that of enabling an outsider pupil to comprehend an insiders' conceptual framework (Line 1). The teacher's role is to facilitate the pupil's ability to use these concepts in ways that reflect their meaning within that religion's conceptual structure. The diagram does not distinguish between different types of outsider, but clearly some outsiders might be closer to particular insiders than others. For instance, monotheistic pupils may find other forms of monotheism simpler to grasp; indeed Copley and Walshe (2002) found that Muslim pupils easily accepted some aspects of Christology, such as the virgin birth, when compared with agnostic or secular pupils, or Hindu or Sikh pupils (p. 33). Line 2 presents the process of enabling an insider's conceptual development, for whom this may be a more fluid process, but which nevertheless requires support (Court 2010; Rymarz 2013). Line 3 represents a conception of religious education as enabling an outsider to become like an equivalent insider – an unstructured empathy –

Task design in learning about religions **179**

|  | **Insiders (e.g. Sikhism)** | **Outsiders** |
|---|---|---|
| Generic concepts | Religious language and ideas, e.g. *Guru, haumai, manmukh, gurmukh*[1] | Philosophical/comparative concepts *Afterlife, ethics, rites of passage* (Other insiders' conceptual frameworks) |
| Everyday concepts | Terms that a Sikh child encounter in everyday contexts *Guru, kesh, gurdwara*[2] | Everyday outsiders' concepts *Family, love, good* (But also *Allah, puja, prayer, Torah*) |

1) Appropriation of insiders' conceptual framework by outsider
2) Appropriation of insiders' conceptual framework by insider
3) Appropriation of everyday insider language by outsider
4) Appropriation of outsiders' conceptual framework by outsider
5) Appropriation of outsiders' conceptual framework by insider
6) Appropriation of insiders' conceptual framework from outsiders' conceptual framework

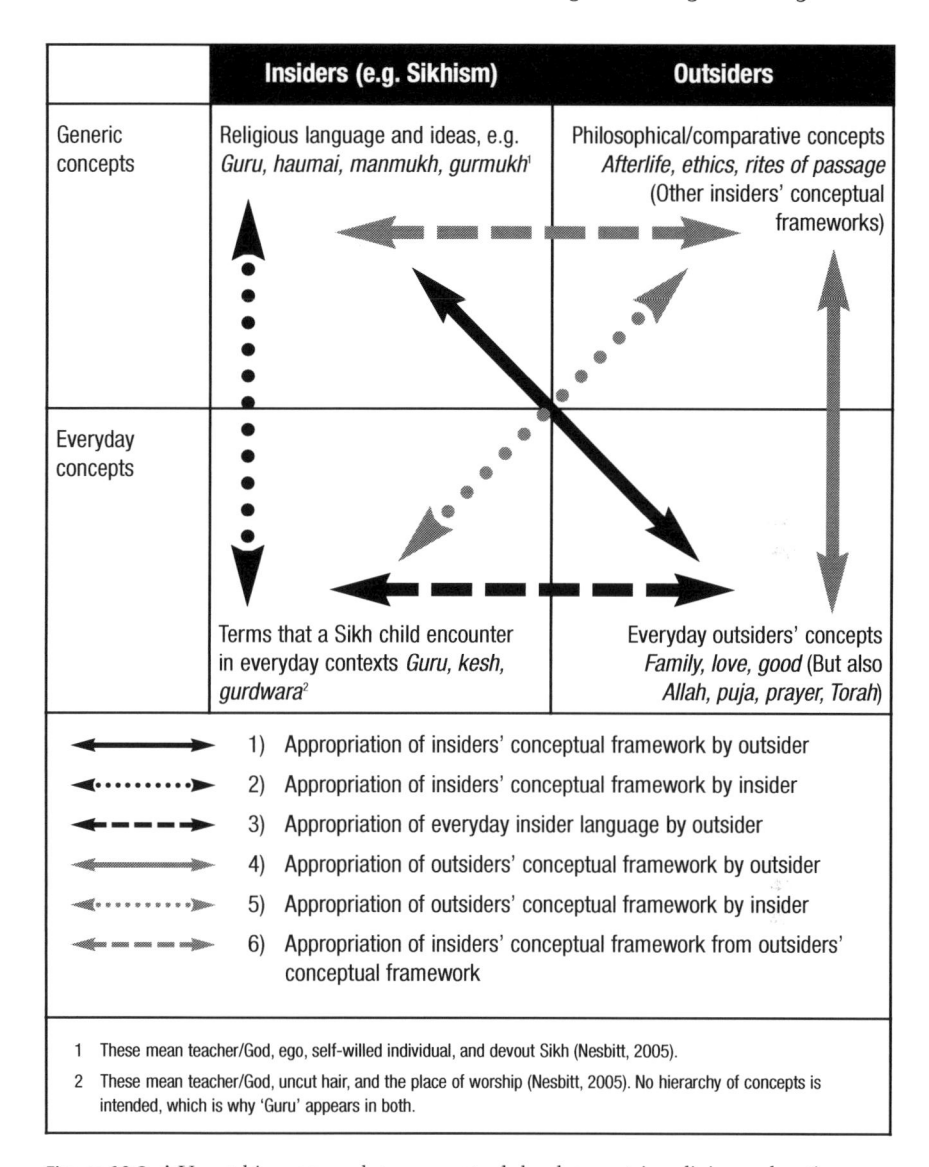

1 These mean teacher/God, ego, self-willed individual, and devout Sikh (Nesbitt, 2005).
2 These mean teacher/God, uncut hair, and the place of worship (Nesbitt, 2005). No hierarchy of concepts is intended, which is why 'Guru' appears in both.

**Figure 10.3** A Vygotskian approach to conceptual development in religious education

without any attempt to grasp insiders' wider conceptual framework; this quadrant can be seen as the target of Barnes' (2001) and Wright's (2004) critiques.

One approach is to use an external conceptual framework as a way of classifying and analysing religious concepts (Line 4). This can apply at the level of task design in a lesson: pupils might be introduced or asked to reflect on a non-specific equivalent to the specifically religious concept, such as selfishness, before being introduced to the Sikh concept of *manmukh*, or forgiveness before considering the

Islamic notion of Allah's mercy. Moreover, it could be in the sense of learning a non-religious framework for the analysis of religions, such as the language of religious studies, to identify and describe them: festivals, rites of passage or worship. Sometimes naïve versions of the phenomenology of religion appear, in which entire modules are structured around such themes; the study of festivals could include Christmas, Divali, Wesak, and Eid. While these do provide a coherent set of generalisable generic concepts, the problem is that the internally embedded narratives and concepts which underpin each festival are ignored, with a tendency to focus on superficial similarities and differences: festivals of light rather than Christmas as an incarnational, salvific event. However, it could also represent approaches to religious education that shy away from enabling pupils genuinely to grasp the insiders' frameworks, such as some philosophical and ethical dilemma approaches in which pupils simply consider, for example, debates about abortion, without addressing insiders' perspectives thoroughly (Jackson *et al.* 2010). There is also the related process whereby an insider is asked to appropriate outsiders' perspectives of their religion – thus a Sikh has to grasp outsiders' perspectives on Sikhism (Line 5). This process of distanciation can be troubling, and can be handled inappropriately. Ipgrave (1999) shows how Muslim pupils disagreed with their teacher's secular interpretations of Islam (also, Moulin 2011). Overall, this strategy is clearly an important part of a non-confessional approach to the subject, in enabling pupils to develop the wider conceptual tools to analyse the religious concepts for themselves. The issue is getting the balance right in enabling pupils to oscillate between the specificities of each religion and these more generic concepts (Line 6); for example, teachers may want pupils to develop their use of a cluster of Muslim concepts relating to prayer with more general ideas, or ideas from a different religion.

## Concepts, experience and dialogue

This quadrant model overcomes some difficulties in conceptualising such learning solely within either of the two dichotomies. Clearly this is not inculcation of shared generic concepts that flow into pupils' everyday concepts; there is a need to grasp the interior modalities of others' conceptual frameworks. Furthermore, it is not simply about enabling outsiders to grasp insiders' everyday perspectives. Pupils are not asked to be like pupils of a particular religion, as if they were an equivalent believer. Instead, pupils are required to grasp the insiders' generic concepts, across both the vertical and horizontal axes of the diagram (Figure 10.3). More importantly, it highlights the role of the teacher because he or she has to identify, on the conceptual plane, both the specific religious concepts and the non-specifically religious concepts, and, on the plane of pupils' everyday concepts, their starting points in the process of learning, as insider or outsider. Having identified these elements, teachers have to scaffold the learning appropriately.

Moreover, developing this four-fold typology of concepts avoids over-reliance on the notion of experience, which permeates much discussion in religious education, as discussed above. The notion of experience is used in three ways, which can be conflated. First, it refers to the pupils' experience, for instance:

> The ideas involved in Christian beliefs are largely alien to children in the western world because they do not form part of their everyday experience... The skill is to find a way of building a bridge between the world of Christian belief and the world of children's experience.
> 
> *(Cooling 1994: 8)*

This is wise strategy, but pedagogically it is more sensible to conceive of it as a movement from their everyday concepts, rather than the more nebulous idea of pupils' experience. It is simpler to envisage conceptual development as a movement between different types of concept, rather than between experience and concept, as if pupils did not have any prior concepts. The second use of experience is in the notion of 'shared human experience'. For example, Grimmitt (1987) linked religious belief systems to pupils' lives in a model of human development, and accordingly, pupils and religions are seen as both sharing 'Core human values' (p. 256). This approach has the merit of focusing on the inter-relationship between religions and pupils' lives, but shared human experience is used to dissolve the distinction between insiders and outsiders, and indeed between different religions, which may simply be seen as varying manifestations of general existential concerns. Further, this approach downplays the need for a coherent understanding of different religions' conceptual frameworks, replacing it with a sense of the pupils' general development. The third use of experience is in the notion of religious experience. This is discussed above in relation to Barnes' (2001) critique of empathy, and other approaches are based on the principle that all humans have an innate religiosity (Hay 2000), or spirituality (Ota and Erricker 2005), which all religions exemplify. Such approaches have helped develop a wide variety of innovative classroom techniques (Hay 2000), but they are also problematic in dissolving the insider/outsider distinction, and in under-emphasising the value of education as aiding pupils' conceptual development.

Sometimes these different types of experience are elided. For instance, Erricker (2010) incorporates them in his model of conceptual development, suggesting that pupils should work through:

- 'concepts that are within children's own experiences' in kindergarten/foundation
- 'concepts that are common to religious and non-religious experience' in Lower Primary
- 'concepts that are common to many religions' in Upper Primary
- 'concepts that are particular to specific religions' in Lower Secondary.

*(Erricker 2010: 84, emphasis added)*

This model not only conflates pupils' experience, non-religious experience and religious experience, it also assumes an interrelationship between these experiences and different types of concept. Why for instance, are pupils' experiences no longer relevant beyond the first stage? Further, while his model set outs a clearly structured process of moving from pupils' (outsiders') everyday concepts to outsiders' generic concepts, and from there to insiders' concepts, combining Lines 4 and 6 in Figure 10.3, it is unclear why this cannot be conducted each lesson. He also argues that more generalisable concepts are easier to understand than specific ones: thus 'festivals' would be easier to grasp than 'Christmas', but it is hard to see how pupils would grasp the more abstract concepts without examples. While he is right to take conceptual development seriously, he nevertheless draws on a hazy subsidiary pedagogical principle.

Finally, in terms of task design, a Vygotskian approach to conceptual development means focusing on the insiders' concepts for each lesson, how they inter-relate, and considering how they relate to the particular pupils' everyday concepts, so that pupils can develop their own mature thinking. It is worth highlighting some Vygotskian implications about *how* learning should happen in the classroom, though there is not space to develop this fully. One criticism of naïvely focusing on learning about religions is that it has tended towards a narrowly descriptive, and potentially indoctrinatory, model of learning (Eke *et al.* 2005; Stern 2010). However, Vygotsky (1978) was insistent both that pupils had to construct their own knowledge by engaging with the generic concepts through activities, especially through classroom talk, and that the teacher's role was to mediate this learning. Indeed the notion of mediation is central in Vygotskian pedagogy, and his work has underpinned a wide variety of recent studies of effective classroom talk (for example Alexander 2000; Mercer and Littleton 2007; Mercer and Hodgkinson 2008). In this respect, Rymarz's (2013) use of Vygotsky's ideas to combat simplistic versions of constructivism and argue for 'direct instruction' in religious education does not do full justice to the importance of mediation. Research has shown how pupils effectively appropriate these concepts for themselves through discussion (Eke, Lee nad Clough 2005; Ipgrave 2013), and there is also exploration of the value of discussion between pupils of different perspectives in itself, from England (Fancourt 2009) and across Europe (ter Avest, Jozsa, Knauth, Roson and Skeie 2009). Indeed, the insights from much more generic work on classroom talk could provide the basis for a more effective understanding of discussion in religious education. Put another way, to highlight learning about religions is very definitely not to imply a teacher-led didactic approach, but to encourage teachers to consider carefully the internalisation of insiders' concepts through a range of tasks.

In conclusion, this chapter has begun to sketch out how the application of Vygotskian pedagogical principles can shed light on aspects of how pupils learn about different religions. It has shown how it can be combined creatively and coherently with an interpretive approach to the distinction between insider and outsiders. The chapter has presented a coherent model of conceptual learning, which recognises what pupils' may bring to their learning, but also the potential epistemic distance between them and the religions studied. A wide range of other issues have not been fully explored, notably the ways that pupils respond to these ideas for themselves reflexively, or how classroom dialogue can contribute to this process, but there is considerable potential for Vygotskian approaches to contribute to these too. Learning about religions is not something difficult or to be feared, but it does require a methodical approach to pedagogy which draws both on general educational principles as well as the demands of the subject discipline. While the demands for such a skill are often ethical and instrumental, such as open-mindedness in a religiously diverse society, the educational process must be pedagogically sound.

## References

Afdal, G. (2010) *Researching Religious Education As A Social Practice.* Münster: Waxmann.

Alexander, R. 2000. *Culture and Pedagogy: International comparisons in primary education.* Oxford: Blackwell.

Álvarez, A. and del Río, P. (1999) Cultural mind and cultural identity: projects for life in body and spirit. In S. Chaiklin, M. Hedegaard and U. Jensen (eds) *Activity Theory and Social Practice.* Aarhus: Aarhus University Press.

American Academy of Religion. (2010) *Guidelines for Teaching About Religion In K-12 Public Schools in the United States.* Atlanta: American Academy of Religion

Australian Curriculum and Assessment Reporting Authority (2013) *General Capabilities in the Australian Curriculum* [Downloaded from www.acara.edu.au]

Banks, J. (ed.) (2009) *The Routledge International Companion to Multicultural Education.* London: Routledgefalmer.

Barnes, P. (2001) What is wrong with the phenomenological approach to religious education? *Religious Education*, (96)4: 445–61.

Barnes, P. (2006) The misrepresentation of religion in modern British (religious) education. *British Journal of Educational Studies*, (54)4: 395–411,

Barnes, P. (2007) The disputed legacy of Ninian Smart and phenomenological religious education: a critical response to Kevin O'Grady. *British Journal of Religious Education*, (29)2: 157–68.

Barnes, P. (2009) An honest appraisal of phenomenological religious education and a final, honest reply to Kevin O'Grady, *British Journal of Religious Education*, (31)1: 69–72.

Barton, K. and Levstik, L. (2004) *Teaching History for the Common Good.* Marwah: L. Erlbaum Associates.

Blanck, G. (1990) Vygotsky: the man and his cause. In L. Moll (ed.) *Vygotsky and Education*, Cambridge: Cambridge University Press.

Bozhovich, E. (2009) Zone of proximal development. In *Journal of Russian and East European Psychology*, (47)6: 48–69.

Chidester, D. (2003) Religion education in South Africa: teaching and learning about religion, religions and religious diversity. In *British Journal of Religion Education*, (25)4: 261–78.

Cooling, T. (1994) *Concept-cracking: exploring Christian beliefs in school.* Nottingham: Stapleford Centre.

Copley, T. and Walshe, K. (2002) *The Figure of Jesus in Religious Education.* Exeter: University of Exeter Press.

Court, D. (2010) What happens to children's faith in the zone of proximal development, and what can religious educators do about it? In *Religious Education: The official journal of the Religious Education Association*, (105)5: 491–503.

Davie, G. (1994) *Religion in Britain since 1945: Believing without belonging.* Oxford: Blackwell.

Davis, D. and Miroshnikova, E. (eds) (2012) *The Routledge International Handbook of Religious Education.* London and New York: Routledge.

Debray, J. (2002) *L'Enseignement du Fait Religieux Dans l'Ecole Publique: Rapport au ministre de l'Éducation Nationale.* Paris: Odile Jacob.

Derry, J. (2004) The unity of intellect and will: Vygotsky and Spinoza. *Educational Review,* (56)2: 113–20.

Eke, R., Lee, J. and Clough, N. (2005) Whole class interactive teaching and learning in religious education: transcripts from four primary classrooms. *British Journal of Religious Education,* (27)2: 159–72

Ellis, R. ( 2005) Principles of instructed language learning. *System,* 33(2): 209–24.

Endacott, J. (2010) Reconsidering affective engagement in historical empathy. *Theory and Research in Social Education,* (38)1: 6–47.

Erricker, C. (2010) *Religious Education: A conceptual and interdisciplinary approach.* London and New York: Routledge.

Fancourt, N. (2009) The 'safe forum': difference, dialogue and conflict. In J. Ipgrave, R. Jackson and K. O'Grady (eds) *Religious Education Research through a Community of Practice.* Münster: Waxmann.

Fancourt, N. (2013) Religious education across Europe: contexts in policy scholarship. In G. Skeie, J. Everington, I. ter Avest, S. Miedema (eds) *Exploring Context in Religious Education Research: Empirical, methodological and theoretical perspectives.* Münster: Waxmann.

Fowler, J. (1981) *Stages of Faith: The psychology of human development and the quest for meaning.* San Francisco: Harper and Row.

Gearon, L. (2013) *Masterclass in Religious Education: Transforming teaching and learning.* London: Bloomsbury.

Geaves R. (2005) The dangers of essentialism: South Asian communities in Britain and the 'world religions' approach to the study of religions. *Contemporary South Asia,* (14)1: 75–90.

Geertz, C. (1983) *Local Knowledge.* New York: Basic Books.

Goldman, R. (1966) *Readiness for religion.* London: Routledge and Kegan Paul.

Gorsky, J. (2004) Beyond Inclusivism: Richard Harries, Jonathan Sacks and The Dignity of Difference. *Scottish Journal of Theology,* 57: 366–376.

Grimmitt, M. (1987) *Religious Education and Human Development: The relationship between studying religions and personal, social and moral education.* Essex: McCrimmons.

Grimmitt, M. (ed.) (2000) *Pedagogies of Religious Education.* Great Wakering: McCrimmonds.

Haakedal, E. (2012) Voices and perspectives in Norwegian pupils' work on religions and world views: a diachronic study applying sociocultural learning theory. *British Journal of Religious Education,* (34)2: 139–54.

Hay, D. 2000. The religious experience and education project: experiential learning in religious education. In M. Grimmitt (ed.) *Pedagogies of Religious Education.* Great Wakering: McCrimmons.

Hedegaard, M. (1999) Institutional practices, cultural positions, and personal motives: immigrant Turkish parents' conceptions about their children's school life. In S. Chaiklin, M. Hedegaard and U. Jensen (eds) *Activity Theory and Social Practice.* Aarhus: Aarhus University Press.

Hunter-Henin, M. (ed.) (2011) *Law, religious freedoms and education in Europe.* Farnham: Ashgate.

Husserl, E. (1931) *Ideas: General introduction to pure phenomenology.* London: Routledge.

Ipgrave, J. (1999) Issues in the delivery of religious education to Muslim pupils: perspectives from the classroom. *British Journal of Religious Education,* (21)3: 147–58.

Ipgrave, J. (2013) The language of interfaith encounter among inner city primary school children. *Religion and Education,* (40)1: 35–49.

Jackson, R. (1997) *Religious Education: An interpretive approach.* London: Hodder and Stoughton.

Jackson, R. (2004) *Rethinking Religious Education and Plurality: Issues in diversity and pedagogy.* London: RoutledgeFalmer.

Jackson, R., Ipgrave, J., Hayward, M., Hopkins, P., Fancourt, N., Robbins, M., Francis, L. and McKenna, U. (2010) *Materials Used to Teach About World Religions in Schools in England.* London: DCSF.

Jackson, R., Miedema, S., Weisse, W. and J.-P. Willaime (eds) (2007) *Religion and Education in Europe: Developments, contexts and debates.* Münster: Waxmann.

Jawoniyi, O. (2012) Children's rights and religious education in state-funded schools: an international human rights perspective. *The International Journal of Human Rights*, (16)2: 337–57.

Keast, J. (2007) *Religious Diversity and Intercultural Education: A reference book for schools.* Strasbourg: Council of Europe Publishing.

Kiblinger, K. (2003) Identifying inclusivism in Buddhist contexts. *Contemporary Buddhism: An Interdisciplinary Journal*, (4)1: 79–97.

Kozulin, A. (1990) *Vygotsky's Psychology: A biography of ideas.* Hemel Hempstead: Harvester Wheatsheaf.

Kozulin, A. (1997) *Psychological Tools: A sociocultural approach to education.* Cambridge, MA: Harvard University Press.

Kozulin, A. (2003) Psychological tools and mediated learning. In A. Kozulin, B. Gindis, V. Ageyev and S. Miller (eds) *Vygotsky's Educational Theory in Cultural Context.* Cambridge: Cambridge University Press.

Lantolf, J. and Thorne, S. (2006) *Sociocultural Theory and the Genesis of Second Language Development.* Oxford University Press, Oxford.

Leganger-Krogstad, H. (2011) *The Religious Dimension of Inter-cultural Understanding: Contributions to a contextual understanding.* Münster: Lit.

Lovat, T. (2012) Interfaith education and the phenomenological method. In T. van de Zee and T. Lovat (ed.) *New Perspectives on Religious and Spiritual Education.* Münster: Waxmann.

Luria, A. (1976) *Cognitive Development: Its cultural and social foundations* [M. Cole (ed); M. Lopez-Morillas and L. Solotaroff, Trans.]. Cambridge, MA: Harvard University Press.

Lynch, M. (2001) Religion's influence on culture and psychology. *American Psychologist* (56)12: 1174–5.

Mercer, N. and Hodgkinson, S. (eds) (2008) *Exploring Classroom Talk.* London: Sage.

Mercer, N. and Littleton, K. (2007) *Dialogue and the Development of Children's Thinking.* London: Routledge.

Miller, J., O'Grady, K. and McKenna, U. (eds) (2013) *Religion in Education: Innovation in international research.* New York: Routledge.

Moll, L. and Greenberg, J. (1990) Creating zones of possibilities: combining social contexts for instruction. In L. Moll (ed.) *Vygotsky and Education.* Cambridge: Cambridge University Press.

Moore, D. (2007) *Overcoming Religious Illiteracy: A cultural studies approach to the study of religion in secondary education.* New York: Palgrave.

Moser, P. (2010) Religious exclusivism. In C. Meister (ed.) *The Oxford Handbook of Religious Diversity.* Oxford: Oxford University Press.

Moulin, D. (2011) Giving voice to 'the silent minority': the experience of religious students in secondary school religious education lessons. *British Journal of Religious Education*, (33)3: 313–26.

Nanbu H. (2008) Religion in Chinese education: from denial to cooperation. *British Journal of Religious Education*, (30)3: 223–4.

O'Grady, K. (2005) Professor Ninian Smart, phenomenology and religious education. *British Journal of Religious Education*, (27)3: 227–38.

O'Grady, K. (2009) Honesty in religious education: some further remarks on the legacy of Ninian Smart and related issues, in reply to L. Philip Barnes. *British Journal of Religious Education*, (31)1: 63–6.

Organisation for Security and Co-operation in Europe (2007) *Toledo Guiding Principles on Teaching about Religions and Beliefs in Public Schools.* Warsaw: Organization for Security and Co-operation in Europe.

Ota, C. and Erricker, C. (eds) (2005) *Spiritual Education: Literary, empirical and pedagogical approaches.* Brighton: Sussex Academic Press.

Qualifications and Curriculum Authority (2004) *Religious Education: The non-statutory national framework.* London: QCA.

Riegel, U. and Ziebertz, H.-G. (2009) Germany: teachers of religious education – mediating diversity. In H.-G. Ziebertz and U. Riegel (eds) *How Teachers in Europe Teach Religion.* Münster: Lit.

Robbins, M. and Francis, L. (2010) The teenage religion and values survey in England and Wales: an overview. *British Journal of Religious Education,* 32: 307–320.

Rymarz, R. (2013) Direct instruction as a pedagogical tool in religious education. *British Journal of Religious Education*, (35)3: 326–41.

Sampson, E. (2000) Reinterpreting individualism and collectivism: their religious roots and monologic versus dialogic person–other relationship. *American Psychologist*, (55)12: 1425–32.

School Curriculum and Assessment Authority (1994) *Model Syllabuses for Religious Education: Model 1: Living faiths today.* London: School Curriculum and Assessment Authority.

Schools Council. (1971) *Religious Education in Secondary Schools.* London: Methuen International.

Sharma, A. (2010) A Hindu perspective. In C. Meister (ed.) *The Oxford Handbook of Religious Diversity.* Oxford: Oxford University Press.

Sim J. (2008) What does citizenship mean? Social studies teachers' understandings of citizenship in Singapore schools. In *Educational Review*, (60)3: 253–66.

Smart, N. (1986) Phenomenology of religion. In J. Sutcliffe (ed.) *Dictionary of Religious Education.* London: SCM.

Stern, J. 2010. Research as pedagogy: building learning communities and religious understanding in RE. *British Journal of Religious Education*, (32)2: 133–46.

ter Avest, I., Jozsa, D.-P, Knauth, T., Roson, J., and Skeie, G. (eds) (2009) *Dialogue and Conflict on Religion: Studies of classroom interaction in European countries.* Münster: Waxmann.

Thompson, I. (2012) Stimulating reluctant writers: a Vygotskian approach to teaching writing in secondary schools. *English in Education* (46)1: 85–100.

Van der Veer, R. (2007) *Lev Vygotsky.* London: Continuum.

Van der Zee T., Hermans, C. and Aarnoutse, C. (2008) Influence of students' characteristics and feelings on cognitive achievement in religious education. *Educational Research and Evaluation*, (14)2: 119–38.

Vygotsky, L. (1978) *Mind in Society: The development of higher psychological processes* (M. Cole, V. John-Steiner, S. Scribner, and E. Souberman eds). Cambridge, MA: Harvard University Press.

Vygotsky, L. (1986). *Thought and Language.* Cambridge, MA: MIT Press. (First published in 1962.)

Walshe, K, and Teece, G. (2013) Understanding 'religious understanding' in religious education. *British Journal of Religious Education*, (35)3: 313–25.

Watson, A. 2010 Shifts of mathematical thinking in adolescence. *Research in Mathematics Education*, 12(2): 133–148.

Watson, J. (2010) Including secular philosophies such as humanism in locally agreed syllabuses for religious education. *British Journal of Religious Education*, (32)1: 5–18.

Weisse, W. (2007) The European research project on religion and education 'REDCo'. In R. Jackson, S. Miedema, W. Weisse and J-P. Willaime (eds) *Religion and Education in Europe: Developments, contexts and debates*. Münster: Waxmann.

Willaime, J.-P. (2007) Teaching religious issues in French public schools: from abstentionist *laïcité* to a return of religion to public education. In R. Jackson, S. Miedema, W. Weisse and J-P. Willaime (eds) *Religion and Education in Europe: Developments, contexts and debates*. Münster: Waxmann.

Wright, A. (2004) *Religion, Education and Post-modernity*. London: RoutledgeFalmer.

# INDEX

accountability system 19–20, 24
active learning 70–1, 75, 80–3
active reading 100–2, 103
activity, definition of 47
Alexander, Robin 6
Applebee, Arthur N. 92, 194, 196
assisted performance 8–9, 97–8
automaticity 133

Barber, Michael 33
Barnes, Douglas 3, 6, 88
Bernstein, Basil 81–2
Bloom, Benjamin 191
book clubs 102
Bourdieu, Pierre 39
Bousted, Mary 39
Brice-Heath, Shirley 90
Bruner, Jerome 7–8, 14, 39, 88
Bullock Report (1975) 92
Burgess, Tony 88–9, 90

Carter, Kathy 6, 74, 161–2
Chaiklin, Seth 8, 17–18
classroom environment: academic and organisational aspects 6–7; conceptual framework 90, 95–6
classroom tasks: learning through discussion 113–14, 182; task demand and instruction 18–20; task sequencing model *21*, 21–4
Claxton, Guy 15, 16, 154
Clive of India debate 157–8
Cole, Michael *see* Newman, Denis

collaborative writing 97–100
concept development: literacy skills 88–9, 90; religious education 176–80, *179*, 182; support frameworks 7–8, 176; teaching of 5–6, 89–90, 182; Vygotsky's theory 176, *177*
conceptual units of instruction: practical assignments 196–7, 198; principles of 194–5; process of unit construction 198–202; teaching unit design 202–5
constructivism, influence of 71–2, 75
Counsell, Christine 156, 159–60
Cox Report 92
cultural censorship 39
curriculum design: class factor 40; dialectical relationships 41–2; England's national framework 31–2; international review 32; knowledge-based approach 38–41, 75–6; knowledge/learner interaction 76; neo-liberalism, impact of 29–30; perennial challenges 35–6; political interference 33, 38–41, 86, 93

Daniels, Harry 8
Daniels, Harvey 101–2
Dearing, Ron, Sir 32
'deliverology' 33
Derry, Jan 90
*Development of Writing Abilities* (Britton *et al*) 96, 98–9
disciplinary constraint 73, 78, 79–80, 83
disciplinary knowledge: constructivist approach 76 7; disciplinary critique

80–1, 83; disciplined judgement 79–80, 83; epistemes 77–8; role of 72–3
Dixon, John 91–2
Doyle, Walter 6–7, 18–19, 23, 74, 161–2

Eagleton, Terry 91
Education Reform Act (1988) 31, 94
Edwards, Anne 8, 9, 96, 159, 164, 165
Egan, Kieran 5
Ellis, Rod 131
Ellis, Viv 5
English (as subject): conceptual learning 88–90, 196–7; government categorisation 92; historical and cultural development 90–4; interpretation of purpose 86–7; models of teaching 91–2, 93; purpose of 95; task design for reading 100–2, 103; task design for writing 96–100, 103
epistemes 78
epistemology 72
everyday knowledge 6
explanation skills: explanations activity 128; practical theorising 117–19, 122–3; subject knowledge 110–11; teacher/mentor interaction 119–22; theoretical framework 111–13

Ford, Michael J. 71, 80–2, 83

genre theory 93
Geographical Association 78
geography: disciplinary knowledge 81, 83; plurality of approaches 78–9; task design elements 74
Gibb, Nick 37, 38, 40
Gove, Michael 37–40, 95–6, 158
Griffin, Peg *see* Newman, Denis
Gunnarsdottir, Rosa 23

Hall, Catherine 158
Hedegaard, Mariane 20
history, teaching of: disciplinary focus 158–9; enquiry question 157–8, 166; historical significance 164; interpretative value of sources 159–61, *160*; knowledge, contested discipline 152–3; public debate, impact of 156–7; student perceptions and engagement 162–5; teacher preconceptions 154–5

*Importance of Teaching, The* (DfE) 2010 75
Initial Teacher Education (ITE) 115–16
instruction, direct and indirect 18–20

internalisation 20, 24, 89, 98, 159
internship: developing explanations (practice) 119–20, 122–3; developing explanations (theory) 117–19, 122; novice science teachers 115 16; pedagogical content knowledge 116–17

Jackson, Robert 171–2, 174–5

Kingman Report (1988) 92
knowledge: everyday 6; powerful 75–6, 155–6, 157; production of 77–8, 82–3; schematic 197; subject 4–5, 14–15; substantive 14, 87, 108; syntactic 14–15, 87, 108
knowledge differentiation 81–2

Language in the National Curriculum 93
language learning: classroom language task evaluation 143–6; decoding task evaluation 140–3; dialogical model of planning 138–9, *139*; distinctive attributes 132–3; individual learners 136; negative perceptions 129–30; recognised principles 135; skill development 146; task-based language teaching 130–1; task objective, design approach 136–7, 147; teacher education 147–8; theoretical research, interpretation of 133–7
learning strategies: affective aspects 24–5; knowledge gathering 14–15; metacognition 15; quadrant model *21*, 21–5; self-regulation 16; split-screen thinking 15–16
Leavis, F.R. 91
literature circles 101
Longino, Helen 79

Mason, John 49
mathematical tasks: design approaches explored 50–4, **51**, *52*; design purpose and processes 58–9, **60–3**, 63–6; learning new methodology 53–6, *54*; mathematics-related pedagogy tasks 49; task formulation planning 56–7, *57*; teaching methods, effect of 48–9
mathematics teachers: didactic awareness 49–50; mathematical activity, adaptable design 58–9, **60–3**, 63–6; task design course 47–50; task design exercises 50–7, **51**, *52*, *54*, *57*, **58**; task design reassessed 66–8

mediated learning 7, 22, 182
Mercer, Neil 4
metacognition 15
Morrow, Wally 72
Mortimer, Eduardo 111, 112, 113–14, 117
Muth, William *see* Stemhagen, Kurt

national curriculum (England): 2007 revisions and aims 33–6; coalition's knowledge-based reforms 36–40, 75; knowledge/learner interaction 76; main concepts 94; prescriptive design 31–2, 39–41, 74–5; reforms in the 90's 32
National Foundation for Education Research 32
neo-liberalism, impact of 29–30
Newbolt Report (1921) 91
Newman, Denis 4, 8, 95
Nisbet, John 15
novice teachers: conceptual units of instruction 196–7, 198–202; English (as subject) 196–7; history 154–5; languages 147–8; science 114–15, 116; teacher/mentor interaction 119–22, 155, 162
Nunan, David 131

*Of Mice and Men* (Steinbeck) 100–1
Ofsted: curriculum evaluation 35; English, teaching of 94; history, teaching of 159–60; teaching style 75
Ogborn, Jon 107, 111–12, 113
Orr, David 30
Oxford Internship scheme 4, 116–17, 154–5

pedagogical content knowledge: concept of 108–10; novice and non-specialist issues 114–15, 116; science teaching 117–22
Perkins, David 77–8
phronesis 153, 162–3, 166–7
powerful knowledge 75–6, 155–6, 157
Pring, Richard 33
process writing 92
pupil agency 20, 23

quadrant model *21*, 21–2
Qualifications and Curriculum Authority 32, 34

Reich, Gabriel *see* Stemhagen, Kurt
Reiss, Michael 32

relativism 76–7
religious education: belief frameworks, understanding of 171–5, *172*; empathy approach 173–4; experiences, types of 180–2; external concept framework 179–80; Vygotskian approach 176–8, *179*, 182–3

scaffolding, concept of 8
Schama, Simon 157, 158
schematic knowledge 197
Schwab, Joseph 5, 14, 87, 108
science, teaching of: experience differences 114–15; explanation, key skill 110–13; internship and practical theorising 116–22, 123; learning through discussion 113–14; pedagogical content knowledge 108–10, 122
Scott, Philip *see* Mortimer, Eduardo
Secondary National Strategy 75
second language acquisition (SLA): research, interpretation of 134–7; theory, practical applications 133–4
self-regulated learning: pupil response 23–4, 25; self-assessment 22; teacher responsibilities 16, 20, 24–6
Shavelson, Richard J. 7
Shucksmith, Janet 15
Shulman, Lee 108, 109
Smagorinsky, Peter: conceptual units, task analysis 198–202; conceptual units, teaching of 202–5; 'construction zone' 95, 203; design principles, adoption of 191–2, 194–5; teacher education 195–8; writing, teaching of 96
split-screen thinking 15
Stemhagen, Kurt 71, 73, 78, 79–80, 83
Stern, Paula 7
structured process approach 194–5
Stylianides, Andreas J. 49, 50–1
Stylianides, Gabriel J. 49, 50–1
subject knowledge: learning tools 14–15; pedagogical content knowledge 108–9; task of teaching 4–5
substantive knowledge 6, 14, 87, 108
syntactic knowledge 6, 14–15, 87, 108
systematic functional linguistics 93

task analysis: principles of 192–3; process of unit construction 198–202
task-based language teaching 130–1
task demand 18–20
task design: active reading 100–2; assisted performance 8–9, 97–8; dialogical

approach 138–40, *139*; enquiry question, construction of 157–8, 164–5; external concept framework 179–80; fundamental elements 6–7, 74; interpretative value of sources 159–61, *160*; mathematical tasks exercises 50–7, **51**, *52*, *54*, **58**; novice teachers 147–8; performance related 94; structured process approach 194–5; student perceptions and engagement 162–3; task objective, working towards 136–7; writing, teaching of 96–100
task, interpretation of 47, 70
teachers: career aims 13; knowledgeable resource, role as 23; positive support 24–6; professionalism undermined 33; pupil engagement 13–14, 71; *see also* novice teachers
three part lesson 22–3
Traille, Kay 163
Tyler, Ralph 191

vocabulary knowledge 136–7
Vygotsky, Lev: concept development 5–6, 89–90, 176; mediated learning 7, 22, 182; social interaction in learning 6, 89; theological influences 175–6; zone of proximal development 8, 17, 89

Watson, Anne 49
Wheelahan, Leesa 76–7
White, John 32
Wilson, Suzanne *see* Wineburg, Samuel
Wineburg, Samuel 153, 158, 159
Wrenn, Andrew 164
writing, teaching of: historical perspective 92; processes involved 98–9; process writing 93; task design 96–100, 103

Young, Michael 75–6, 155–6, 157

Zimmerman, Barry 16
zone of proximal development 8, 17–18, 89

Printed in Great Britain
by Amazon